When Marriage Goes Wrong...

Biblical Answers on Divorce and Remarriage

When Marriage Goes Wrong...

Biblical Answers on Divorce and Remarriage

Concise Studies in the Scriptures
Volume Six

Raymond C. Faircloth

First edition 2017
Second edition 2018
Third edition 2019

Marriage must be highly valued by all,
and husbands and wives must remain faithful in their marriage,
because God will judge the sexually immoral and the adulterers

Hebrews 13:4

Contents

Introduction to the Third Edition

PART ONE
CHRISTIAN MARRIAGE

1. Background to Bible-Based Marriage 3

2. The Relationship between Husband and Wife 7

3. How Married Couples Should Treat Each Other 11

4. The Basics for Maintaining a Good Marriage 20

PART TWO
BACKGROUND TO DIVORCE

5. The Biblical Terms for Divorce and Its Grounds 29

6. The Issues and Problems in Understanding Biblical Divorce 33

7. Did Jesus Make the Mosaic Law of No Value? 37

8. Mosaic Case Law Concerning Divorce 43

9. Case Law for Divorce Based on Deuteronomy 24:1-4. 46

10. Case Law for Divorce Based on Exodus 21:10-11. 55

11. God's Example in Divorce 60

12. God Does Not Hate All Divorce – Malachi Two 65

13. The Rabbinic Background to Christian Divorce Issues 71

PART THREE
JESUS ON DIVORCE

14. The Four Passages Concerning Jesus' Teaching on Divorce 81

15. Understanding Jesus on Divorce in Matthew 5:31-32. 89

16. Understanding Jesus on Divorce in Matthew 19:1-6. 96

17. Understanding Jesus on Divorce in Matthew 19:7-9. 105

18. Why Was Exodus 21:10-11 Not Discussed with the Pharisees?   111

19. Understanding Jesus on Divorce from Mark and Luke   114

20. Failure of Past Understanding of Jesus' Teaching on Divorce   119

PART FOUR
PAUL ON DIVORCE

21. Paul's Teachings on Marriage Obligations   126

22. Paul's Teachings on Divorce in Relation to the Gentile World   130

23. Can Two Believers Ever Divorce?   135

24. Two Situations for a Believer Married to an Unbeliever   142

25. What Constitutes Abuse and Neglect?   146

26. Final Thoughts on Bible-Based Divorce   155

PART FIVE
JESUS AND PAUL ON REMARRIAGE

27. Background to Remarriage for Christians   159

28. Did Jesus Forbid Remarriage?   162

29. Paul's Teachings on Remarriage   170

30. Don't Paul's Words on Marriage Apply Only to the Betrothed?   178

31. "The Unmarried" with Strong Sexual Desire Should Marry   180

32. Putting the Record Straight on Remarriage   182

33. Anomalies and Injustices in Current General Church Policy   186

34. Concluding Comments   188

APPENDICES

A. Homosexuality as Grounds for Divorce   195
B. Can Divorced Men Serve as Overseers or Deacons?   198
C. Summary of Biblical Teaching on Divorce   200
D. Summary of Biblical Teaching on Remarriage   209
E. Will the Institution of Marriage Exist in God's Kingdom?   212

Index of Theological, Hebrew, and Greek Terms   219
Suggested Reading   221
Scripture Index   223
Subject Concordance   228

———— ❑ ————

Bible Translations Referenced

CEB	Common English Bible
CEV	The Contemporary English Version
CJB	The Complete Jewish Bible
CSB	Christian Standard Bible
ESV	English Standard Version
GWT	God's Word Translation
KNT	Kingdom New Testament by N.T. Wright
LEB	Lexham English Bible
LXX	Septuagint (Greek Version of the Old Testament)
MOFF	The Moffatt Translation of the Bible
NAB	New American Bible
NASB	New American Standard Bible
NET	New English Translation
NJB	New Jerusalem Bible
NIV	New International Version
NLT	New Living Translation
NRSV	New Revised Standard Version
OGOMT	The One God the Father, One Man Messiah Translation
REB	Revised English Bible
S&G	Smith and Goodspeed–An American Translation
UBS	United Bible Societies Interlinear

For New Testament quotations I have substantially referenced my own version: *The Kingdom of God Version–The New Testament (KGV)*

Dedication

This book is dedicated to all those Christians who have suffered the various kinds of persistent and serious abuses and neglect from an uncaring and unloving spouse. This includes my loving Christian wife Cherie, who previously experienced a marriage which became intolerable until divorce was inevitable.

———— ❑ ————

Introduction to the Third Edition

The reasons for the third edition of this book are: firstly, because much more needed to be said concerning Jesus' position in relationship to the Mosaic Law and therefore, the principles relevant to divorce and to remarriage. This information can be found in a new chapter entitled, "Did Jesus Make the Mosaic Law of No Value?" Secondly, a number of chapters now contain additional and new information with more facts and reasoning on this complex subject of divorce. Thirdly, there is one point expressing a corrected view related to 1 Corinthians 7:10. Fourthly, much more is said about how to maintain a good marriage. And lastly, I have attempted to improve the layout of the book while expressing some thoughts clearer and more logically than in the previous editions. So, this third edition is a substantial revision and reworking of the book.

Nevertheless, there is no change to the earlier presented facts that there is much confusion and contradiction in the so-called "orthodox" understandings of grounds for divorce and whether or not remarriage can take place. In fact, there is no single position as presented by the various Christian denominations that is truly orthodox. These different positions taken by these denominations range from: "no divorce allowed under any circumstances" to "divorce may be allowed and then followed by remarriage for both the innocent party and the guilty party if repentant." Indeed, more detail will be given on this confusion in the book.

However, for a long time, scholars have asked the question: what about persistent serious abuse and neglect that a marriage partner may be suffering as caused by their spouse? Can this be grounds for divorce? Indeed, it is only in the last part of the twentieth century and this current century that this aspect of divorce has been seriously addressed. So, this book sets out to show from the Scriptures that God has great concern for those who are suffering persistent serious abuse and neglect in their marriages. Therefore, our key question is: what can a Christian legitimately do under such terrible circumstances when a marriage goes irreparably wrong? The answer must come from taking note of the entire background of the Scriptures and the context to the statements on this subject made by Jesus and the Apostle Paul. Indeed, for clarity and completeness on this issue it is imperative that one obtains the greatest possible amount of biblical and background information that is currently available on the subject.

Theologian Craig Keener speaks of Christians who have been "wounded by spouses they trusted, only to be wounded again by fellow Christians." It appears that these rather harsh fellow Christians have gained their understanding of the subject of divorce and remarriage by the quotation of a few so-called proof-texts—texts which have been taken out of context. They have also failed to read this complex biblical subject in light of its cultural background. Evidently, the subjects of divorce and remarriage are highly controversial in the world of Christianity and with many Christian divorcees being ostracized by other Christians. In fact, during most of my life I believed that divorce could happen for one reason only, namely, the adultery of one's marriage partner, after which an innocent partner could remarry. I understood that any other reason used by a Christian spouse, as grounds for divorcing their partner, would have put such a person outside of Christian fellowship.

However, in the mid-1990s I became aware of a situation which was problematic to my Christian sensibilities. It was that of hearing about a Christian sister who was often physically beaten by her unbelieving husband; and yet her church would not allow her to divorce him because he had not committed adultery. She was advised to move out of the family home and to lead a celibate life-style, but with no hope of her divorcing her bullying husband or any hope of remarriage unless and until the day he committed adultery, if ever! I now realize that similar situations are quite common.

Later, in the early 2000s, I was asked to counsel a couple concerning their very narrow view of divorce and remarriage. This couple had come from a church background which taught that there should be no divorce and no remarriage under any circumstances, and that all divorcees must return to their first partner. This prompted me to make an in-depth study of this subject. In doing so I was initially astonished to find out how many different views of divorce were held by the many scholars and denominations. (I have presented these in Chapter 6).

In my searching I found that the research and presentations by certain leading scholars most enlightening and for the most part contextually Scriptural. In particular, both David Instone-Brewer and Craig keener show that divorce is biblically allowable when one spouse persistently seriously abuses another, as well as the other generally recognized grounds of adultery and desertion. However, it is not only because of my concerns for fairness that I now believe this to be correct, but because I understand this view as totally provable from the Scriptures when one takes into account all of the biblical statements, that is, all their harmonious evidence. Unfortunately, it seems that the way in which many people come to their conclusions on this subject is rather like the "six blind men of Hindustan" who describe an elephant using only one part of the animal to define the remaining parts, but overlooking the entire animal i.e., all the evidence for what the creature actually looks like. In the same way, when looking at the subject of divorce and remarriage it seems advisable for many Christians to broaden their thinking to gain a rounded-out perspective on this subject.

Nevertheless, I do not believe that any one writer on this subject is absolutely correct on all points and so I have endeavoured to present what I understand as the biblical view—yet I am certainly open to valid correction on various points, even though expecting to be verbally attacked by those religious teachers who hold to very restricted views on this subject. I simply ask them to open their minds to a more godly and biblical approach. The key questions on the subject of divorce and remarriage that are answered in this book are:

- Is divorce ever allowable according to the Bible?
- If so, what are the biblical grounds for divorce?
- Does the sexual adultery of one partner form such grounds for divorce?
- Does the persistent serious abuse or neglect of a partner form such grounds for divorce?
- Is remarriage ever allowed according to the Bible?

In Appendix A I touch on the subject of homosexuality. Although this subject is controversial, it is important to understand it with special reference to its occurrence within a marriage. This is because of the great difficulties that are caused if one partner has that orientation, and even more so if he or she engages in homosexual activities—such a situation is almost certain to ruin the marriage. (I use the term marriage only as being between a man and a woman and never as between two same-sex partners). So, I ask the question: could even a homosexual orientation in one partner be biblically allowable as grounds for divorce?

So, to begin our study of divorce and remarriage it is vital that we establish for ourselves what the real purposes of marriage are from a biblical perspective and then to understand what exactly is involved in the respective roles of husbands and wives in maintaining a good marriage.

——— ❑ ———

PART ONE

Christian Marriage

1

Background to Bible-Based Marriage

The Greek philosopher Socrates is reported as saying, "By all means marry; if you get a good wife, you'll become happy; if you get a bad one, you'll become a philosopher," and indeed there are many people, including some Bible commentators and other Christians who have developed their own philosophies about marriage—much of it not particularly healthy. More healthful are the words from the book *Princess Ben* by Catherine Gilbert Murdock when she gives her mature opinion that:

> Every fairy tale, it seems, concludes with the bland phrase "happily ever after." Yet every couple I have ever known would agree that nothing about marriage is forever happy. There are moments of bliss, to be sure, and lengthy spans of satisfied companionship. Yet these come at no small effort, and the girl who reads such fiction dreaming her troubles will end ere she departs the altar is well advised to seek at once a rational woman to set her straight.

So, before examining what Bible-based marriage should look like we need to look briefly at the ancient background to this subject. Firstly, money was always involved.

Marital Monetary Considerations in the Ancient Near-East

THE BRIDE PRICE

Called the *mohar* in Hebrew, this price, which amounted to approximately ten month's wages, was paid by the groom to the bride's father (Ex. 22:16). In the event of a divorce this price was retained by the bride's father. This showed how serious this man was about his bride and the value he was putting on her.

THE DOWRY

Called the *nedunyah* in Hebrew, this amount, paid by the father (Jud. 1:14-15; 1 Kings 9:16), was far in excess of the bride price and was regarded as the bride's share of the estate. If, later, the husband was the **cause of** a divorce he had either to pass the dowry over to his wife or return it to the wife's father. On the other hand, if the wife was the cause of the divorce, then the husband could keep the dowry.

Monogamy and Polygamy in Bible Times

In the sinless conditions of the Garden of Eden the Genesis record holds out the ideal for marriage as being monogamous. So, for Adam: *"...he must hold fast to his wife, and they shall become one flesh" (Gen. 2:24 ESV)*. Yet the rest of the Hebrew Scriptures give no criticism of the fact that many husbands in the imperfect world had more than one wife i.e., they were polygamous (more correctly called polygyny). In fact, these Scriptures make no issue out of this practice, even though the excesses are condemned. However, the women were expected to have only one husband and so to be monogamous. This meant that only a wife could be accused of adultery i.e., having a sexual relationship with a man who was not her husband. Interestingly, the first divorce was that of polygamous Abraham in divorcing his secondary wife Hagar at Sarah's insistence (Gen: 21:10) and yet Hagar had committed no serious wrong!

Nevertheless, in time, the Jewish Qumran community (using Leviticus 18:18) condemned polygamy. Indeed, in Matthew 19:5-6 Jesus (using Genesis) also showed monogamy to be God's original ideal prior to sin entering into the world.

Prime Factors of a Bible-Based Marriage

Marriage is, of course, a union of two people, and should be of one man and one woman. It is a union of hearts, minds, and bodies— what is commonly called "being soul-mates." This union has several primary purposes. So, from a biblical perspective, the following separate aspects of the purposes of marriage as a bonded relationship frequently cross over into the other aspects of marriage. These prime purposes are:

1. Companionship. Fundamentally and primarily marriage is so that men and women will not be alone (Gen. 2:18). In the perfect and sinless condition of Adam and Eve marriage should have been life-long as the ideal.

4

2. A loving relationship. Such is a relationship of total care, cherishing, and commitment to each other (Eph. 5:28-29). Indeed, the couple should show significant interest in each other and in each other's interests (Gen. 29:31-34; Mal. 2:14; 1 Cor.11:9; Eph. 5:22-23). This includes being in love (Gen. 24:67) with the enjoyment of each other physically/sexually (1 Cor. 7:2-5; the Song of Solomon)—the "one flesh" union (Gen. 2:24; Matt. 19:4-6; 1 Cor. 6:16). The intention is that the couple should be in love throughout their life-long marriage.

3. Procreation (Gen.1:28; 4:1; Ps. 127:3). Since the perfection of the Garden of Eden this, of course, lasts only whilst the couple still have their procreative powers or until a family is considered complete.

In all ancient Near East nations, including Israel, marriage was by definition **a conditional contract** (*Heb. ketubah)* or <u>covenant</u> that specified conditions that both parties agreed to fulfil. This involved vows to that effect made by the two parties. So basically, it involved agreed **obligations**, **payments**, and **penalties** and was, in some senses, like every other business or diplomatic covenant. If one of the parties to the contract broke it, the wronged party could take action. In the case of a marriage covenant this could result in divorce. So, clearly a complete breaking of the marriage covenant was the lawful basis for divorce in Israel. However, the usual views of divorce generally fail to recognize that the contractual relationship of marriage has broken down when vows are persistently broken and no longer any companionship and love.

CHRISTIAN MARRIAGE VOWS

So just as with Israel, Christian marriage today is a contract/covenant between a man and a woman and with God Himself as a witness to each truly Christian marriage.

At weddings a marriage contract—a covenant—is enacted. This means that both parties agree to keep the Bible-based vows which they express at the time of the wedding. This makes it a bi-lateral and conditional covenant. In fact, with the exception of the "to obey" and the "till death do us part" vows, modern marriage vows in the churches substantially follow the biblical vows of sexual faithfulness and cherishing along with the provision of and proper use of necessary materials and love for each other.

The Scriptures do not give a single complete list of the obligations that two candidates for marriage would vow to keep. So, the Jewish Rabbis had to glean what these obligations would be from the relevant texts. These primarily involved Exodus 21:10-11 and were later confirmed in Paul's words stated in 1 Corinthians 7:2-5 and Ephesians 5:21-33. So, once the marrying couple had contracted their marriage, based on these vows, any persistent breaking of the vows by either party could serve as the basis for divorce.

NOTE: Marriage is not a sacrament as taught in Roman Catholicism. Indeed, Erasmus, in the 1500s showed that this Roman Catholic idea originated from the faulty translation of Ephesians 5:32 in the Vulgate version of the Bible. It concerns the Greek word *mysterion* which was rendered wrongly in Latin as *sacramentum.*

Why "Marry Only in the Lord"?

The Apostle Paul counsels that, "*a wife is bound to her husband as long as he is living. But if her husband should fall asleep [in death], she's free to marry anyone she wishes; **only in the Lord**"* (1 Cor. 7:39 KGV). Other less literal translations render this last phrase as "but only if the man is a Christian" (GWT—similar in GNT and WE) or "provided he is a believer in the Lord" (CJB). By extension this counsel applies, not only to widows, but to all Christians who are seeking a marriage partner.

But why does God command us not to marry outside of the Christian family? Well, just as He commanded Israelites not to marry the "foreign women" because of their pagan beliefs which would likely influence them and corrupt them, so, too, for Christians. Yet, even if one's beliefs were not being corrupted, living with an unbeliever is far more of a struggle for the Christian because the goals in life of the two are running in different directions. Of course, this means that the Christian who is seeking a marriage partner should seek God's help and guidance in finding the right person.

2

The Relationship Between Husband and Wife

In his book *Time Enough for Love* Robert Heinlein commented that: "A woman is not property, and husbands who think otherwise are living in a dreamworld." Sadly, some Christian men view their wives in this way or in some way to be controlled.

Is a Wife to Be Subordinate to Her Husband?

The ancient Gentile view of women was quite derogatory. The Greek Philosopher Plato (424-347 B.C.) held the view that: "It is only males who are created directly by the gods." And Aristotle (384-322 B.C.) stated that: "Women are defective by nature." Sadly, this was a common view throughout the ancient world, even among some rabbis of Judaism. In time these views came to be part of the culture of the churches of Christendom, especially as certain misunderstood statements in the standard translations of the Bible were used to promote a view of women which treats them as secondary i.e., subordinate to men and restricts what they may do as Christians. However, the term "subordination" is quite different in meaning to the biblical term "submission," the latter referring to when one may consent to the wishes of another; whereas "to be subordinate" means that one is of lower rank or secondary and subservient—a lesser person!

SCHOLARS WORDS AND TRANSLATIONS
One of the difficulties for truth-seeking Christians is that our standard Bible translations let us down—sometimes badly. There seems to be no translation that completely says what the scholars in the lexicons and commentaries etc., tell us the text should say on all points on this subject. For instance, very early on in the biblical account Eve is made to look like a lesser person—a subordinate! Is this the actual biblical picture for women?

Was Eve Subordinate to Adam?

Most translations render Genesis 2:18 as if God says: "I will make a helper fit for him" and so indicating that the woman was a kind of 'add on' to the man. Much better are the translations in the NAB: "*a suitable partner for him*" and in the REB: "a partner that suits him." However, the Hebrew word *ezer* means "strength" or "power" and so this verse is really saying: "*I will make a power corresponding to man*" so that the woman is really man's equal although in a different role. According to Adam she was: "*bone of my bones, and flesh of my flesh*" *(Gen. 2:23)*. So, Walter Kaiser, professor of Old Testament, informs us that:

> The idiomatic sense of this phrase "bone of my bones" is a "*very close relative*" "*one of us*" or in effect "*our equal.*" The woman was never meant to be an assistant or "helpmate" to the man. The word mate slipped into English since it was so close to Old English *meet*, which means "fit to" or "corresponding to" the man... What God had intended then was to make a "power" or "strength" for the man who would in every way "correspond to him" or even "be his equal" *Hard Sayings of the Bible* p. 94.

There is nothing in the account recorded in Genesis Two to indicate that Adam was placed in a leadership role over Eve. Even when they both had to answer to God for their wrong-doing by breaking God's command regarding the tree, Eve was not judged for any insubordination toward Adam. This is because the passage never shows her as having to be subordinate to him. Furthermore, if Eve had been required to be subordinate to Adam, then he alone, as the leader, would have been questioned and held responsible by God. However, this was not the case. As we shall see later in the study of 1 Timothy 2 the key difference between them in this situation was that Adam had considerably greater knowledge of God than Eve did, so that she alone was later deceived by the Serpent.

A Wife's Status After Eve Sinned

Many Christians have said that, even if Eve was not subordinate before the Fall, she certainly was since that event, and so putting all woman-kind in that same position. This is based on God's words to the woman that: *"I will greatly increase your pains in childbearing; with pain you will give birth to children. Your **desire** will be for your husband, and he will **rule over** you"* (Gen. 3:16 NASB). Nevertheless, rather than the word "desire" the modern renderings of the LXX use the word "recourse" which means "a source of help." Also, in the book *Hard Sayings of the Bible* Kaiser tells us that:

> The Hebrew word *tesuqah*, now almost universally translated as "desire," was previously rendered as "**turning**." The word appears in the Hebrew Old Testament only three times: here in Genesis 3:16, in Genesis 4:7 and in Song of Songs 7:10. Of the twelve known ancient versions almost every one renders these three instances of *tesuqah* as "turning," not "desire." ... Furthermore, the Latin rendering was *conversio* and the Greek was *apostrophe*, words all meaning "a turning." With such strong and universal testimony in favour of "turning," how did the idea of *desire* ever intrude into the translator's agenda? ... Katherine C. Bushnell...traced its genesis to an Italian Dominican monk named Pagnino ... It is time the Church returned to the real meaning of this word. The sense of Genesis 3:16 is simply this: as a result of her sin, Eve would turn away from her sole dependence on God and turn to her husband ... We may conclude, that *tesuqah* does not refer to the lust or sexual appetite of a woman for a man. Neither does the verb to rule over her express God's order for husbands in their relationships to their wives. pp. 97-99.

From this it is clear that this is not a command from God that husbands must rule over their wives, but rather, because of a woman's turning away from Him and to have recourse to her husband he will take advantage of her.

But Isn't It Only Man Who Is in God's Image?

Thousands of years after God's pronouncement upon Eve in the Garden of Eden, Paul wrote: *"For a man ought not to cover his head, since he is **the image** and **glory** of God, but woman is **the glory of man**"* (1 Cor. 11:7). From this it has been assumed that women are no longer in God's image.

9

WOMEN ARE ALSO IN GOD'S IMAGE

However, this is not the case as Professor Manfred Brauch explains. He notes that although Paul:

> ...does not say that woman is the image of man; she is only his glory. For Paul knew that, according to Genesis 1:26-27, human beings as male and female were created in God's image...Thus the woman as man's glory is only in recognition of the temporal sequence of God's activity, since her being is derived from the being of Adam. But no less than man, woman is the glory **and image** of God since she too is "from God" (11:12) (emphasis mine). *Hard Sayings of Paul* p. 145.

Clearly, at the very beginning of the Bible it is made clear that both men and the women were made in God's image:

> *"Then God said, 'Let us make man in our image, according to our likeness ... God created man in his own image, in the image of God he created him; male and female he created them'"*
>
> *(Gen. 1:26, 27).*

This reference to mankind—both male and female—shows both sexes to be in "the image of God" and so Eve obviously was equally "the glory of God" along with the man **even though Paul doesn't mention that fact** in the context of 1 Corinthians 11:7. So woman is both "the glory of man" and "the glory of God." Therefore, there is no reason for men to treat women as subordinate to them.

3

How Married Couples Should Treat Each Other

The Male Controlling Type of Headship
Is Not Biblical

In scholarly circles there is an issue over exactly what the Greek word for "head" i.e., *kephale* actually meant in New Testament times when Paul wrote, "...*I [Paul] want you to understand that **the head (Gk kephale) of every man is Christ, the head of a wife is her husband**, and the head of Christ is God" (1 Cor. 11:3)*. This verse is generally understood as demonstrating a chain of command with levels of authority. Certainly, the Greek word *kephale* means "head" in its literal physical sense; but in its metaphorical sense it has the meanings of 'taking priority over,' 'source,' or 'origin' as well as 'authority.' However, it does not mean 'having harsh authority over' in any domineering sense. The metaphorical usage of *kephale* in the Koine Greek is stated in *Liddell and Scott's Lexicon* to be that of 'source' or 'origin' and several leading scholars have adopted this viewpoint. Yet, in contradiction of that fact conservative scholar Wayne Grudem writes that: "A new search of 2,336 examples of *kephale* from a wide range of ancient Greek literature produced no convincing examples where *kephale* meant "source."" Also, linguist D. A. Carson states that: "Although some of the New Testament metaphorical uses of *kephale* could be taken to mean "source," all other factors being equal, in no case is that the required meaning; and in every instance the notion of "headship" implying authority fits equally well or better" *Exegetical Fallacies* p.37.

Evidence for "Head" As Meaning "Source"
As Well As "Authority Over"

However, in spite of the above comments, there is strong evidence that 'source' was certainly one of the meanings of *kephale* or, at least, part of its meaning as the following theologians have said. For instance, Professor Manfred Brauch shows regarding the word *kephale* that:

> The linguistic evidence points strongly, if not overwhelmingly, away from the common reading of "head" as "chief," "ruler," "authority over," though there are many conservative scholars who would challenge this. The most exhaustive Greek-English Lexicon covering Greek literature from about 900 B.C. to A.D. 600, among numerous metaphorical meanings for *kephale*, does not give a single definition which would indicate that in common ordinary Greek usage, *kephale* included the meaning "superior rank" or "supreme over" or "leader" or "authority." ... However, among the range of meanings which *kephale* had in ordinary Greek were: "origin" or "source" or "starting point" and "crown" or "completion" or "consummation."
>
> *Hard Sayings of Paul* pp. 136-137

Brauch then goes on to explain that the Hebrew word *ro'sh* has the figurative meaning of "leader" or "chief" or "authority figure." Yet he notes that in producing the Septuagint that:

> when the translators, however, sought the appropriate Greek word to render this figurative meaning, they used not *kephale*, but *archon*...It is clear from this data that the Greek translators were keenly aware that *kephale* did not normally have a metaphorical meaning equivalent to that of *ro'sh;* else they would have used it for most, if not all, occurrences of *ro'sh* when it carried the meaning "chief" or "leader"...Another factor to take into consideration is that nowhere else in the New Testament is *kephale* used to designate a figure of authority.
> *Ibid.* pp. 137, 138.

Also regarding *kephale* in 1 Corinthians, Emeritus professor Gordon Fee explains that:

> The metaphor itself is often understood to be hierarchical, setting up structures of authority. But nothing in the passage suggests as much ... Paul's understanding of the metaphor, and almost certainly the only one the Corinthians would have grasped, is "head" as "source," especially "source of life." This

12

seems to be corroborated by vv. 8-9, the only place where one of these relationships is picked up further in Paul's argument. There he explicitly states that man was the original source of the woman (cf. v.12). Thus Paul's concern is not hierarchical (who has authority over whom), but relational (the unique relationships that are predicated on one's being the source of the other's existence).

The First Epistle to the Corinthians pp. 502-503.

Also, with reference to 1 Corinthians 11:3 *The NIV Theological Dictionary of New Testament Words* states:

> "Here *kephale* should probably be understood not as ruler but **as source** or origin. The creation narrative of Gen.2:21-23 assigns a priority to the male." (p. 679).

In fact, there is abundant evidence that in New Testament times there was no such thing as headship in the sense of dominant 'ruler' with those who are subordinate to him, but rather the indications are that it is in the sense of his being a source for his wife, but with his taking priority. Furthermore, it is clear that a husband should never be authoritarian or domineering; but rather that he has a God-given responsibility to work within his family in a loving way as demonstrated in Philippians 2:3, 4 and in Ephesians 5:25 as the context of verses 21-24 shows. So here my conclusion is that there is enough evidence to show that the metaphorical term "head," as used in the New Testament, has the meaning of the husband being the source of good things but with a certain priority in the family in loving leadership.

Submission Is an Attitude Not a Role of Subordination

In Ephesians 5:21-24 Paul directs Christians to:

> "*Be submissive to one another out of reverence for Christ. Wives, [submit] to your own husbands, as to the Lord. For the husband is the head (loving authority as source) of the wife even as Christ is the head of the church, his body, and is himself its Saviour. Now as the church submits to Christ, so also wives should submit in everything to their husbands*" (Moffatt) *Also see the NAB, NJB, The Unvarnished New Testament, REB, NLT, NKJV.*

13

Please note that verse 21 says: *"**Be submissive to one another** out of reverence for Christ."* Accordingly, there is no rule that one category of Christians must be any more submissive than any other category. So, in imitation of Jesus this is an attitude that a Christian must develop. As well as his submissiveness to God, Jesus was submissive to his disciples in many ways including the washing of their feet. So, a wife's submission to her husband does not mean she is subordinate to him i.e., of a lower rank, but rather it means that she is willing to yield or consent to something if it does not contradict what is true or go against a biblical principle. However, husbands are equally to submit to their wives according to Ephesians 5:21 as with submitting to all the other brothers and sisters in Christ. In fact, in the phrase "Wives, [submit]," the word 'submit' is missing from the Greek text and is only implied from the previous phrase, which therefore means that the subject concerning submission by wives is connected to the phrase *"...submitting to one another <u>out of reverence for Christ.</u>"* Indeed, the following are a few of the many examples of Christ's own submission to others and which all Christians should imitate. For instance, he said: *"Take my yoke on you and learn from me, because I am gentle and humble in heart, and you will find rest for your souls"* (Matt. 11:29); and *"It must not be this way among you! Instead whoever wants to be great among you must be your servant, ... just as the Son of Man did not come to be served but to serve, and to give his life as a ransom for many""* (Matt. 20:26, 28); *"But I am among you as one who serves"* (Luke 22:27); *"If I then, your Lord and Teacher, have washed your feet, you too ought to wash one another's feet"* (John 13:14).

After Jesus had ascended to heaven the Apostle Paul, in quoting Jesus said, *"...we must help the weak, and remember the words of the Lord Jesus that he himself said, 'It is more blessed to give than to receive'"* (Acts 20:35) and *"even Christ did not please himself, but just as it is written, "The insults of those who insult you have fallen on me""* (Rom. 15:3-5). Consequently, it is "out of reverence for Christ" (Eph. 5:21) that a wife is submissive to her husband in the same way the Congregation is to be submissive to Christ i.e., in its a humble response to Christ's own self-giving or self-sacrificing attitude. It has nothing to do with control, power, coercion or the making of demands by a husband; but rather it is submission "as to the Lord" *(vs. 22)*.

14

This Is a Relative Submission to a Husband

Certainly, the Apostle Peter says, *"wives, be subject to your own husbands" (1 Pet. 3:1)*. However, when Paul says in Ephesians 5:24 that, *"wives should submit **in everything**,"* he is not meaning for this submission to be in any absolute, universal sense. This is because a sincere Christian woman would want to do only what is in harmony with the holy Scriptures and not do what is out of harmony with those Scriptures. Clearly this is a relative subjection because any unbelieving husbands may attempt to dissuade their wives from scriptural truth or conduct. So, with the above information is there any Scriptural way that could sustain the principle of authoritarian headship rather than the relationship being simply that of different roles for husbands and wives?

But What Does "Law of Her Husband" Mean?

According to the King James Version Romans 7:2 reads: "For the woman which hath an husband is bound by the law to her husband so long as he liveth; but if the husband be dead, she is loosed from the law of her husband." However, modern translations express this as:

- *"she is released from the law concerning the husband"* - NASB.
- *"she is released from the law of marriage"* - ESV and NIV.
- *"she is discharged from the obligations of the marriage-law"* – NEB.
- *"the laws of marriage no longer apply to her"* - NLT.

For this reason, just as a husband has obligations to his wife so, too, she has obligations to him. Indeed, this passage does not indicate that a husband has any right to make harsh and unreasonable rules for his wife that must be obeyed. This phrase in Romans 7:2 refers to the normal reasonable obligations in a marriage.

A Husband Must Love His Wife

In fact, Ephesians 5:21-24 is set in the context of the husband loving his wife as himself and sanctifying her as well as his being the source, like the head of a river, of necessary material, emotional and spiritual good things. Accordingly, the Apostle Paul explains that:

15

*"In the same way a husband **should love his wife** as his own body. He who loves his wife loves himself, because no one ever hated his own body, but rather he <u>nourishes it</u> and <u>cherishes it</u>. This is just the same as Messiah does for the community of believers ... 33In any case, each husband should love his wife as he loves himself"* (Eph. 5:28-29, 33a).

Although the Greek word used here for "love" is *agape* (self-sacrificing love), the most important facet of love for a wife is that of being shown affection. So, the admonition of "submitting to one another" shows that a husband should fulfil his wife's material, emotional and spiritual needs and take into account her concerns and wishes, rather than putting his selfish interests first (Phil. 2:3, 4). From this we can see that Christianity elevated women's position far above that of the general attitude of the time. However, over time male dominated Christian society has misused the Scriptures in the area of Bible mistranslation to put women in a secondary position. However, a correct translating of terms and phrases and an understanding of the culture of the time give us the picture that Jesus and the apostles would want us to live by.

From the above examination of the Scriptures, their language, and their background the best view of this issue shows that men and women are equal in God's eyes but have different, yet complementary, roles in all aspects of life and with the husband as "head"—he being a source of good things for his wife as well as taking priority over the direction in which the family unit should go, but in a considerate way. So, as pointed out earlier, the major factor in good marriage is simply that the couple truly love each other. This may take some amount of hard work because any two people will come from different backgrounds and some different ways of thinking. In his book *I, Isaak, Take Thee Rebekah: Moving from Romance to Lasting Love* Ravi Zacharias wrote:

"Love is a commitment that will be tested in the most vulnerable areas of spirituality, a commitment that will force you to make some very difficult choices. It is a commitment that demands that you deal with your lust, your greed, your pride, your power, your desire to control your temper, your patience, and every area of temptation that the Bible clearly talks about. It demands the quality of commitment that Jesus demonstrates in His relationship to us."

16

A Husband Is to Be Respected and Loved in Practical Ways by His Wife

As Jesus' emissary, the Apostle Paul gave several instructional statements concerning how a Christian wife was to view her husband and how she was to treat him. These are found in the letters Paul wrote to the Ephesians, the Colossians, and to Titus:

> *"Also be willingly submissive to each other out of reverence for Messiah—²²wives to your husbands as to the Lord. ... ²⁴But, just as the community of believers is willingly submissive to the Messiah, so also wives should be willingly submissive to their husbands in everything. ... ³³In any case, each husband should love his wife as he loves himself; and the wife should <u>respect her husband</u>" (Eph. 5:21, 22, 24, 33 KGV).*

Paul further said, *"Wives: continue willingly to be subject to your husbands, as is fitting in the Lord" (Col. 3:18 KGV).* And *"in this way they may show the younger women how to love their husbands and their children, and how to be self-controlled, virtuous, good homemakers, kind, and willingly submissive to their own husbands. This is so that the message of God may not be spoken of badly" (Titus 2:4-5 KGV).* In confirmation of the above instructions and guidance, the Apostle Peter later wrote similarly, but also included more details on the qualities of a Christian wife as well as giving the Hebrew Bible's example of Sarah and how she responded to Abraham as her husband:

> *"In the same way, you wives should willingly submit yourselves to your husbands. Even if some are not obedient to the message, they could be won over through your behaviour as wives, without any words being said, as they observe your pure and reverent lives. ...⁵In this same way the holy women of the past, who hoped in God, made themselves beautiful by willingly submitting to their husbands. Sarah obeyed Abraham, her husband, and called him her master. And you women are true daughters of Sarah if you always do what is right and don't fear any threats" (1 Pet. 3:1-2, 5-6 KGV).*

Adding to this biblical picture is the famous passage in Proverbs 31:10-31 which describes the wonderful qualities to be found in a

17

good wife such that any husband would be honoured to have such a loving and caring wife. All of these characteristics show that her love is something that finds its expressions in her actions. The passage really speaks for itself saying:

>""*Who can find a wife with a strong character? She is worth far more than jewels. Her husband trusts her with all his heart, and he does not lack anything good. She* <u>helps him</u> *and* <u>never harms him</u> *all the days of her life. "She seeks out wool and linen with care and works with willing hands. She is like merchant ships. She brings her food from far away. She wakes up while it is still dark and gives food to her family and portions of food to her female slaves. "She picks out a field and buys it. She plants a vineyard from the profits she has earned. She puts on strength like a belt and goes to work with energy. She sees that she is making a good profit. Her lamp burns late at night. "She puts her hands on the distaff, and her fingers hold a spindle. She opens her hands to oppressed people and stretches them out to needy people. She does not fear for her family when it snows because her whole family has a double layer of clothing. She makes quilts for herself. Her clothes are made of linen and purple cloth.*
>
>*"Her husband is known at the city gates when he sits with the leaders of the land. "She makes linen garments and sells them and delivers belts to the merchants. She dresses with strength and nobility, and she smiles at the future. "She speaks with wisdom, and on her tongue there is tender instruction. She keeps a close eye on the conduct of her family, and she does not eat the bread of idleness. Her children and her husband stand up and bless her. In addition, he sings her praises, by saying, 'Many women have done noble work, but you have surpassed them all!' "Charm is deceptive, and beauty evaporates, but a woman who has the fear of the* LORD *should be praised. Reward her for what she has done, and let her achievements praise her at the city gates""* (GWT).

Of course, all of these activities are in a relatively primitive setting of around 2,800 years ago, but the principles set out above apply equally well to today in terms of the modern-day activities a wife would engage in. Certainly, the passage shows how the truly godly wife will demonstrate her love for her family in many practical ways.

Loving Submission in Making Decisions Together

Almost every day Husbands and wives need to make decisions about certain things, that is, they should decide the best thing to do in any particular situation. For example, what if it is a matter of choosing where to live—a new home? There should be agreement on the top price to pay, on what size of house is needed, and on many other factors. This is where submitting i.e., deferring where possible to one another comes into play and so the couple are able to grow together as husband and wife as they come to these decisions. However, when there are problems in arriving at a particular decision that's when it is time to be praying together over the particular matter to seek God's guidance. But if there is still some uncertainty in one partner's mind, but the other is more certain then one could submit to the other as Abraham submitted to Sarah, his wife regarding the divorcing of Hagar (Gen. 21:12).

Ultimately, all, including those who are married, should pray as Paul did, asking:

> "...may the God of **peace** Himself cause you to become completely dedicated to Him. May **y**our spirit, soul, and body be preserved entirely blameless at the royal coming of our Lord Jesus the Messiah" (1 Thess. 5:23).

There really is no true marriage without peace, they go hand-in-hand, so that peace must rule any married couple. However, it must be worked at and with each spouse doing their part.

On a lighter note, Albert Einstein once commented on marriage that, "Men marry women with the hope they will never change. Women marry men with the hope they will change. Invariably they are both disappointed." So, along with lovingly submitting to one another and working toward peace, how else does one keep a marriage in good shape?

§

19

4

The Basics for Maintaining a Good Marriage

Firstly, I must say that I am not a marriage counsellor and, like many others, in my earlier life I failed on some of the basics in maintaining a good marriage. Nevertheless, it "takes two to tango" and so generally, although not always, both parties to a marriage can be at fault to varying degrees. However, there are some basic principles and advice that we might consider in making for a good marriage and in solving the various problems that arise in marriage. Nevertheless, marriage is not an easy road and requires significant investment of time, energy, and thoughtfulness. Certainly, all that was said in the first three chapters in this book on headship, submissiveness, love, and respect, as based on the Scriptures, must be vital factors toward a good marriage.

Love Is Foundational for a Good Marriage

So, now we will note just how big a part true love is foundational for a great marriage, rather than just a functioning marriage. Interestingly, in the ancient Greek language there were four different words for "love" representing four different kinds of love. Three of these come from the overlapping Greek words of—*agape, phileo*, and *storge*—with *agape* and *phileo* being used in the New Testament, but minimally interchangeable. The fourth word—*eros*, although not appearing in the Bible is, nevertheless, also essential in a marriage. So just how does the application of these four aspects of love actually work toward building and maintaining a great marriage?

Agape: As used in the New Testament is godly <u>unconditional, self-sacrificing love</u> shown to a person. It encompasses the mind, the will, and the emotions in its unselfishness. It continues despite the faults and shortcomings of that person, even if one does not like him or her. This is the primary love that our heavenly Father shows, as the Apostle Paul stated that, *"God confirms His love (Gk agape) for* us by the fact that the Messiah died in place of us while we were sinners" (Rom. 5:8).

Phileo: This is the showing of <u>tender affection</u> toward one's partner or friend. This kind of love is because of the good qualities one sees in the other person that draws you to be their friend. In fact, *"The Father loves (Gk phileo) the Son" (John 5:20)* i.e. has tender affection for him. Similarly, for Christians as Jesus stated that, *"the Father Himself loves (Gk phileo) you! He loves (Gk phileo) you because you have loved (Gk phileo) me, and have believed that I came from God" (John 16:27)*. Certainly, God wants husbands and wives to show this kind of tender affection for each other as well as to apply *agape* love for each other by overlooking each other's faults and shortcomings.

Storge: This is not just one's feelings from the heart, but is a physical show of affection e.g., a hug, a kiss, or another expression of genuine affection.

Eros: This is physical love that brings about the fulfilment of one's sexual desire that a husband and wife have for each other. Although the word is not used in the Bible the idea of it is demonstrated in the Song of Solomon.

So, in a marriage all four types of love are important for it to be a complete marriage. Because a marriage relationship is built over a lifetime these kinds of love must be continually worked at so that both partners may feel fulfilled and that the marriage can cope with all of the vicissitudes of life. Indeed, if there is failure in any one of these kinds of love the marriage will begin to drift onto shaky ground. For example, if *agape* love diminishes, then selfishness will come to the fore in the relationship. If *phileo* love diminishes then friendship and its expression in *storge* love will fade. If *storge* love diminishes then an imbalance in the sexual relationship may develop with passion only occurring when sex is involved or the sexual relationship becomes just a matter of duty. With age comes a natural diminishing of *eros* love in terms of physical ability, but this should never diminish in terms of desire for one's partner. Helpfully, the magazine *Focus on the Family* provided a wonderful internet article on maintaining a good marriage by suggesting that, "If you think of marriage as a house, there are four kinds of love that can be thought of as representing the basic components of the structure. **If one of these components is missing, the house is incomplete.**

First, there's **unconditional love**. This is *the foundation* of the house. It's the kind of love that gives without expecting anything in return. It's the agape love of the New Testament writers (see 1 Corinthians 13), the self-sacrificial love that Christ demonstrated on the cross. When a realtor writes a house listing, he rarely comments on the quality of the foundation. But that's the first place a home inspector looks when assessing the longevity of the dwelling. This "in spite of" love is urged upon us in Ephesians 5:25, where the apostle Paul writes, "Husbands, love (Greek *agapate*) your wives, just as Christ loved the church." This provides the stability needed for a lasting covenant.

- *The frame* of the house can be compared to **companionship love**. Open communication, shared activities, laughter, and even tears provide the structured living space within which a couple's love can be nurtured and grow. It's significant that the most happily married couples usually describe themselves as "best friends." In the same way, the passionate bride in Song of Solomon refers to her husband not only as "my lover" but as "my friend" *(Song of Solomon 5:16).*

- Once the foundation and frame of the house are in place, *the roof* has something to rest upon. The roof represents **romantic love** because this kind of love is a "peak" experience. It's supported by the first two loves; without them it has no way to sustain itself. Romantic love is a direct response to and celebration of the qualities of the loved one – beauty, charm, strength, tenderness. It's characterized by the emotional excitement expressed by the bride in Song of Solomon 2:5—"I am faint with love." It gleams in the sunlight at the top of the house. But it can't stand alone. On the contrary, basing a marriage on romantic love by itself would be like unloading a pile of shingles on an empty lot and calling it a house. And to junk the house simply because the roof leaks would be foolish. The proper thing to do in that situation is to make the necessary repairs.

- When the roof is on and the house is finished, *the furniture* can be brought in to decorate the house and make it luxurious. The furniture symbolizes **sexual love**—the physical union between husband and husband and wife that is consummated only after the marriage has been sealed. This love is praised and exalted in Proverbs 5:19, where the writer urges a young man to "rejoice in the wife of his youth": "As a loving deer and a graceful doe, let her breasts satisfy you at all times; and always be enraptured with her love."

If romance has faded in your marriage, put it in perspective. By all means, work at renewing it. Set aside a regular date night so that you can spend more time together, even if it means paying a babysitter. Write a love letter to your husband. Buy your wife a rose. Be creative in the ways you show affection to each other. But remember that God's design for your marriage includes all four loves, each in its proper place. Don't damage your house by expecting the roof to support more weight than it's designed to bear."

The following are the most wonderful of biblical descriptions of how real love works for all, but in particular for a married couple:

> "*Love is patient; love is kind. Love isn't envious or boastful or arrogant; it doesn't behave shamefully or insist on its own way. It is never easily provoked to anger and it **never bears a grudge**. Love doesn't take pleasure in injustice, but is thrilled with the truth. It bears everything, believes everything, hopes everything—endures everything*" (1 Cor. 13:3-7).

Later Paul added that Christians should:

> "*...serve each other through love; because the entire law can be summed up in a single statement, namely, "You must love your neighbour as yourself" (Lev. 19:18). But if you continue to bite and devour each other, watch out that you're not annihilated by each other*" (Gal. 5:13-15).

All of this also involves the showing of affection which the couple show through their words, loving glances, holding hands in public or even across a restaurant table. Indeed, there are many Bible texts that are applicable to all Christians, but which are most applicable to the relationship that is our closest, namely, our marriage partner. For instance, all Christians should, *"constantly pursue covenant justice: godliness, faithfulness, love, endurance, and meekness" (1 Tim. 6:11)*.

Further Factors in Maintaining a Good Marriage

As just highlighted, for a marriage to work well there must be friendship where there is a sharing of similar interests and beliefs. This will keep the couple connected in spending quality time together involving regular significant conversation and laughter together. And finally, the disciple James says that we should, *"practice confessing [our] deliberate offences to each other, and praying for each other" (Jas 5:16)*. This involves more than just saying sorry, but actually taking responsibility for our failures. As one commentator stated on their personal relationship in marriage:

> We have learned to confess to one another, to take ownership and responsibility of our sins, flaws, and weaknesses, and to apologize specifically for how we have hurt each other. As humbling as this can be, confession has brought an intimacy between us that is far greater than any prideful "rightness" could ever bring. We've learned to confess to one another, and then to forgive one another.

Furthermore, the husband's significant role in the marriage is that of developing unity in the relationship. If he fails to do his part, failure of the marriage becomes possible, even likely. As the loving head of the household, a great responsibility is placed upon him by God to show self-sacrificing love to his wife just as Jesus did to his wife—the congregation of believers (Eph. 5:23-28). Indeed, the primary needs of each partner differ, so that, the primary needs of the husband are those of companionship and respect, but those are not the primary needs of the wife, which are those of love and affection. So, there is great danger of each partner neglecting these needs of the other. The biblical solution to this problem is that the husband must lead in showing love and affection. Indeed, he must be prepared to sacrifice his primary needs to be able to satisfy those of his wife. This will draw her toward sacrificing her primary needs to satisfy his i.e., it becomes a very "giving" relationship with the result that both partners' needs are satisfied and there is unity between them. Also, if there are children in the family, they too will experience this unity and feel that self-sacrificing love.

KEEPING GOD IN THE MARRIAGE

However, if there is tension in the marriage husbands are told to, "*love your wives, and stop being bitterly harsh with them*" *(Col. 3:19)*. Yet, the reverse is a great problem for husbands when it is the wife who is quarrelsome. Indeed, for him it is, "*better to live in a desert, than with a quarreling and angry woman*" *(Prov. 21:19)*. Yet, for both partners they should "*not let the sun go down while [they] are still angry*" *(Eph. 4:26)*. Whatever the issues are they, "*should be kind to each other, compassionate, forgiving one another as God, through Messiah, forgave you*" *(Eph. 4:32)*.

If, however, there is a breakdown in communication then both partners should, follow James' counsel that, "*if any one of you falls short in wisdom, let them ask God, and it will be given to them*" *(Jas 1:5)* and that one should be, "*forgetting the past and straining forward toward what is ahead*" *(Phil. 3:13)*. Also, if there is fault-finding between the partners then Jesus humorously puts things in perspective when he asks, "*Why do you keep focusing on the speck of saw-dust in your brother's or sister's eye, but then overlook the beam of wood in your own eye?*" *(Matt. 7:3)*.

Of course, there is much more that could be said about good marriage and there is a vast array of helpful books available. Indeed, a harmonious marriage is a wonderful thing. But what should be done when that wonderful experience begins to have seriously bad things happening in it? What should be done after all attempts at reconciliation have failed? As referred to earlier, biblically it is the significant and perpetual breaking of the marriage vows that is the real sin which may well lead to a divorcing of one partner from the other.

Balance Concerning the Marriage Institution

Throughout much of church history, most Christian denominations have taken the position that the institution of marriage is more important than the couples who make up the marriage. In the Bible, God is never shown to take that position. God loves people more than He loves institutions. In fact, any marriage is only as good as the couples who make up their marriage, just as the nation of Israel was only as good as the people who made up that nation at any one time. When the people were courageous for doing what was right their nation was strong. Similarly, with a marriage! Indeed, most denominations and many married couples have often displayed a misplaced emphasis on the marriage institution to the exclusion of those who are in the marriage i.e., they care more about the marriage than the state of the relationship between the couple. Certainly, if one must choose, it is more important to save the people in the marriage than the marriage itself. If Christians don't do that then they have failed to see the very purpose of the marriage institution. Evidently, the horrendous shunning of divorcees does not come from God!

PART TWO

Background to Divorce

5

The Biblical Terms for Divorce
and Its Grounds

The Terms Used Concerning Divorce in Bible Times

From the various Hebrew-English lexicons and Greek-English lexicons we find that there are a variety of terms used for divorce:

THE HEBREW TERMS
Shalach, (salah) has the basic meaning of "sending away" or "putting away" and is rendered so in the LXX, the KJV, the ASV, Young's Literal, and several other older translations.

K'rithuth occurs only four times in the Hebrew Scriptures. Each time it is part of the phrase "certificate of divorce" (Deut. 24:1, 3; Isa. 50:1; Jer. 3:8). It means "cut off" as if dead to the former spouse. Therefore, <u>divorce, as a punishment, became a substitute for the death penalty</u> in cases of adultery.

THE GREEK TERMS
Apoluo . The basic meaning is "to send away, dismiss, divorce."
Chorizo. This was a well-used verb for divorce in a divorce context with the basic sense of "to separate."
Aphemie. The basic sense is "to release."
Apostasion. This was the nearest Greek word to describe the Hebrew *k'rithuth*, and which the lexicons show to involve relinquishment, abandonment, and giving up of one's claim i.e., a notice of divorce, commonly called **a certificate of divorce**.

All such terms could refer to **legitimate divorce**, but they could also refer **to unjust/treacherous divorce and so be invalid** as divorce in God's eyes. Such unjust divorce would leave neither party legitimately free to remarry. Additionally, in early Greek civilization there were some fifty words used for representing the concept of divorce.

Biblical Law on Sexual Adultery

The first obvious command against adultery can be found in the Ten Commandments (Ex. 20:14). Next, we find the law that if a man "... *commits adultery with the wife of his neighbour...both the adulterer and the adulteress shall surely be put to death" (Lev. 20:10 ESV. Also Deut. 22:22-24).* Nevertheless, it appears that the death penalty for adultery was rarely carried out because of the requirement for two or three witnesses to adultery—a situation that was virtually impossible. So, divorce became the solution to this, thereby completing the "death of the marriage."

THE PENALTY FOR ADULTERY IN LATER TIMES

The Greek term for adultery is *moichia* as meaning "to commit adultery" for which the original penalty had been death. However, only a woman could have been accused of committing adultery unless a man did so with a married woman. But in later centuries, in cases of adultery, some of the rabbis may have applied the quality of mercy in imitation of God's example in Hosea. In fact, the records show that in the early first century the Shammaite and Hillelite rabbis viewed divorce, rather than the death penalty, as being the consequence of and punishment for committing adultery. This however, does not preclude that the death penalty for adultery may rarely have been carried out officially, at least, until the beginning of the first century when the Romans took over administration of Palestine and possibly even up to 30 C.E (T.B. Sanhedrin 41a).

If John 8:1-11, concerning the adulterous woman, is definitely part of the inspired record, then the event of the bringing of her to Jesus was staged by the Law teachers to trap him. Rather than actually stoning this woman, which they were not allowed to do by Roman law, they brought her to Jesus (John 18:31). So, the trap for him was that if he had said that she should be executed by them then he would have run into trouble with the Roman authorities. If, on the other hand, he had said that she should not be executed he would have been accused of failing to support the Mosaic Law as stated in **Leviticus 20:10.** But Jesus' very cleaver answer to these people of, *"the person here who is sinless should be the first one to throw a stone at her"* completely dealt with this situation and destroyed their trap. Nevertheless, **this event shows that Jesus was not insistent upon the death penalty** for an adulteress because no potential executioner was free from sin, but rather the woman was to *"sin no more."*

Many words in the New Testament have both a literal and a metaphorical usage. This usage originally referred to Israel's **breach of covenant** with God because of her idolatry in the sense of adulterating her relationship with God. Later, Jesus used the term metaphorically as referring to **non-sexual** "adultery." For example, in Matthew 12:39 Jesus declares the people to be, *"an evil and* **adulterous** *[Gk moichalis] generation [that] seeks for a sign,"* but they were not literally sexually adulterous. So, in the circumstances of divorce this usage referred to a person's unfaithfulness or breach of their marriage covenant thereby adulterating it i.e., adding something to it to make the relationship of poorer quality.

Divorce - a Solution Invented by God

As we endeavour to understand the subject of divorce, we will get a great amount of understanding from the Old Testament (the Hebrew Scriptures) statements on this subject. So, we should not discount what is said in this major section of the Bible for the reason that, *"all Scripture (i.e., the Hebrew Bible) is breathed by God" (2 Tim. 3:16).* So, when we read the passages in the Hebrew Scriptures concerning divorce as stated in Deuteronomy 24:1-4 and Exodus 21:10-11 and other passages, we must realize that divorce and its arrangements to give freedom to a seriously wronged person come from God—these are His thoughts and so showing that He invented the concept of divorce to rescue such a person in a very bad marriage. This arrangement for Israel included the loving provision of the giving of a **"certificate of divorce"** to a divorced wife to allow her the right to remarry.

THE IMPORTANCE OF DIVORCE

Although it is a priority to save any marriage, yet when it goes seriously wrong and, over a significant period of time all attempts to fix it have failed, then the choice for each party in the marriage is to either live in an intolerable and damaging situation or to divorce. This is rather like finding out that one has gangrene and having the choice to lose the gangrenous limb or to lose one's life. The sensible

31

choice is obvious! So, too, with the surgical operation of divorce! Even though that procedure is very painful it may be necessary for the preservation of the spiritual life (or even the physical life) of, at least, one of those partners.

§

6

The Issues and Problems in Understanding Biblical Divorce

As shown in the preface to this book there is no such thing as a truly "orthodox" understanding of the biblical grounds for divorce. So now we must begin to look at all the issues and difficulties involved in this controversial subject. Indeed, the subject of Bible-based divorce and remarriage is the most complex of Christian ethical issues. As we shall see this subject is not a matter of turning to one or two Bible passages and thinking that one has the complete answer concerning what grounds there should be, if any, regarding divorce for Christians—simplistic answers are absolutely inadequate! For this reason, I have presented a large amount of scriptural and background information, so that in later chapters we will see what Jesus meant in context on this subject, and several further chapters will show what the Apostle Paul meant in context on this subject. In fact, there are, within the Christian world, a number of different positions taken in regard to divorce and remarriage, most of which can lead to a great amount of suffering for at least one of the parties to a bad marriage. The main positions are:

1. No divorce and no remarriage.

This is the Roman Catholic position, but which opts for a policy of annulment only, as if the marriage never took place. A few other denominations and cults take this position. This was also originally the policy within Anglicanism.

2. Divorce, but no remarriage.
   a) On the grounds of adultery only.
   b) On the grounds of **adultery** or **desertion** by an unbeliever.
   A diminishing number of Bible scholars take these positions.

3. Divorce followed by remarriage for the innocent party (and sometimes for the repentant guilty party).
   a) On the grounds of adultery only.
   b) On the grounds of adultery or desertion by an unbeliever.
   Many Bible scholars and churches take these positions.

4. Divorce followed by remarriage for both the innocent party and the guilty party if repentant.

On the grounds of:

Adultery. Or

Desertion by an unbeliever or an unrepentant believer being treated as an "unbeliever." Or

Persistent and significant **marital neglect or abuse**

A small, but growing, number of Bible scholars and churches take this position.

5. Divorce followed by remarriage for both the innocent party and the guilty party on any grounds. This is the "no fault" divorce position taken by very few churches.

~

As a result of the above facts, it is very evident that the picture in the various denominations concerning divorce and remarriage is very uncertain, confused and clouded. This is generally because of tradition based on many misunderstandings of Jesus' and Paul's words on the subject as well as a failure to examine the context involving the Hebrew Scripture background.

Misunderstanding of the Subject from the Second Century

Emeritus professor James Dunn notes that:

> "The first task of exegesis [explaining the Bible] is to penetrate as far as possible inside the historical context(s) of the author and of those for whom he wrote. So much of this involves the taken-for-granteds of both author and addressees. Where a modern reader is unaware of (or unsympathetic to) these shared assumptions and concerns it will be impossible to hear the text as the author intended it to be heard (and assumed it would be heard). In this case, a major part of that context is the self-understanding of Jews and Judaism in the first century and of Gentiles sympathetic to Judaism. **Since most of Christian history and scholarship, regrettably, this has been unsympathetic to that self-understanding, if not downright hostile to it, a proper appreciation of Paul in his interaction with that self-understanding has been virtually impossible."**
>
> *Romans 1-8, Word Biblical Commentary,* pp. xiv, xv.

Therefore, if we are to gain a complete understanding of the various Christian Scripture statements concerning divorce and remarriage it is necessary to understand the background knowledge and assumptions of a first-century reader. Sadly, this background had already been forgotten by the second century because:

1. Early Jewish Christians were either expelled from the synagogues or formed their own house churches and so later generations became less aware of relevant Jewish teaching, especially concerning the ongoing debate on divorce by the two main groups of rabbis at that time—the Hillelites and the Shammaites (see later).

2. The destruction of Jerusalem and its temple system in A.D. 70 meant that later there were no Shammaite rabbis around whose teachings were a little closer to those of Jesus on marital matters.

3. The second century Christian Congregation was largely comprised of Gentiles who also were unaware of Jewish issues concerning divorce.

4. Only the Jewish Hillelite 'for any cause' type of divorce was known to the Christians. They rejected this because they knew that it contradicted their narrow understanding of the teachings of Jesus on divorce/remarriage.

5. The Hebrew Scriptures were essential for a correct understanding of Jesus' and Paul's statements on divorce. However, there was a mindset of rejection of the Hebrew Scriptures on the part of some early Christian groups—the most heretical being the Marcionites who accepted only the Sermon on the Mount; an edited version of the Gospel of Luke, with its Jewish elements removed; and the Pauline letters.

6. The "taken-for-granteds," the exceptions, and the hyperbole in places were not fully noted by these Gentile Christians.

This situation meant that the Early Church Fathers misunderstood the texts of the Christian Scriptures concerning divorce and remarriage; and for this reason, they taught variously that either:

35

- There could be divorce only for the adultery committed by a marriage partner, or,

- There could be **no divorce or remarriage for a Christian at all**, or,

- That only with the death of their spouse could any Christian remarry.

The following chapters will attempt to demonstrate that, although the emphasis of the holy Scriptures is against divorce, there are four basic grounds whereby a divorce may scripturally take place, after which there can be remarriage.

The Basis for Better Understanding

If we read the New Testament texts through the eyes of Church tradition or of a modern reader, we will come to different conclusions about divorce than if we read these texts **in a culturally sensitive way**. So, because the inspired Scriptures were mainly not dictated, one has to attempt to understand the mindset of the people of the time if one is to grasp the meaning of what they said and wrote. In recent decades there has been rigorous historically contextual biblical research to correct the misunderstandings of the past. Nevertheless, one major statement that must be made before going any further is that: divorce must be **the absolutely last resort**. Every possibility must be made by the couple to save their marriage! Nevertheless, to say that divorce is a bad thing is rather simplistic and does not take account of the harsh and painful realities involved when marriage goes wrong.

However, before examining the results of this biblical and background research it is necessary to look at the subject of marriage and divorce from the perspective of the Mosaic Law, Jesus' view of it, and later the description of God's metaphorical marital relationship with Israel/Judah as described by the Prophets.

§

7

Did Jesus Make the Mosaic Law of No Value?

Readers on the subject of divorce may wonder why, in Chapters 5 and 6, there was mention made of the Mosaic Law when God had, *"erased the written record of debt that stood against us with its legal regulations. He took it away by nailing it to the cross" (Col. 2:14).* This means that God's people are no longer under the regulations of the Mosaic law (Rom. 7:6; 1 Cor. 9:20; Gal. 3:24-25; Heb. 7:18; 8:13). Certainly, the Apostle Paul directly said, *"I am not under the law" (1 Cor. 9:20).* Furthermore, Jesus' authority has superseded that of Moses as shown in Hebrews 3:5-6 where it states that, *"Moses was faithful in [God's] entire house as a servant...but Messiah is faithful over God's house as a son."*

As we consider the question of whether or not the Mosaic Law has any bearing on the subject of divorce for Christians we first of all realize that Jesus was *"born under law" (Gal. 4:4),* and after the age of twelve, he became "a son of the Law," and so continued under that law fully obedient to his parents (Luke 2:51-52). Nevertheless, after his receiving of God's spirit at his baptism he was outwardly recognized by God as being His Son, i.e., the Messiah for Israel and the rest of the world, he clearly superseded Moses in authority and teaching and indicated that the legal regulations of the Mosaic Law were to be replaced. Evidence for this can be seen in the following biblical examples:

1) In regard to the Mosaic food laws Jesus declared that, *"There's nothing outside of a person that can contaminate them by entering into them. Rather, it's what comes out from a person that contaminates them" (Mark 7:15)* and then the text informs us that, *"in saying this he declared every kind of food clean" (Mark 7:19).* However, we must remember that the principle to be taken from such food laws was that of the 'purity' of God's people and Jesus certainly was not abolishing that principle. Indeed, Jesus' statement here does not change the fact that all the Bible's ethical teachings are grounded in the Hebrew Scriptures.

37

2) John 8:3-11 records the event when the scribes and Pharisees brought a woman caught in adultery to Jesus to see if he would condemn her to death by stoning according to the regulation stated in Deuteronomy 22:22, although there is no recorded case of this being implemented. In fact, Jesus does not condemn her, but simply tells her to "sin no more" while indicating that the scribes and Pharisees were just as much sinners as she was!

3) Jesus also made the claim to the Jews that he was the temple, which was another way of saying that he has now superseded Moses and therefore, the Mosaic Law in regard to the sacrificial system.

So, along with his correction of the Jewish religious leaders concerning their regulation-based approach to the keeping of the Sabbath, rather than applying its spirit, the above details show that Jesus was attempting to correct the Jews for their failure to apply **the spirit of the law** as well as his start on moving the Jews away from their being supervised by the regulations of the law of Moses (a form of immaturity) and toward maturity which concerns living by God's spirit and so requiring faith, rather than legal regulations. In all of these actions and teachings of Jesus we find that he was paving the way—transitioning—toward the placing of God's people into the New Covenant arrangement which was to be initiated by his death.

Jesus' Approach to the Mosaic Law

It is certainly evident that, during his ministry, Jesus highly valued the regulations of the entire Mosaic law along with its spirit and the principles contained within it. In fact, he used all of these in countering the wrong views of the religious leaders. One example is recorded in Matthew 15:3-6 where he quotes from the Mosaic law in Exodus 20:12 and 21:17 and shows that these statements are "God's commandment" and that the religious leaders had *"nullified God's word for the sake of their tradition."* He even told a certain Jew to *"practice keeping the commandments"* and then he lists several of these from the Ten Commandments (Matt. 19:17-19). Certainly, Jesus never ignored or denigrated the Mosaic Law or played off one Scripture against another when commenting on issues or in debating with the religious leaders. So, it is clear that Jesus had no

38

intention of destroying the *torah*, at least, in terms of its original meaning of divine instruction and guidance. This is as he said during his Sermon on the Mount:

> *"Don't think that I have come to destroy the Law or the Prophets. I haven't come to destroy, but to show them in their fullness (or "fulfil them"). [18]I can assure you: until sky and land pass away, not one dot or one stroke of a letter will pass from the Law until everything has happened. [19]So anyone who rejects one of the least of these commands, and teaches others to do the same will be called least in the Kingdom of Heaven. But anyone who practices them and teaches others to do so will be called great in the Kingdom of Heaven. [20]That's why I tell you: unless your covenant faithfulness goes beyond that of the experts on Jewish teachings and the Pharisees, you will never get into the Kingdom of Heaven"*
> (Matt. 5:17-20).

Throughout the Sermon on the Mount Jesus was correcting the failure of the religious leaders to apply the Mosaic law correctly— that is to apply it to the inner person. He used divine wisdom to discern the essential meaning of each relevant law i.e., its spirit and so to draw out the personal moral implications from each law. In fact, even after his resurrection, when the "legal code" of regulations had been taken away by its being nailed to the cross (Col. 2:14) Jesus spoke respectfully of Moses' teachings. Luke tells us, *"So beginning with Moses and all the prophets, [Jesus] explained to them the things written about himself in all the Scriptures"* (Luke 24:27). These are the same Scriptures of which the Apostle Paul says are, *"all...breathed out by God and profitable for teaching, for reproof, and training in righteousness..."* Certainly, in Matthew 5:17-20 Jesus explicitly said that he did not intend to abrogate the law i.e., to rescind or annul it.

Paul's View of the Law

Although the Apostle Paul directly said, *"I am not under the law"* (1 Cor. 9:20) as just noted, this does not mean that he did not value the Mosaic law as the *"all scripture breathed by God."* In fact, in its deeper principles and true meaning he rated it as *"holy...and good"* (Rom. 7:12) and asked, *"Does that mean faith in God does away with the law? Of course not! In fact, we are affirming and fulfilling the* law" *(Rom. 3:31 OGOM Translation)* or more literally, *"Do we then nullify the Law through faith? May it never be! On the contrary, we establish the Law"* (NASB). So, certainly there is no repealing of the principles, truths, and deeper meaning of the law on the issues it deals with, even though its regulations have been superseded. Otherwise, the Sermon on the Mount would be useless to us and we may as well never read the details of the law again! In fact, anyone who promotes the idea that Christians must not reference the Mosaic law at all is sliding dangerously close to heretical Marcionism of the first century.

APPLICATION FOR THE CHRISTIAN
The Apostle Paul stated that:

> *"In fact, whatever things that were written beforehand were written for our instruction, so that through patient endurance, and through the encouragement of the Scriptures, we can maintain our hope"* (Rom. 15:4).

Although not under the regulations of the Law, Christians should live by **the spirit and learn from the principles of the Mosaic Law** just as Jesus showed in the Sermon on the Mount. The fact is that Jesus wants his disciples to do better than the regulation-keeping religious leaders in regard to the Mosaic law, which is why he said, *"unless your righteousness exceeds that of the scribes and Pharisees, you will never enter the Kingdom of Heaven"* (Matt. 5:20 ESV). So, from Jesus' example in the Sermon on the Mount it is evident that the Christian should take the law of Moses seriously in discerning the moral principles which underlie each text and then apply the relevant principle to the various situations in life. For example, take Moses' words in Deuteronomy 22:8 that, *"whenever you build a new house, put a railing around the edge of the roof. Then you won't be responsible for a death at your home if someone falls off the roof"* (GWT). So, bearing in mind that this speaks of the flat roofs of the day in Israel we can see that the principle the Christian would take from this text, in our modern-day setting, is that of making anything that one is responsible for safe in all respects for anyone who might enter our property e.g., one's car—this is an act of love toward one's fellow-man. This same biblical approach helps Christians with their understanding of the subject of divorce and remarriage and which

40

comes in the form of the principles and truths drawn from the case law as presented primarily in Deuteronomy 24:1-4 and Exodus 21:10-11, although there are other relevant passages on this subject. So, Christians are to discern the principles applicable to divorce and remarriage as much today as in Hebrew Scripture times just as Paul indicated in 2 Timothy 3:16.

SHOWING LOVE FULFILS THE LAW
Indeed, *"love is the fulfilment of the law"* *(Rom. 13:10)* and so, all Christians should be demonstrating love to those who have had the misfortune to have been divorced for no good reason or have had to divorce their partner because of their sexual immorality or other seriously bad actions (see later). Christian sympathy and empathy should be demonstrated to these ones in the same way as toward those who are bereaved because they are now widowed (see later).

God Does Not Change His Moral Standard

Certainly, Jesus made **no radical reversal to the ethics or morality** of the Hebrew Scriptures, as if God changes on what is correct morality. However, Jesus did correct the numerous misinterpretations of the Scriptures by the religious authorities of the time. In fact, through Moses, Jesus, and Paul, God was regulating divorce rather than forbidding it because he recognized that divorce may be necessary at times e.g., when there has been sexual immorality, but the injustices to wives also had to be stopped. However, if the principles, which are higher than laws, were changed in Jesus' time, then it would suggest that marriage or humanity had changed significantly; but obviously this is not the case. So, we cannot simply discount the principles given by Moses or discount the spirit of that law when we are analysing Jesus' quotations from Leviticus and Genesis as noted in Mathew 5:31-32 and 19:4-6, 8 and then conclude that Moses' words were simply a **temporary permission for all divorce.** The fact is that there is **no contradiction between the Old Testament and the New Testament** on the principles involved in marital standards and in being against hard-hearted divorce. Furthermore, in analysing these matters, we must take note of the principles by which interpreters understand biblical issues. These are as Professor James Dunn and others show that this means that the Scriptures should be read

41

through the filters of the language and the culture to which it was first addressed. This means that the primary meaning is the plain sense, as it would be understood by an ordinary person in the culture for which it was written.

Certainly, there are further factors to be analysed concerning Matthew 19:4-6, 8 where Jesus referenced the Scriptures taken from Genesis and his statements in 19:8b. These will be examined in detail in later. So, because of the relevance of the principles and great truths contained in the Mosaic Law to this subject we will now examine the details of the various case laws concerning marriage and divorce and note the background to Jesus' statements and the principles that can be gleaned from them. This is especially true of details found in Deuteronomy 24:1-4 as involved in the debate Jesus had with the religious leaders (Matt. 19:1-12; Mark 10:2-12. However, we will firstly note a couple of situations set out in the Mosaic law where God did actually remove the right to divorce. This shows that divorce was the norm whenever there was a valid reason for a marriage to end. (Please see my book: *The Veil Removed by Turning to Christ*).

8

Mosaic Case Law Concerning Divorce

The Cases Where the Mosaic Law
Did Not Allow for Divorce

There are just two hypothetical situations described in the Mosaic Law whereby a man was not allowed to divorce his wife. This shows that divorce was a regulated, but fully accepted part of life in Israel. The first situation was when a husband claimed that his new wife was not a virgin when, in fact, she was proved to be a virgin. The passage states that:

> "If a man takes a wife and, after lying with her, dislikes her and slanders her and gives her a bad name, saying, 'I married this woman, but when I approached her, I did not find proof of her virginity,' then the girl's father and mother shall bring proof that she was a virgin to the town elders at the gate. The girl's father will say to the elders, 'I gave my daughter in marriage to this man, but he dislikes her. Now he has slandered her and said, 'I did not find your daughter to be a virgin.' But here is the **proof of my daughter's virginity.**' Then her parents shall display the cloth before the elders of the town, and the elders shall take the man and punish him. They shall fine him a hundred shekels of silver and give them to the girl's father, because this man has given an Israelite virgin a bad name. She shall continue to be his wife; he **must not divorce** [lit. dismiss] **her as long as he lives**"
>
> (Deut. 22:13-19).

The second situation was when a man had sex with a single woman who was a virgin. The passage states that:

> "If a man happens to meet a virgin who is not pledged to be married and rapes her and they are discovered, he shall pay the girl's father fifty shekels of silver. He must marry the girl, for he has violated her. **He can never divorce her as long as he lives**"
>
> (Deut. 22:28, 29).

Here it is shown that this man must pay a fine, namely, the dowry of a bride to her family, and that by his having sex with her he has

43

taken her as his wife and can never divorce her. However, this was to be only with her father's consent (Ex. 22:17). These two cases clearly imply that divorce was not forbidden under the law in Israel in normal circumstances and it follows that, under those circumstances, such persons may remarry and, in fact, were encouraged to remarry to fulfil the Genesis 1:28 mandate to multiply.

Case Law for Marriage and Divorce

Case law, in contrast to statute law, means that the principles from a case or series of cases are more important than the details. So, any particular case may establish a legal principle for judging new cases that share something in common with it. Therefore, the teachers in Israel, in studying the Mosaic Law, used the exegetical rule called *qol vahomer*. This showed that: "if this is true, then surely this is also true." So, when applied to divorce this meant that if *a slave wife* has the rights stated in certain places in the Law, then surely *a free wife* would have, at the very least, the equivalent rights. As an example, in 1 Corinthians 9:8-11 the apostle Paul uses this exegetical rule when he says:

> *"Do I say these things from a mere human perspective? Doesn't the law also say this? Yes, it's written in the law of Moses, "You must not muzzle an ox while it is treading out the grain" [Deut. 25:4]. Surely God isn't just concerned about oxen, is He? Rather, isn't He speaking entirely for our benefit? Yes, He is—it was written for our sake, because the one ploughing and the one threshing should work in hope of sharing in the crop. If we've sown spiritual things among you, is it too much if we reap some material support from you?"*

This is called an *a fortiori* argument; that is an argument from the lesser to the greater. If God cares for animals He cares at least as much for slaves. So, *"When a man strikes the eye of his slave, male or female, and destroys it, he shall let the slave go free because of his eye" (Ex. 21:26 ESV).* Certainly, if God cares that slaves are not abused, then He cares at least as much that free persons are not abused. Indeed, if the one-flesh wife of a slave status (i.e., a concubine) has certain rights, then the free wife (i.e., the companion) has at least those rights in marriage and divorce and so **this text** applies even more so for a wife who is physically abused.

44

Case Law for Divorce Based on
Deuteronomy 21:10-14

This is expressed to Israel by Moses in the situation that:

> *"When you go out for battle against your enemies, and Yahweh your God gives them into your hand, and you lead the captives away, and you see among the captives a woman beautiful in appearance, and you become attached to her and you want to take her as a wife, then you shall bring her into your household, and she shall shave her head, and she shall trim her nails. And she shall remove the clothing of her captivity from her, and she shall remain in your house, and she shall mourn her father and her mother a full month, and after this you may have sex with her, and you may **marry her**, and she may **become your wife**. And then if you do not take delight in her, then **you shall let her go** to do whatever she wants, but you shall not treat her as a slave, since you have dishonored her" (LEB).*

Even though the woman here is a prisoner of war, the Israelite who captures her is to show her respect by allowing her to mourn her relatives for a month. In this hypothetical situation the man later, *"no longer delights in her"* and so he divorces her as stated in the phrase *"you shall let her go."* This does not mean that God encourages divorce, but that if it should happen then the law regulated it by blocking the man from treating this woman as still a slave and making a financial gain from her by means of divorce. In other words, the law was concerned with the fair treatment of a wife. Furthermore, although a slave who becomes a wife is in the lowest status in society, the Jews would see the principle of this law as also applying to the free wives of greater status (1 Cor. 9:8-10).

With this information we are now ready to study the first of the two primary case laws related to divorce—the first of which is found in Deuteronomy 24:1-4.

NOTE: According to **the Mishnah** the Jewish rabbis themselves had taken the principles concerning marital responsibilities from the key texts of Exodus 21:10-11, Deuteronomy 21:10-14, and 24:1-4 to form their necessary case law for divorce. However, in some of their views there appears to be a certain amount of misinterpretation and misapplication.

§

9

Case Law for Divorce Based on Deuteronomy 24:1-4

This passage describes the hypothetical case of a man's divorcing his wife for "some indecency" on her part. We will discuss the meaning of this phrase a little later. The passage in the LEB says that:

> "When a man takes a wife and he marries her and then she does not please him, because he found something objectionable (**some indecency** ESV. Heb. erwat dabar) and writes her **a letter of divorce** and puts it in her hand and sends her away from his house, and she goes from his house, and she goes out and **becomes a wife for another man**, and then the **second man dislikes her** and he writes her **a letter of divorce** and places it into her hand and sends her from his house, or if the second man dies who took her to himself as a wife, her **first husband who sent her away is not allowed to take her again** to become a wife to him after she has been defiled, for that is **a detestable thing** before Yahweh, and so you shall not mislead into sin the land that Yahweh your God is giving to you as an inheritance"

The meaning of this passage has been much debated. Many commentators view the first husband as having the grounds of "some indecency" as a valid reason for divorce, just as the Pharisees and earlier rabbis did. However, others view the first husband as perpetrating **a** treacherous divorce upon his wife attributing to her "some indecency" i.e., **something viewed as serious but, in fact, something that she did not actually do.** This latter view seems the more likely because the passage is in a context, from Deuteronomy 23:15 to 24:7, of protection of individuals so that they are not viewed as a mere chattel. So, this seems to be true also of the divorced wife in 24:1-4 where she is protected by a certificate of divorce and so allowing her to remarry and to receive her necessary food, clothing, and love (Ex. 21:10). Nevertheless, it seems that the second husband is definitely perpetrating a treacherous divorce upon his new wife and so does not have valid grounds. This is indicated by the phrase "he hates her," which   is a technical term meaning **divorces without adequate grounds** as in Malachi 2:16 i.e., treacherously so that he unjustly breaks the marriage contract with her.

To What Did *"Erwat Dabar"* Originally Refer?

Although this Hebrew term found in Deuteronomy 24:1 is easy enough to translate, it is exceedingly difficult to interpret. It seems to be a vague catch-all and non-specific term. The notes in the NET Bible, on the phrase *"**something offensive** or **indecent*** (Heb. **erwat dabar**),* state:

> *Heb* "nakedness of a thing." The Hebrew phrase עֶרְוַת דָּבָר ('ervat davar) refers here to some gross sexual impropriety (see note on "indecent" in Deut. 23:14). Though the term usually has to do only with indecent exposure of the genitals, it can also include such behavior as adultery (cf. Lev. 18:6-18; 20:11, 17, 20-21; Ezek. 22:10; 23:29; Hos. 2:10).

In Deuteronomy 23:13, 14 the word *erwat,* means 'excrement' *('anything indecent').* So, in that Israelite culture *erwat dabar* may have concerned a matter that is too distasteful, shameful, personal, and serious to mention in public. It appears to have been a cover-all term used instead of naming the specific offence and as a legal term it, therefore, breaks the marriage covenant. However, as D. A. Carson says, "the original meaning of indecency could not have been limited to infidelity, since the provision of the Mosaic law for adultery was death (Lev. 20:10)" *Commentary on the New Testament Use of the Old Testament* p.23. So, it is evidently **unlikely that this term originally referred directly to actual adultery**, whereas in this case the woman was to be given a certificate of divorce and sent away as her punishment. Furthermore, in other forms, *erwat* means **"nakedness"** and **"shame"** in numerous scriptures, including Exodus 28:42. So the rabbis interpreted this such that a woman could be divorced for **engaging in illicit sexual activity** and even for encouraging adultery with her by revealing too much of her beauty. According to *m. Ketub 7.6* and *t. Ketub 7.6* rabbinic teaching saw this as being done if the woman were to:

1. Do spinning in the street; thereby showing her bare arms to men.

47

2. Having her garments slit on both sides and so being provocative.
3. Speaking with any man and particularly joking with young men.
4. Bathing in a public bath with any man, even though fully dressed.

So, it would appear that for the early Jewish interpreters *erwat dabar* may have had an original meaning of **unfaithful sexual behaviours** whereby a woman was purposely engaging in **practices that could lead to adultery**, even though not actually committing adultery. So, because *"she should find no favour in his [her husband's] eyes...he must also write her a certificate of divorce."* However, in time there seems to have been a shift in the interpretation of the term *erwat dabar* by the rabbis, so that it referred only to **"extramarital sexual intercourse."**

A Hard-Hearted Husband Divorces for an Alleged Offense

As mentioned above, a number of modern writers on this subject understand this passage to concern unjust divorce i.e., for no good reason, so that a hard-hearted husband is using *erwat dabar* as a pretext to divorce his wife. (This is the "hard-heartedness" mentioned later by Jesus in Matthew 19:8). Therefore, Jesus is understood as also not agreeing with the rabbinic interpretation of Deuteronomy 24:1-4 so that it does not give genuine grounds for divorcing a wife, but he saw this as unjust divorce because of male hardheartedness (Matt. 19:8). So, commenting on Deuteronomy 24, Bible educator Rick Walston notes that:

> Verses 1-3 simply document what it was that hard-hearted men were doing. Note the conditionals in this passage set off by the word "if" and the repetitious use of the word "and," and then there is the concluding conditional set off by the word "then"
> ... *Something Happened on the Way to "Happily Ever After"* p. 66.

It is also noteworthy that the second man who marries her also divorces her because he "dislikes" her and gives her a certificate of divorce—again this seems to be an unjust divorce i.e., for no significant reason. So, this indicates that the first husband has fabricated grounds for divorcing his wife simply because, *"she finds no favour in his eyes"*—this phrase being used as a parallel to the phrase *"some indecency"* (Heb. *erwat dabar*). This would then indicate that he is merely **making the allegation that she committed this "indecency"** or at most it is a trivial excuse in reality. Therefore, the "indecency" does not seem to involve any actual unfaithful sexual behaviour on her part or perhaps only a minor slip—it is simply an unjust excuse used by the hard-hearted husband to divorce her. This makes some sense because:

1. The penalty for adulterous actions was death (Lev. 20:10, Deut. 22:22-24), rather than divorce as was the case for *erwat dabar*. So, this term must refer to something less than adultery.

2. The double standard here is seen inasmuch as the wife cannot be accused by the first husband of being "unclean" enough to be divorced (vs. 1) and then "clean" enough to be married again by him (vs. 4). This indicates that the real reason for the divorce was not actually a very serious one and may be a pretext.

3. The passage is in a context, from Deuteronomy 23:15 to 24:7, of protection of individuals, so that they are not viewed as a mere chattel. Certainly, the certificate of divorce in verse one was for the woman's protection. This concept makes more sense if she were unjustly divorced, and not guilty of any unfaithful sexual behaviour.

4. When Jesus speaks of men's "hardheartedness" it is almost certainly a reference to Deuteronomy 24:1. This is because that was the original subject of discussion raised by the Pharisees in their debate with Jesus (Matt. 19). This is indicated by the use of the terms *"any cause"* and *"certificate of divorce."* Indeed, these terms were mentioned only in Deuteronomy 24:1 and Jesus called this divorce action hard-heartedness on the man's part.

5. Because God legitimately divorced Israel (see chapter 11) and with a purpose of remarrying her after her repentance, it seems clear that the restriction of remarriage on the first husband in Deuteronomy 24 indicates that this was his trivial or treacherous divorcing of his wife.

An Objection to It Being an *Alleged* Offense

Some may say that because the text says, *"she finds no favour in his eyes **because** he has found some indecency,"* that he discovers some actual seriously bad conduct on her part and which then results in her finding "no favour in his eyes." This is a very good point! However, because of the above points it is more likely that the phrase "he found" means that he searched out in his mind and "found" or fabricated a serious reason as grounds for divorce or exaggerated one of her failings so that he could divorce her. Indeed, researcher on the subject of biblical divorce, Barbara Roberts, comments on Deuteronomy 24:1-4 that:

> In fact, the text is much more a warning and restriction to husbands than a degradation of wives. Let us first observe that verses 1-3 contain no commandment or regulation, they merely narrate a hypothetical situation. They indicate that in the Israelite community some men were divorcing their wives because they found *no favour* in their eyes, *found some uncleanness* in them, or even *detested* them. Only in the fourth verse is there a regulation: the first husband cannot remarry the woman should her second marriage terminate.
>
> *Not Under Bondage* p. 64.

Why Was the First Husband Not Allowed to Remarry His Ex-Wife

Barbara Roberts' comment that this is the only actual regulation in this passage is confirmed by famous commentators Keil and Delitzsch who state that:

> The law that the first husband could not take his divorced wife back again, if she had married another husband in the meantime, even supposing that the second husband was dead, would necessarily put a check upon **frivolous divorces**...The thought, therefore, of the impossibility of reunion with the first husband, after the wife had contracted a second marriage, would put some restraint upon a frivolous rupture of the marriage tie: it would have this effect, that whilst, on the one hand, the man would reflect when inducements to divorce his

50

wife presented themselves, and would recall a rash act if it had been performed, before the wife he had put away had married another husband; on the other hand, the wife would yield more readily to the will of her husband, and seek to avoid furnishing him with an inducement for divorce.

Biblical Commentary on the Old Testament.

Another possible reason for this arrangement is given by D. A. Carson who states that, "It is possible that the original motive behind this law was to protect the woman from having to provide the same man with two dowries" *Commentary on the New Testament Use of the Old Testament* p.23. However, although there are various views concerning why the first husband could not remarry the divorced wife, it seems most likely that it concerns the first husband's hard-heartedness in the first place and that he has already declared her "unclean." So, it would be wrong for the wife to return to a man who has already declared her "unclean"—one who could easily mistreat her once again and divorce her again on a whim. Furthermore, if the second marriage ended with an unjust divorce (*the term "**hates her**" being a technical term for a groundless divorce*) then she, as the innocent party, would have been awarded the equivalent of a dowry from that second marriage even if she had not brought a dowry into this second marriage. If then the first husband had been allowed to remarry her, he would have unfairly gained access to this second dowry. So, the law that was stated in Deuteronomy 24:4 was put in place to prevent any previous husband from getting such an unjust financial benefit by such a remarriage. These financial restrictions and penalties were not unusual in the Mosaic Law as for example the case of a man who made a false accusation about his new wife's virginity (Deut. 22:13-18).

NOTE: Because there has been a process in some Muslim cultures of "pimping" a wife by a first husband to a second husband for the night, and then receiving her back, a few theologians think that it is possible that God was protecting Jewish wives from this practice by providing this law in Deuteronomy 24:1-4.

What Does "She Has Been Defiled" Mean?

The most common understanding of this is that when the woman enters the second marriage this morally defiles her, and so prevents the first husband remarrying her. The problem with this interpretation is that God would then be seen as allowing for marriages that defile, and so He has approved of children being born into such defiled marriages. Another and better explanation given is that **her first husband originally declared her to be "defiled" to him** and so she must not return to him. So, although it is difficult to know with certainty why "she has been defiled" or made unclean, it works toward the debarring of the first husband from remarrying her i.e. she would be out of bounds only to him, so that he gets no chance to mistreat her once again and gets no unjust financial benefit. However, she is not out of bounds to any other man because she has a certificate of divorce in both instances. So, it seems that the restriction God arranged for through Moses was to hold back the sins of serial divorce and remarriages that were already happening at that time.

NOTE: David was reunited to his "defiled" wife Michal. However, David had not divorced her. In fact, she had been taken from him by Saul. Also, Hosea was reunited to his "defiled" wife Gomer who had been chosen to picture Israel's spiritual adultery.

The Certificate of Divorce
Allowed a Woman to Remarry

Many of the rabbis in the early centuries seem to have taken note only of the first husband's right to divorce; whereas the main purpose of this law seems to be **to protect a wife** who is **unjustly divorced** by a hard-hearted husband—one who may have had another woman lined up for marriage (Mal. 2:14-16). Therefore, he uses the grounds of "some indecency" as a false reason to divorce his wife. Such a wife was given the protection of the God-prescribed certificate of divorce (Deut. 24:1), so that she would be able to remarry and therefore not become destitute. Indeed, the husband was **required by law** to write her this certificate (Deut. 24:1, 3). Once in her hand the certificate showed that the marriage was completely ended, so that her previous husband now had no hold on her. The woman divorcee had a **full right to remarry** and so justice for women was safeguarded. This provision of the certificate put the law for Israel head and shoulders above the marriage laws of the surrounding nations. But one caveat was that although the document might say "that you may be married to any man you wish"

52

it was understood that this would be any Jewish man. This assumption moves on in Christianity for widows and by extension to divorcees to become in Paul's words: *"free to be married to whom she wishes, only in the Lord" (1 Cor. 7:39).*

NOTE: There were a couple of categories of men that an Israelite woman could never marry namely: a former husband who had declared her unclean (Deut. 24:4) or a priest (Lev. 21:7).

A Woman's Position if No Divorce Certificate Was Provided

However, the divorcing of a wife where no certificate was ever provided did not constitute a valid divorce. This situation was comparable to a husband's abandoning of his wife, likely leaving her destitute and so leading to her great need to remarry quickly. Indeed, if the husband neglected to provide or refused to provide her with a certificate of divorce, she would have no proof of her freedom from any marital obligations to the husband who had divorced her. Without it she was left as either destitute because of not being able to remarry or if she did remarry, she could be charged as an adulteress. Additionally, her ex-husband could reclaim her at a later date at his whim.

An Ex-Husband's Position Concerning the Certificate of Divorce

For a man the situation was different because of the practice of polygamy which Israelite law did not condemn. Therefore, he would not need a certificate of divorce from his divorcing wife before marrying another woman. However, he would be an adulterer if he: *"...commits adultery with the wife of his neighbour...both* **the adulterer** *and* **the adulteress** *shall surely be* **put to death***" (Lev. 20:10 ESV),* whereas a man, married or single, who seduced a single girl had to offer to marry her, pay the bride price, and was never allowed to divorce her (Ex. 22:16, 17; Deut. 22:28, 29).

The Benefits of the Certificate of Divorce

1. It helped prevent impulsive divorce by an angry or capricious husband.
2. It declared to the woman "you are free to marry any [Jewish] man."
3. It removed ambiguity concerning the marital status of the parties, preventing any charge of adultery if the woman should enter into a new marriage.
4. It removed the man's power to annul the woman's vows (Num. 30).
5. It was proof of the parentage of any children.

A further text which shows that a divorced woman in Israel had the right to remarry is Numbers 30:9 because her vows and promises from the point of divorce onward could not be vetoed by her ex-husband. Nevertheless, Deuteronomy 24:1-4 is not about reasons that would justify or not justify divorce. It has the singular goal of protecting women. So, we now come to the second primary case law related to divorce which is found in Exodus 21:10-11.

10

Case Law for Divorce Based on Exodus 21:10-11

This passage contains a law about how a male Israelite should treat a slave wife when he later marries a second wife—one who is a free wife—and so giving the man two wives in harmony with the polygamy of the times so that:

> "When a man sells his daughter as a slave ... *8If she does not please her master, who has* **designated her for himself**, *then he shall let her be redeemed. He shall have no right to sell her to a foreign people, since he has* <u>broken faith with her</u>. *9 If he designates her* **for his son**, *he shall deal with her as a daughter.* *10If* <u>he</u> *takes* **another wife** *to himself, he shall not diminish her* **food**, *her* **clothing** *and her* **marital rights**. *11And if he does not do these three things for her,* <u>she shall go out</u> *for nothing, without payment of money"* (Ex. 21:7-11 ESV).

This rather literal translation leaves one in some confusion concerning who is the man who "takes another wife" in verse 10. Is the "he" the father or the son? The context favours it as being "the son" as shown in the *God's Word Translation (GWT)* because she has just been given to him as his wife. Furthermore, if verse 10 referred to the father, then why does it say that he must give this slave woman her conjugal rights i.e., sexual intimacy? This would be immoral! Therefore, the reference must be to "his son." So, the rendering in the *GWT* gives this greater contextual clarity to verses 10 and 11 when it says:

> "**If that son** *marries another woman, he must not deprive the first wife of food, clothes, or sex ("conjugal rights" in Moffatt and in Smith & Goodspeed, or "sexual intimacy" in the NLT)* *11 If he doesn't give her these three things, she can go free, without paying any money for her freedom."*

It is also helpful to read this passage from other dynamic equivalence translations so that we may catch even more of the meaning. So, the following translations express the text as:

> "If a man sells his daughter as a slave, she is not to go free like the men-slaves. ⁸ If her master **married her** but decides she no longer pleases him, then he is to allow her to be redeemed. He is not allowed to sell her to a foreign people, because he **has treated her unfairly.** ⁹ If he has her **marry his son,** then he is to treat her like a daughter. ¹⁰ If he ("that son" GWT) **marries another wife,** he is not to reduce her food, clothing or marital rights. ¹¹ If he fails to provide her with these three things, she is to be given her freedom without having to pay anything"
>
> (The Complete Jewish Bible).

> "If a man sells his daughter as a servant, she is not to go free as male servants do. ⁸ If she does not please the master who has selected her for himself, he must let her be redeemed. He has no right to sell her to foreigners, because he has **broken faith with her** ("dealt treacherously" in the LEB). ⁹ If he selects her for his son, he must grant her the rights of a daughter. ¹⁰ If he [the son] **marries another woman,** he must not deprive **the first one** of her food, clothing and marital rights. ¹¹ If he does not provide her with these three things, she is to go free, without any payment of money" (NIV).

This passage concerns a female slave who becomes the wife of her master, but is then passed on to his son as a wife and this son then marries again. However, because this son fails to provide the first wife with the necessaries of "her food, her clothing, or her marital rights" she can divorce him. Even though the first man is called her master, this is not about a woman who simply remains as a slave, but she becomes a concubine in the system of regulated polygamy as allowed in Hebrew Bible times. This is because the master has also "selected her" as a wife for himself or "betrothed her" as in the KJV. In fact, the meaning is more likely that of "married her" as most modern translations show. In any case, in Bible times there was almost no difference in status between betrothed and married, and so he was considered as her husband as was Joseph who wanted to "divorce" Mary. The proof that this is about "a wife" in verse 8, as either betrothed or married, is the fact that verse 10 says, "if he takes another wife" or "marries another woman" (NIV). So please note that the master has "treated her unfairly," or "broken faith with her" or "dealt treacherously with her" as meaning broken his marriage contract with her. This is his sin inasmuch as he has reneged on his promise to treat her as a wife, and it is certainly a wife rather than an ordinary female slave that is spoken about here. This is because sexual intimacy is one of the key requirements in the marriage and a master should not have sex with his slave! Even the fact that this woman must not be sold to foreigners shows that her status has changed so that she is not merely a slave, but a concubine—a secondary wife.

A Free Wife Can Divorce If She Is Not Provided With the Necessaries

Based on the above information and based upon Jewish exegetical principles, it would be unreasonable to think that the full wife had fewer rights than the concubine wife. Indeed, the same argument counts when a male or female slave is physically abused by the master and so must be given their freedom (Ex. 21:26-27) with an **emancipation certificate**. Even more so would this apply to a wife on the principle of "from the lesser to the greater," and therefore allowing her to get a divorce from a husband who persistently fails her in providing the necessaries of life! So, from the above case law principles found here in Exodus 21:10-11, the meaning is that, if a slave wife must not be neglected in the three fundamental areas of life—food, clothing, and marital rights/sexual intimacy, then the free wife must also never be neglected in these three features of life. In fact, this passage of case law in Exodus 21:10-11 became a vital passage the principles of which were used by the Jewish teachers regarding the subject of marriage and divorce as well as its connection with other texts on divorce, namely, Deuteronomy 21:10-14; 24:1-4. Indeed, the phrases "she shall go out" or "she may leave as a free woman" mean that she has actually **divorced her husband** for his persistent failures in these key areas of marriage. So, this passage became the basis for understanding the obligations and stipulations of a husband in the marriage contract. It showed that persistent failure by him to provide his wife with: **sustenance, clothing** and her **marriage due/rights (sexual intimacy)** would be **neglect or even abuse** and would serve as the basis for divorce. These obligations on the husband were later emphasized by the

Apostle Paul when he said that a husband is responsible to be concerned as to *"how he may please his wife" (1 Cor. 7:34).*

A Wife's Marital Obligations in Ancient Israel

Furthermore, the principle in this case law would apply to a husband, so that in the marriage contract/covenant the wife would agree to use the materials that the husband provided for the benefit of the family. This would mean the preparation of the meals, the turning of materials into garments and the general housekeeping. Such a good wife is described in Proverbs 31:16-27. She would be concerned as to *"how she may please her husband" (1 Cor. 7:34).* This would mean she would lovingly engage in their sexual intimacy (subject to any mitigating circumstances) in response to her husband's loving advances and at times to initiate such intimacy with her loving husband to show her desire for him, and so following the pattern in the Song of Solomon and as later emphasized by the Apostle Paul in 1 Corinthians 7:2-5. Indeed, if she significantly and persistently failed in any of these areas she would be breaking her part of the marriage contract and thereby giving cause for her husband to divorce her. *The Jewish Mishnah. Ketub.5.5* lists the woman's material obligations as "grinding flour, baking bread, laundry, preparing meals, feeding the baby, making the bed, working in wool."

The Discovered Marriage Contracts
Concerning Exodus 21

Concerning Jewish families living in Elephantine, Egypt in the 500s B.C., a large number of discovered marriage contracts and documents related to divorce show that the basis for marriage was that of Exodus 21:10-11, and so indicating that continual failure to keep these vows served as the basis for divorce. Furthermore, in the 1890s Agnes Smith Lewis and Margaret Dunlop Gibson were permitted to ship many dozens of the most valuable documents from the Synagogue in Cairo back to Cambridge University. These had been kept in the geniza, a room in the synagogue where discarded documents were stored. In this particular case the geniza had not been emptied for about one thousand years. These documents included many Jewish marriage contracts. It took a very long time for experts working in the Cambridge University Library to complete the cataloguing of these, and so it is only in recent decades that they have been properly studied. The results of such studies reveal that the words "honour," "care for," "keep," and "cherish" in the modern -day marriage vows are clearly traced back to the obligations set out in Exodus 21, the persistent breaking of which would give a basis for divorce.

CONCLUSION

From this examination of the Mosaic Law on the subject of divorce it is evident that God, through Moses, **regulated** divorce by means of the passages of Exodus 21, Deuteronomy 21, and 24, and one does not regulate something if it is forbidden. Indeed, it would be wrong to separate the background to the Hebrew Scriptures from Jesus' statements to the Pharisees which were in the context of Deuteronomy 24:1-4. However, Jesus would naturally have accepted the principles in Exodus 21:7-11 because he was a Jew who respected the Mosaic Law as were the rabbis who also accepted these principles and this moral standard. Certainly, Jesus didn't change the moral principles underlying these case laws when he spoke of the hardness of men's hearts which concerned their mistreating of their wives, not just general sinfulness. However, today we are not under such regulations of the Mosaic Law, but the principles still apply, and because of this we get God's mind on the various issues.

One amazing fact, that may shock readers, is to find out that God was a divorcee—at least in a metaphorical sense. So, let's now look at this intriguing subject.

11

God's Example in Divorce

God metaphorically married Israel when the Law covenant was agreed to by the Israelites at Mount Sinai. So, Israel, as the bride, agreed to obey God's laws (Ex. 19:4-8) and God agreed to give them the Kingdom and the marital blessings which included respect, protective care, maintenance, and children. Yet it is the prophet Hosea who was the first to present the details of God's marriage to Israel and its later breakdown precipitating a divorce **as initiated by God**. The drama in Hosea (c.740 B.C.E.) pictures how God has been wronged by the unfaithfulness of Israel—she committed **spiritual adultery** *(idolatry)*, thereby violating the marriage contract. God is seen as putting Israel on trial for this *adultery*. This situation is portrayed by Hosea's divorcing of his wife for her many cases of literal adultery. In neither case is the wife threatened with the death penalty as would be the case if the Law of Leviticus 20:10 had been strictly applied—perhaps because mercy was shown. There is, in fact, no actual case recorded in the Hebrew Scriptures of a putting to death of an adulteress. The case in Hosea is of a trial for adultery where the plaintiff, the husband, shows mercy and is <u>desirous of having a chastened wife</u> rather than seeking divorce. This drama shows that it was Israel's **spiritual adultery** that was the cause of the eventual divorce. Although not putting her to death, God, as her husband, finally threatened to **withdraw all that was normally His legal responsibility to provide her as support**. Indeed:

> "*she did not know that it was I who gave her the **grain** and the **wine** and the **oil**, and who lavished on her **silver** and **gold**, which they used for Baal...I will take back my grain in its time, and my wine in its season, and I will take away my **wool** and my **flax** which were to cover her nakedness*" (Hos. 2:8-9 ESV).

This indicates that the Exodus 21:10, 11 passage is the basis of the marriage contract for what is expected of a husband to provide for his wife. God sets the example. This further shows that legitimate divorce is not sinful because it was something that even God was prepared to do.

60

God Divorces Israel –
Giving Her a Certificate of Divorce

In accordance with the law in Deuteronomy 24:1 God only divorced Israel after giving her a written certificate of divorce as shown by Jeremiah:

> *"'Then Yahweh said to me in the days of Josiah, the king, "Have you seen what apostate Israel has done? She has gone on every high hill and under every leafy tree and she has prostituted herself there. And I thought, 'After her doing all these things to me she will return,' but she did not return. And her treacherous sister Judah saw it. And I saw that for this very reason, that on account of apostate Israel committing adultery I divorced her and gave the letter of divorce to her. Yet her treacherous sister Judah was not afraid and she went and prostituted herself also'"*
>
> *(Jer. 3:6-8 LEB).*

God stated the same in the book of Isaiah:

> *"Thus says Yahweh: "Where is this divorce document of your mother's divorce, with which I dismissed her? or to whom of my creditors did I sell you. Look! you were sold because of your sin, and your mother was dismissed because of your transgressions"*
>
> *(Isa. 50:1 LEB).*

God's Example in Marriage to Unfaithful Judah

This is really one and the same marriage as to Israel at Mount Sinai. God has not really married two wives because:

> *"'...your time of lovemaking had come ... I entered into a covenant with you,' declares the Lord Yahweh, 'and you became mine ...I anointed you with oil. And I clothed you with beautiful finished cloth, and I put sandals on you of fine leather, and I bound you in fine linen, and I covered you with costly fabric. And I adorned you with ornaments, and I put a bracelet on your arms and a necklace on your neck. And I put an ornamental ring on your nose and earrings on your ears and a beautiful crown on your head...you ate finely milled flour and honey and olive oil, and you became exceedingly beautiful; you were fit to be a queen"*
>
> *(Ezek. 16:8-13 LEB).*

61

Here, not only is God fulfilling this marriage covenant according to the law in Exodus 21:10, 11, but He goes far beyond this by lavishing upon Judah the most beautiful of things. Here God gives the ultimate example of the love and care that a husband should give his wife including the demonstration of **love**. Yet for a husband to fail to provide the best that he can for his wife in these areas would show his failure to fulfil his marriage contract; and by such persistent failure he can become the one causing divorce. Yet in this instance it is Judah as a wife who becomes the one who provides grounds for divorce (verses 15-26) because she fails to use her husband's generous provisions for the marriage, but instead misuses those things to engage in her spiritual adultery:

> *"You took some of your **garments** and made for yourself colourful shrines, and on them played the whore...You also took your **beautiful jewels** of my gold and of my silver, which I had given you and made for yourself images of men and with them **played the whore**...Also my bread that I gave you – I fed you with **fine flour and oil and honey**—you set before them for a pleasing aroma ... And you took your sons and your daughters, whom you had borne to me, and these you sacrificed to them [the idols] to be devoured...as an offering by fire..."*

> *(Ezek. 16:16, 19-20 ESV).*

Here Judah had broken her marriage contract/covenant by giving God three grounds to divorce her, namely, the misuse of the food and the clothing provisions, and she committed adultery. A further breach of the marriage covenant was the slaughter of the husband's own children. Deliberate childlessness was a breach of the Mosaic Law and yet to actually slaughter them was almost inconceivable. Any one of these breaches of the marriage contract served as a basis for divorce. And so, God as the innocent party had the right to divorce her as he did with Israel, but here he continued to appeal to her. He endeavoured to be forgiving more than ever.

God's Intention to Remarry Israel

Because there were no financial issues involved, as in Deuteronomy 24:4, between God and Israel it was acceptable for Him to remarry Israel, and so, *"on that day—a declaration of Yahweh—you **will call me, "My husband**;" you will no longer call* *me, "My Baal." And I will* **take you as my wife** *forever; I will take you as a wife for myself in righteousness and in justice, in steadfast love and in mercy. I will take you as my wife in faithfulness, and you will know Yahweh" (Hos. 2:16, 19-20 LEB).*

However, this does not mean that God would be breaking His own law in Deuteronomy 24:4 i.e., for a first husband not to remarry the wife whom he divorced, and who had remarried a second man. Firstly, God's divorce was a legitimate one, whereas the man noted in Deuteronomy 24 divorced for no substantial reason—an unjust/treacherous divorce. Furthermore, in one sense, God would be marrying a new person inasmuch as it would be "the sons" of a combined Judah and Israel. Nevertheless, God's commands to **Hosea** contradicted the law about taking back a former wife. This prohibition was to protect her from an unscrupulous man which Hosea was not. So, this cautions us against playing off one rule against a different rule in another text regarding divorce because we have mistakenly read the Bible as a legal manual.

Divorcing of a Wife as Approved by God

Not only does the Pentateuch never speak against legitimate properly motivated divorce, but a number of divorces are described including that of **Abraham's divorcing of Hagar, and with God's approval** (Gen. 21:12). As is seen in God's dealings with Israel and Judah, there is no condemnation of the person who is seeking a divorce on valid grounds or who initiates such a divorce. The fault lies with the one who significantly and persistently **breaks a stipulation** of the marriage contract. Therefore, if a wife became an adulteress or persistently failed in her other wifely duties (although absolute perfection is not required) she could be divorced. However, because of the acceptance of polygamy in ancient times a husband could not be accused of committing **adultery** against his wife. But as shown earlier concerning a husband who persistently failed to provide his wife with **food**, **clothing** and **love** (including all sexual intimacy—Ex. 21:10, 11) she would have valid grounds for a divorce, but it would be the husband who had <u>caused the divorce</u>, and so he would suffer the various penalties. But whoever was the innocent party should keep the dowry.

God Approved Joseph's Intention to Divorce Mary

The only narrative example in the New Testament concerning divorce is that of Joseph's wish to divorce Mary. Had it happened it would have been a betrothal divorce—a strange concept to Western ears. Matthew records that: *"Because Joseph, her [Mary's] future husband, was a man approved of by God, and because he didn't want to disgrace her, he intended to **divorce** her privately"* (Matt. 1:19). This passage indicates how we are to understand exceptions, even though it concerned a betrothal. This exception concerned helping Mary to avoid shame. However, some interpreters see this last phrase *as if this concerned a completed marriage*. Indeed, as shown earlier the Jewish betrothal was a legal contract just as binding as marriage (Deut. 20:7; 22:24) and legal action could be taken to divorce a person who was sexually immoral with a third party prior to the wedding. So, following this custom, Joseph's discovery that Mary was expecting a child while betrothed to him, led him, out of kindness to her, to decide to divorce her privately with an "any cause" divorce (more on this later), rather than exposing her to public shame (Matt. 1:18, 19). Accordingly, this was **not a marital divorce but a betrothal divorce** and so does not mean that later divorces described in the New Testament concerned only betrothal divorces. In fact, because Joseph was intending this privately, it seems that there was no public documentation required because none was needed in an "any cause" divorce case. Therefore, this was technically an invalid betrothal divorce, but for a valid reason and would indeed be seen as valid in those times.

~

But doesn't God's own divorce and his approval of Abraham's divorce contradict God's apparent hatred and therefore banning of all divorce as mentioned in Malachi 2?

§

12

God Does Not Hate All Divorce - Malachi Two

Divorce Itself Cannot Be a Sin – Bad Treatment of a Marriage Partner Is a Sin

Nowhere in all of the many lists of sins in the Scriptures is legitimate well-motivated divorce classified as sin. There certainly can be a wrong motive for a divorce as seen in the case law of Deuteronomy 24:1-4. Furthermore, Bible commentator Rick Walston makes the point that:

> James 1:13b says, "For God cannot be tempted by evil, nor does he tempt anyone." If divorce is the evil that many people think it is, then it is all the more astounding that God would voluntarily place Himself in that picture! It is simply unthinkable that He would picture Himself as a sinner.

Sadly, it can often be heard from Christians who are not fully enlightened about the subject of divorce that "God hates divorce." However, after our examination of God's own metaphorical divorcing of Israel one can hardly believe that God must hate all divorce to the point of condemning all cases of divorce. Certainly, there are many things that God hates as Proverbs 6:16-19 shows:

> "There are six things Yahweh hates, and seven things are abominations of his soul: haughty eyes, a lying tongue, and hands that shed innocent blood, a devising heart, plans of deception, feet that hurry to run to evil, a false witness who breathes lies and sends out discord between brothers" (LEB).

From all of these we can see that wrong or perverted motives are in the heart of one who does these things. When God observes a seriously bad marriage with numerous sins being committed within that marriage, He surely hates that marriage. This is also true of some divorces so that God certainly hates the divorce of any self-seeking divorcer whose motive is treacherous, for instance, if they

65

wish to dump their marriage partner for someone else they think will be better for them. Nevertheless, God does not hate all divorce although many translations give renderings of Malachi 2:16 as if He does? So, when people say, "God hates divorce" is that what the Hebrew text of Malachi 2:16 really says?

Correct Translation of Malachi Two

Contrary to modern-day popular opinion, the words of Malachi 2:16 do not give a basis to believe that God hates **all** divorce so that divorce is a sin. There is a significant translation issue in verse 16, and below is a typical, but incorrect, rendering of Malachi 2:14-16:

> *"And you ask, 'Why?' Because Yahweh stands as a witness between you and the wife of your youth, with whom you* **have broken faith**, *even though she was your partner and your wife by covenant. Did he not create a single being ('made them one' NIV), having flesh and the breath of life? And what does this single being seek? God-given offspring! Have respect for your own life then, and* **do not break faith with the wife** *of your youth. For I* **hate divorce** *(Heb. shalach), says Yahweh, God of Israel, and people* **concealing their cruelty** *under a cloak (or "covers his garment with violence" ESV), says Yahweh Sabaoth. Have respect for your own life then, and do not break faith ("Do not be unfaithful to your wife" NLT)" (Mal. 2:14-16 NJB).*

GRAMMATICAL POINTS

The Hebrew Interlinear does not actually read: 'God hates divorce' as many Christians often quote as a kind of slogan. It reads: *"he hates and divorces (Heb. shana),"* yet most translations wrongly render this as God saying of Himself: "I hate divorce." Apart from being grammatically wrong this does not fit the context because it is "he (the husband)...who covers his garment with violence." Such a wrong rendering as "'I hate divorce,' says Yahweh" contradicts the rest of the Hebrew Scriptures on this subject, including God's encouraging of Abraham to listen to Sarah and so to divorce Hagar.

THE RENDERING OF VERSE 16 IN the HEBREW, and the LXX

The Lexham English Septuagint renders verse 16 as: ""*But if, while hating, you dismiss your wife," says the Lord God of Israel, "you will conceal the wrongdoing of your thoughts..."* Indeed, up-to

66

date scholarship and 18 translations show that this concerned the action of the husband rather than an expression of God's feelings, and so it is rendered in the following versions as:

> "For the man who does not love his wife but divorces her, [lit. hates and divorces" Heb. shalach "dismisses"] says the LORD, the God of Israel, covers his garment with violence..." (ESV).

> "'If he hates and divorces his wife,' says the LORD God of Israel, 'he covers his garment with injustice,' says the LORD of Hosts. Therefore, watch yourselves carefully, and do not act treacherously" (CSB).

> "The man who hates and divorces his wife," says the Lord, the God of Israel, "does violence to the one he should protect," says the Lord Almighty. So be on your guard, and do not be unfaithful"
> (NIV).

Indeed, starting with a translation by Ewald in 1868 this phrase has also been rendered similar to the above by the following scholars: Van Hoonacker (1908), Lattey (1934), Rene Vuilleumier (1981), Westbrook (1986), Glazier-McDonald (1987), Hugenberger (1994), D.C. Jones (1994), C. John Collins (1994), Sprinkle (1997), Stuart (1998), and Zehnder (2003). It is also rendered as showing that the man hates and divorces his wife in the following Bible translations: The Smith and Goodspeed Translation (1927), NEB (1970), REB (1989), as well as the HCSB (1999) and the ESV (2001) set out above.

God Hates Treacherous Divorce

What God hates are divorces of a particular type. Even the context of verse 16 in Malachi 2 is that of Jewish men who had **broken faith** with their wives by each taking another wife—a pagan wife—and treacherously divorcing their first wife without a scriptural cause (Mal. 2:11-12). Clearly, these wives had not failed in their duties to prepare the material things for the family, nor had they failed to respond to their husbands' need for sexual intimacy and so leading to the conclusion that this was divorce for weak, unjust, and invalid reasons, that is, the husbands were acting treacherously. So evidently in verse 16 it is the husband who hates his wife and desires someone else. So, he cruelly, treacherously, and unfaithfully divorces her without adequate scriptural grounds, and so making it an unjust divorce. Notably the passage in Malachi 2 is the last recording in the Hebrew Scriptures on matters concerning divorce prior to the debate between the Pharisees and Jesus. So, Malachi's statements on **treacherous divorce**, no doubt, had some bearing on that New Testament situation.

God Approves of Legitimate Divorce

In the previous chapter we saw a number of divorces, noted in the Hebrew Scriptures, of which God approved, including His own divorce from Israel as a metaphorical divorce. In each instance these required major surgery by God, so that the individual marriage partners could be spiritually preserved. In other words, as important as the institution of marriage is, the individuals in that marriage are more important to God.

As said earlier, it is very sad that the various denominations, generally, have not grasped God's intention in His providing of divorce as the best solution to a very bad marriage. Many have turned Jesus into a legalist who has little feeling for those in terrible marriages and indeed many leaders of denominations and their congregations are also rather heartless in regard to those in such bad marriages—often using the phrase—"well you made your bed and now you have to lie in it." Certainly, attempts to save the marriage at the expense of those who are in it simply results in many husbands and wives having to live a joyless life and with a very subdued spirit—perhaps even falling away from other Christians or even from God. This wrong-headed approach has been presented as rather like trying to save a burning house and not trying to rescue the people who live in the house. As we have seen God's concern is people rather than institutions. So, the question we must ask ourselves is: Do we save the couple in the marriage, or do we appear to save the marriage itself just for the sake of saving marriages? Of course, the best scenario is the saving of both, if that is possible!

God Does Not Approve of All Marriages

Even though it was God who instituted marriage, He does not approve of all marriages. This is seen in Ezra (chapters 9 and 10) when certain Israelite men married women from the surrounding pagan nations as contrary to God's will—a shameful iniquity. So, in prayer these men were brought by God to a realization of their sin and so that they would correct this situation by their divorcing of those foreign women. These men came before God in shame saying, *"We have broken faith with our God and have married foreign women from the peoples of the land" (Ezra 10:2)*. Then these men made a covenant with God to divorce those women. A similar situation occurred later when Nehemiah had to break up the marriages of certain Jews to pagan women (Neh. 13:23-27).

GOD'S USE OF DIVORCE AS PUNISHMENT

Because of the many bad attitudes of the Judeans living in Jerusalem, including the rejection of "the word of Yahweh"— without any repentance, He threatens them with corrective punishment, saying: *"Therefore **I will give their wives to others**...because from the smallest to the greatest, all of them make profit for unlawful gain, from prophet to priest, all of them practice deceit" (Jer. 8:10)*. Please note that, here God intended to break up those marriages and therefore, the marriage itself was not of prime concern to Him, but secondary. He was not concerned about maintaining those marriages, but brought a curse upon them because of their continual disobedience. (See Deut. 28:30). Possibly there was mistreatment of the wives by these Jewish husbands. So, here, there is no statement of providing any certificate of divorce, but God simply plans to give these wives to new but foreign partners.

MODERN-DAY BAD CHRISTIAN MARRIAGES

The above noted situations have a bearing on Christians today so that God no longer approves of certain modern-day marriages because the marriage vows are regularly being broken. Nevertheless, the true Christian can be assured of God's support through the traumatic time of a divorce. In fact, He even leads an innocent and rightly motivated person through the divorce because of their prayers and so helping them in the broken relationship to make the best decisions for themselves.

One key quality that such a victim of a marriage break-up needs is that of forgiveness, so that in the end they will be at peace without further bitterness, resentment, or continuing blame. In this one must lean heavily on our heavenly Father. Indeed, other Christians could and should be supportive in this, so that emotional healing will take place after the trauma of the whole divorce situation.

~

Regarding marriage and divorce it will now be helpful to know what views were held on this in the period between the close of the writing of the Hebrew Bible and the start of the New Testament.

§

13

The Rabbinic Background to Christian Divorce Issues

Just as it was necessary for us to examine the reasons that it was incumbent on us to study aspects of the Mosaic Law when considering the grounds for divorce, so too, some may wonder why we should bother considering what the later Jewish teachers had to say about grounds for divorce. Indeed, the primary reason for this is that no biblical subject should be analyzed within a vacuum, as if real life does not happen, but only the words of the Scriptures. The fact is that the living background to the Scriptures is what will help us to understand better what was expressed on the subject of divorce in the New Testament. This is especially true because Jesus had to deal with Jewish leaders who held many of the views from the Intertestamental Period.

Marital Issues During the Intertestamental Period

THE JEWISH QUMRAN COMMUNITY
In the Dead Sea Scrolls of the Qumran community there are three references to divorce, two of which are shown below. These references neither condemn divorce nor make any mention of restrictions to remarriage. However, some words are missing from the following documents and so making it difficult for the experts to decipher them:

Temple Scroll 54.4-5:
But any vow of a widow or of **a divorced woman**, anything by which she has bound herself shall stand against her, according to all that proceeded from her mouth.

The Damascus Document CD 13:15-17
Let no man do anything involving buying or selling without informing the examiner in the camp. He shall do it ... and not ... and so for **one divorcing** and he ... humility and with loving mercy.

The marital subject of greater concern to the Qumran community was that of monogamy and the prohibition of polygamy. Because they took the word *'sister'* in Leviticus 18:18 to mean a *fellow female Israelite,* they viewed Leviticus 18:18 as a proof text against polygamy: *"And you shall not take ("marry" NAB and others) a woman as a rival wife to* **her sister,** *uncovering her nakedness, while her sister is still alive." (Lev.18:18 ESV).* However, this may have been a faulty interpretation. Nevertheless, the Damascus document severely criticized **the Pharisees for their practice of polygamy.**
NOTE: All the situations described in Leviticus 18:6-18 are cases of illicit marriage.

THE JEWS AT ELEPHANTINE, EGYPT

The large body of papyri discovered at Elephantine includes Jewish marriage contracts and documents relating to divorce in the fifth century B.C.E. These all indicate an almost total equality of men and women, so that women had the right to divorce just as much as men had that right.

THE MISHNAH

This work, concerning the interpretation of the Scriptures, shows that **all the rabbis** based their understanding of the grounds for divorce on the threefold obligation to <u>feed, clothe and love</u> as set down in Exodus 21:10-11:
m. Ketub. 5.8

> He...may not provide for her less than two *qabs* of wheat or four *qabs* of barley [per week]. And one pays over to her a half-*qab* of pulse, a half-*log* of oil, and a *qab* of dried figs or a *maneh* of fig cake. And if he does not have it, he provides instead fruit of some other type. And he gives her a bed, a cover and a mat. And he gives her a cap for her head, and a girdle for her loins, and shoes from one festival season to the next, and clothing worth fifty zuz from one year to the next.

In Israel only the husband could directly enact a divorce by writing out a divorce certificate and handing it to the wife (Deut. 24:1-4). However, the wife could obtain a divorce when the court of the rabbis would persuade *(by words, fines or beating)* the husband that he must enact this valid divorce because he had failed in his marital obligations. There is evidence in the Mishnah and in a recently discovered divorce document that women did, indeed, bring petitions for divorce in the first century.

The Rabbinic Hillelite/Shammaite
On-Going Debate on Divorce Issues

By the first century there were two different opinions held by the rabbis concerning the interpretation of Deuteronomy 24:1, as to what constituted proper grounds for divorce. One view followed Rabbi Shamma, whilst the other followed Rabbi Hillel. However, both groups assumed that the passage concerned valid divorce:

*THE KEY TEXT OF THE DEBATE – **DEUTERONOMY 24:1***
"When a man takes a wife and marries her, if then **she finds no favour in his eyes** <u>because</u> he has found **some indecency** (Heb. *erwat dabar*) in her, and he writes her a certificate of divorce..."

It seems that both groups of Rabbis missed the point of this passage and focused only on the issue of the meaning and application of the Hebrew term *erwat dabar*, "some indecency" which literally meant "nakedness of a thing" as interpreted by them to mean exposure of ones' sexual organs, and so having sexual connotations.

The Mishnah says:
The **School of Shammai** says: A man should not divorce his wife except if he found a matter of indecency in her, since it says: For he found in her an indecent matter.
And the **School of Hillel** says: Even if she spoiled his dish, since it says: For he finds in her an indecent matter. (m.Git 9.10).

However, an older and fuller account is found in **Sifré Deut. 269** which says:
The **School of Shammai** says: A man should not divorce his wife except if he found indecency in her, since it says: For he found in her an indecent matter.
And the **School of Hillel** said: Even if she spoiled his dish, since it says: [Any] matter.
The School of Hillel said to the School of Shammai, since it said matter [Deut.24:1] why did it [also] say indecency, and since it said indecency, why did it also say matter? Because if it said matter and it did not [also] say indecency I would say: She who is discharged because of a matter is permitted to remarry, but she who is discharged because of indecency may not be permitted to remarry.

Nevertheless, to avoid accusations of illegitimacy of offspring, both schools took a pragmatic view and had a policy of mutual recognition of each others rulings.

RABBINIC ABBREVIATION

The highly abbreviated account of the debate as presented in the **Jerusalem Talmud** indicates that the Shammaites allowed divorce only on the ground of "indecency."

The slightly longer, but still considerably abbreviated, account in the **Mishnah** shows their position to concern their interpretation of only Deuteronomy 24:1.

The **sifre**, although longer, is still so abbreviated as to not mention the fact that the Shammaites allowed for divorce on the grounds mentioned in Exodus 21:10-11, yet these grounds were confirmed in Ketub 5.6 which records the debate the Shammaites had with the Hillelites concerning the length of time a man was allowed to withhold conjugal rights before he could be taken to court and sued for divorce on the grounds of Exodus 21:10.

All of the above shows the types of abbreviation that have taken place in rabbinic literature which **help us to understand the process of abbreviation in the Gospel accounts** as we look at them later.

THE SCHOOL OF THE HILLELITES

The Hillelites took the phrase *"she finds no favour in his eyes"* as something separate to the phrase *"something indecent in her,"* as if his simply disliking her would be reason enough to divorce her. Their mistake was in not recognizing that the *"something indecent in her,"* was the reason why *"she finds no favour in his eyes."* So simply disliking a wife was never a legitimate biblical reason for divorce.

The Hillelites also split the phrase *"something indecent in her,"* into two and so making an additional ground for divorce namely: anything (any matter) = *any cause* (ESV) as used by the Pharisees in their attempt to trick Jesus.

THE SCHOOL OF THE SHAMMAITES

This traditional school of rabbis did not break the phrase "something indecent" into two grounds for divorce. They understood it to mean one thing, namely: adultery.

Summary of Rabbinic Teachings on Divorce

From the above it is clear that in Israel the grounds for the wife to divorce would be the husband's failure to provide "**food, clothing** and her **marital rights**" (Ex. 21:10-11). These three grounds for divorce based on Exodus 21:10 were classified in rabbinic sources under just the two headings of: **Material neglect** and **Emotional/physical neglect.** These became the cultural norm. Indeed, according to rabbinic teaching the grounds for divorce that the husband could claim would be: "**Some indecency** in her (his wife)" (Deut. 24:1) as well as factors from the three grounds mentioned in Exodus 21:10-11. These were the factors in the vows as part of the conditional marriage contract or covenant. So, after the close of the Hebrew Scripture canon, the interpretation of the Scriptures by these Shammaite rabbis gave four grounds *(technically five)* **for divorce**, as well as the grounds of childlessness, as based upon the mandate to Adam and Eve to populate the earth with children. So, all these are summarized as:

1. **Material neglect** (food and clothing) based on Exodus 21:10-11.
2. **Emotional neglect** (failure to love, including sexual relations), also based on Exodus 21:10-11.
3. **Physical neglect/abuse** based on the *a fortiori* argument concerning Exodus 21:26-27
4. **Extramarital sexual sin** i.e., adultery or intent to commit adultery by the wife, based on the rabbinic interpretation of Deuteronomy 24:1.
5. **Childlessness**—her infertility because of the Genesis 1:28 command.

However, because of the acceptance of polygamy the wife was only allowed to divorce her husband on three of those grounds. These were:

1. Material neglect (food and clothing) based on Exodus 21:11.
2. Emotional neglect (provision of love) also based on Exodus 21:11.
3. Physical abuse based on the *a fortiori* argument concerning Exodus 21:26-27.

MODERN COMMENTARY ON THE DEBATE
Since the mid-1800s scholars have become aware of the Hillelite-Shammaite debate of the first century. Henry Alford notes the use of

the phrase "any matter" and writes in his *The Greek Testament:* "This was a question of dispute between the rival Rabbinical schools of Hillel and Shammai; the former asserting the right of arbitrary divorce, from Deut. 24:1, the other denying it except in cases of adultery." Also, many writers in Bible dictionaries and Bible encyclopaedias recognize this debate as the one that Jesus was drawn into by the Pharisees. So, when we look at Jesus' encounter with the Pharisees in Matthew 19:9 he is giving his opinion on rabbinic interpretation of Deuteronomy 24. However, Jesus did not simply take sides with one group against the other. He showed both groups of Pharisees as misinterpreting some parts of the Law. Indeed, most Pharisees had the prime goal of portraying Jesus as contradicting Moses' commandments and so to discredit him in the eyes of the people.

In the First Century "Divorce" Generally Meant "Divorce for Any Cause"

By the first century "**any cause**" whatsoever (e, g. burning his dinner or that he simply no longer liked his wife) was the generally accepted basis or grounds for a man to divorce his wife. Nevertheless, there was still an issue between the Hillelelite and the Shammaite Pharisees which concerned the two phrases: *"a cause of sexual immorality"* and *"any cause."* These phrases had become technical **legal terms** of case law concerning divorce. However, because of the popularity of the new easy-divorce Hillelite interpretation of Deuteronomy 24:1 the Shammaite interpretation was rarely used during the first century, and so there were fewer husbands/wives approaching Shammaite courts in seeking a divorce. However, both schools held firmly to Exodus 21:10, 11 to show what were the marriage contract obligations and the breaking of which formed the grounds for divorce from a bad husband. In fact, this "any matter/**any cause**" Hillelite type of divorce is very similar to the modern-day 'no fault' divorce. Of course, the "any matter" clause encompassed all of the other grounds and therefore required no public trial and so no evidence brought by any witnesses. So, by the time of Jesus the biblical view of the grounds for divorce had been almost entirely replaced by the Hillelite "**any cause**" view of divorce. As we shall see in the next section, it was this view that Jesus showed to be scripturally invalid. Therefore, when the term "divorce" is used in the four passages on this subject found in Matthew 5:31-32; 19:9; Mark 10:11-12; and Luke 16:18, it refers to the generally accepted but biblically **"invalid, unjust, or treacherous divorce."** Certainly, Jewish case law, based on Exodus 21:10-11, spoke of valid divorce, after which remarriage could take place. Nevertheless, both Shammai and Hillel interpreted this issue in a way that moved away from the Law's original purpose.

NOTE: Arguments which deny that Exodus 21:10 is about the rights of a concubine (a slave or secondary wife), are based on retranslating the passage. These have been shown to be faulty and no current version makes such changes.

Later Traditional Judaism

By the time of the writing of the Talmuds in later centuries the wording of marriage contracts had become fairly fixed and can be seen in examples of the **Geniza contracts**:

> I desire of my own will to marry....that I might bring her into my house so that she will be [my wife on condition that I hon]our her, feed her, sustain her, esteem [her] as all [...in the man] ner of dece [ent Jewish] men [who honour, feed, sustain and esteem their wives fa] ithfully.
>
> And she undertook to honour, esteem, attend and [serve him...in the manner of dece[nt women, the daughters of Israel, who attend and serve their husbands in purity and sanctity...].

Additionally, Kairite Judaism, known as the back-to-Scripture movement and whose literature runs from the ninth to the thirteenth centuries A.D., preserves the biblical basis for rabbinic thinking. They discuss the obligations in marriage of food, clothing, and love as based on Exodus 21:10-11. Their ninth century treatise on marriage reads:

> He who says, "I refuse to feed and support my wife," must be compelled to divorce her and pay her the full amount of the marriage contract, as it is written: He shall not diminish her food, raiment and cohabitation. And if he do not fulfil these three for her, she shall go free [Exod. 21:10-11].

Conclusion

From all the information on how the Jews approached the subjects of marriage and divorce in the intertestamental period we have a confirmation of the practice of divorce in the Hebrew Scriptures. From this it is evident that God, through Moses, **regulated** divorce by means of the passages of Exodus 21, Deuteronomy 21, and 24. In fact, the archaeological evidence from discovered documents corroborates the biblical statements concerning divorce, so that for legitimate reasons a husband or a wife could divorce their spouse and then remarry. Certainly, remarriage was the norm and was encouraged. However, God condemned those who divorced their spouses for no good reason i.e., treacherous divorce. Evidently, divorce and remarriage were allowed in the Jewish world up to the time of Jesus, although some of the grounds for divorce were often disputed.

The next several chapters will look in depth at all that Jesus said on this subject and especially so at the time he was approached by the Pharisees, but in the context and setting of those sayings. Please keep in mind that to interpret these issues in a vacuum can and often has led to the making of mistakes in interpretation.

Here, the questions to keep in mind are: did Jesus side with one faction of the Pharisees against another? Did he contradict Moses' teaching which Moses had received from God? Or did Jesus correct the Pharisees interpretation of the relevant Scriptures?

PART THREE

Jesus on Divorce

14

The Four Passages Concerning Jesus' Teaching on Divorce

With the information from the previous chapters in mind we are now in a position to approach Jesus' statements on divorce from a better perspective. His statements are recorded in the four passages found in the parallel passages of Matthew 19:3-9 and Mark 10:2-12 concerning Jesus' major debate with the Pharisees on the subject of marriage and divorce as well as the independent passages in Matthew 5:31-32 and Luke 16:18.

The Apparent Contradictions Created by These Passages

As pointed out earlier, because of a loss of contact with Jewish issues on divorce after the destruction of the temple in A.D. 70, the early church fathers were left with no background information to Jesus' words on divorce, and so had no understanding of the context of these words. Also, their Gentile ascetic mindedness generally seems to have led them to some very restrictive teachings on this subject. Furthermore, because the three Gospels are synopses, a surface reading leaves any later non-Jewish reader in confusion with apparent contradiction in the three Gospels. Indeed, what would have been understood or assumed by a first century Jewish listener or reader is not so easily understood by the modern-day reader. Adding to the confusion is the extra ground for divorce which Paul speaks of in 1 Corinthians 7:8-15, namely, desertion by an unbeliever. So, when reading all these accounts we realize that:

1. From Mark and Luke, Jesus is shown to allow **no grounds** for divorce.
2. From Matthew 5 and 19, Jesus is shown to allow divorce for **sexual immorality only**.
3. From 1 Corinthians 7:15, Paul appears to contradict both of the contradictory statements by Jesus with **desertion by an unbeliever** as grounds for divorce, but not sexual immorality.

81

All these factors have led to a considerable number of different interpretations, so that different scholars and churches take quite different positions on divorce and on the subject of remarriage. All of this uncertainty and lack of logic puts the individual Christian, who is in a seriously damaging marriage, in a very difficult position with many anomalies in life and with impractical solutions to these as offered to them by some Christian counsellors. So, because of the above apparent contradictions we must ask, how do we gain a correct understanding of Jesus' statements concerning divorce?

Firstly, we must **reference the full range of relevant Bible passages as the background and context to Jesus' statements on divorce** along with the first century thinking on this. From the previous study we saw that, by Jesus' time, the view of the Shammaite rabbis as well as the biblical view of the legitimate grounds for divorce had been almost entirely replaced by the Hillelite *"any cause"* view of divorce—a view similar to Roman and modern-day "no-fault" divorce law. It was this *"any cause"* view that Jesus showed to be scripturally wrong because it was often done with a treacherous motive and/or involved what was trivial. So, when we read the term "divorce" as used in the four passages giving Jesus' statements on divorce, it involved **inappropriate or wrongly motivated divorce** just as with each of the other subjects Jesus spoke of in the Sermon on the Mount in Matthew 5. Indeed, this context shows it to be invalid divorce spoken of.

Also, from the information in the previous chapters it is evident that there never was any issue over the lawfulness of divorce or remarriage in Hebrew Scripture (Old Testament) times or during the Intertestamental Period. Indeed, case law, based on the principles of Exodus 21:10-11 speaks of valid divorce by a wife after which remarriage can take place. The question is: Did Jesus discount the principles shown in Exodus 21?

The Two Independent Passages and Grammatical Points

Matthew 5:31-32 (KGV)

"It was said, 'Whoever divorces (Gk apoluō) his wife must give her a <u>certificate of divorce</u>' (Gk apostasion). [32]*But I [Jesus] say to you that anyone divorcing his wife, **except for "a cause of sexual immorality"** (Gk <u>porneia</u>), makes her a victim of [his] <u>adultery</u> (Gk*

moicheuo passive form). And whoever marries a woman <u>who has</u> (middle voice) divorced [in this way], commits <u>adultery</u> (active form)."

This passage in the Sermon on the Mount is likely to have been the first statement Jesus made on divorce. It is the third of six connected examples where Jesus tells his disciples to go *"beyond [the righteousness] of the scribes and Pharisees"* (vs. 20). Indeed, Erasmus, in the 1500s, showed that Matthew 5:31-32 should be interpreted less legalistically than had been done by the Roman Catholic authorities. This was because it was part of Jesus' many hyperbolic statements in the Sermon on the Mount. More will be explained concerning Matthew 5 in relationship to the Sermon on the Mount in the next chapter.

Luke 16:18 (KGV)

"Anyone divorcing his wife for the purpose of (Gk *kai* subjunctive mood. Usually rendered "and," but functions to introduce a result (see Bauer's Lexicon). In the flow of the discussion this presents us with a narrative explanation of why the first, unjustified divorce, occurred) *marrying another woman commits adultery; and anyone marrying a woman <u>who has</u> (middle voice) divorced from her husband [in this way],* **commits adultery** (active form)."

This text in Luke 16:18 most likely concerned the first confrontation Jesus had with the Pharisees over the issue of divorce and has its own context. However, this passage is very similar to the passage detailing the second confrontation with the Pharisees in Matthew 19:3-9/Mark 10:10-12. In fact, this passage is in a context of the poor stewardship of God's teachings by the Pharisees (verses 1-17). So, verse 18 then provides an example of this as given by Jesus when he highlighted and corrected that poor teaching.

The Two Parallel Passages and Grammatical Points

As recognized in many authoritative theological works, the two **parallel accounts** of Matthew 19:3-10 and Mark 10:2-12 concern the Hillelite/Shammaite debate over the interpretation of Deuteronomy 24:1-4, and which had continued through to the time of Jesus. It is in the Matthew and Mark passages that we find the substantially structured accounts wherein the Pharisees raised this issue with Jesus concerning the grounds for divorce:

Matthew 19:3-9 (KGV)

> "Then some Pharisees came and tried to trick him by asking "Is it lawful for a man to divorce a wife **for "any cause"**? (Deut. 24:1)."
>
> 4"Haven't you read," he replied, "that the One who created them from the beginning 'made them male and female' (Gen. 1:27), 5and said, "For this reason a man will leave his father and mother and will be joined to his wife, and the two will become one flesh" (Gen. 2:24). 6So they are no longer two, but one flesh, and no one should break apart (Gk chorizo = divorce) what God has joined together."
>
> 7"Why then," they asked, "did Moses command us to give a certificate of divorce (Deut. 24:1), and so to legally divorce her?"
>
> 8"Moses allowed you to divorce your wives," replied Jesus, "because of your hard-heartedness, but from the beginning it hasn't been this way. 9Now I say to you that whoever divorces his wife, **except for "sexual immorality"** (Gk porneia), and (Gk kai – also implying purpose i.e., "so that he") marries another woman, commits adultery (Gk moicheuo)."

NOTE: The added words in the KJV: "And whoso marrieth her which is put away doth commit adultery" after verse 9 are **not in the Greek text**.

Mark 10:2-12 (KGV)

> "Some Pharisees approached in order to trap him. "Is it lawful for a man to divorce his wife?" they asked. "What did Moses command you?" he replied. "Moses allowed a man," they replied, "to write **a certificate of divorce** (Deut. 24:1), and so to divorce his wife." But Jesus said, "It was **because of your hard-heartedness** that he wrote **this commandment** for you. But from the beginning of creation, 'He made them male and female. (Gen. 1:27); For this reason a man will leave his father and mother, and the two will become one flesh; so that they are no longer two, but one flesh (Gen. 2:24). Therefore, no one should break apart (Gk chorizo = divorce) **what** God has joined together.'" Then in the house, the disciples were again questioning him about this. So he said to them, "Whoever (treacherously) divorces his wife and (Gk kai – also implying purpose i.e., "so that he") marries another woman

*commits adultery **against her** [his first wife]. And if she divorces her husband **and** (as above) marries another man, she commits adultery."*

This statement recorded in Mark 10:11 of: "**divorces** his wife **and** marries **another woman,** commits adultery," was said privately to the disciples after Jesus' encounter with the Pharisees. However, Matthew 19:9 shows this statement was also said to the Pharisees thus linking **the exception clause** to the statement in Mark 10:11. Please note that Jesus says, "**what** God has joined together," rather than "**whom.**" This may be a reference to the institution of marriage, rather than being a reference to individual couples, so that invalid divorce was destructive to the institution of marriage.

Conflation of the Parallel Passages

From these four accounts it can be seen that Matthew 19 is the most detailed. So, concerning the Gospel accounts it is certainly normative and scholarly to interpret the less detailed accounts in the light of the more detailed ones rather than the other way around as some interpret them. Evidently, Matthew 19:3-9 and Mark 10:2-12 are parallel, but present a few different but vital details. Therefore, a conflated presentation is helpful toward getting a complete picture of this event. So, material peculiar to Matthew is presented as boldened; that which is peculiar to Mark is italicised, and common material is in normal type:

> "Some Pharisees approached in order to trap him. *"Is it lawful* for a man to divorce his wife **for "any cause"?"** they asked. *"What did Moses command you?" he replied. "Moses allowed a man,"* they replied, "to write a *certificate of divorce,* and so to divorce his wife." **He replied, "haven't you read that,** *from the beginning of creation,* **the One who created them** 'made them male and female. For this reason a man will leave his father and mother, and the two will become one flesh; so that they are no longer two, but one flesh. Therefore, no one should break apart what God has joined together.'" [7]**"Why then," they asked, "did Moses command us to give a certificate of divorce, and so to legally divorce her?"** But Jesus said, "It was because of your hard-heartedness that he *wrote this commandment for you.* **"Moses allowed you to divorce your wives,"** replied Jesus,

"because of your hard-heartedness, but from the beginning it hasn't been this way. [9]...*Then in the house, the disciples were again questioning him about this.* So he said to them, "Anyone who divorces his wife, except for sexual immorality, and marries another woman commits adultery *against her. And if she divorces her husband and marries someone else, she commits adultery."*

As shown earlier, the Jewish law was not of divorce <u>for men only</u>; but for women who had been wronged too. However, because the Pharisees' question to Jesus concerned only the case law of what "**a man**" might do concerning the divorcing of his wife, it is evident that this debate focused <u>only</u> on **Deuteronomy 24:1** which concerned the divorce grounds of: *"a cause of sexual immorality."* So, it did not touch on the case law from Exodus 21:10-11 which speaks of a wife's rights in marriage and her possible use of the divorce law if she has been persistently mistreated. Evidently, there was plenty of male self-centredness and chauvinism among these Pharisees who approached Jesus on this issue.

THE SPLITTING OF ERWAT DEBAR

Yet, in opposition to the Shammaite Pharisees who accepted the full phrase of *"a cause of sexual immorality,"* as grounds for divorce, the Hillelite Pharisees had split this phrase into two to make two technical legal terms: 1) divorce for *"any cause"* and 2) divorce for *"sexual immorality;"* this latter phrase becoming redundant. Most likely Jesus would never have split this phrase as in the Hillelite system of divorce for men only which system was not evident until around the time when Jesus was born. However, in his debate with the Pharisees it appears that Jesus was correcting all groups of Pharisees on their interpretation of Deuteronomy 24:1-4 and showing that **this passage did not apply as legitimate grounds for divorce**.

Herod's and Herodias' Divorces

These accounts in the Gospels seem to be linked with the background of John the Baptist's condemnation of Herod Antipas (Matt. 14:4; Mark 6:18) who treacherously divorced his innocent wife, so that he could marry Herodias. Although instigated by Antipas, Herodias also initiated her unjust divorce from Philip, so that she could marry Antipas. However, the fact that Herodias obtained a certificate of divorce from Rome did not in any way make her divorce justified. Certainly, this whole sordid event was indeed a major event in the lives of most people of that time, especially for the religious leaders. Indeed, all four passages have this same background and are also based on the last thoughts on divorce in the Hebrew Scriptures, namely, that of the treacherous divorcing of wives in the time of Malachi (Mal. 2:14-16), as well as the current interpretation of the Law on this subject as held and taught by the religious leaders.

The Key Questions to Be Answered in Jesus' Statements on Divorce

To analyse the main factors involved and the key issues to be resolved in Jesus' statements in the Sermon on the Mount and in the debate recorded in Matthew 19:3-9 and Mark 10:2-12 we must answer the following questions about the words, phrases, and thoughts used in this confrontation:

QUESTIONS CONCERNING MATTHEW 5:31-32 AND 19:1-12
1. What is the context of Jesus' statement on divorce in Matthew 5?

2. In the exception clause presented in both Matthew 5:32 and 19:9 what does *"**porneia**"* mean in this context?

FURTHER QUESTIONS CONCERNING MATTHEW 19:1-12
1. In Matthew 19:3 (and Mark 10:2), why and how did the Pharisees propose to trap Jesus in his words?

2. What is the evidence that the Pharisees' question in Matthew 19:3 of, *"Is it lawful for a man to divorce a wife for "**any cause**?"* concerned statements in Deuteronomy 24:1 regarding divorce for men only, and related to the Hillelite/Shammaite debate?

3. Why did the "any cause" policy promote scripturally invalid grounds for divorce?

4. In **Jesus' digression**, what do his quotations from Genesis 1:27 and 2:24 prove in Matthew 19:4, 5 when he summarizes it as: *"So they are no longer two, but one flesh"* (verse 6a)?

5. In **Jesus' digression** what does, *"what God has joined together let no one should break apart"* mean in 19:6b?

6. In Jesus' reference to **Moses' concession** how does the reversal of the verbs "allowed" and "command" in the accounts in Matthew 19 and Mark 10 regarding the giving of the **certificate of divorce** and divorcing a wife, show that the compulsory divorce advocated by the Pharisees was wrong?

7. How should we understand the **Mosaic concession** regarding, *"hard-heartedness"* and *"from the beginning it hasn't been this way"*?

8. Why were the grounds for divorce that are stated in **Exodus 21:10, 11 not discussed** in Jesus' confrontation with the Pharisees as described in Matthew 19:1-9 and Mark 10:2-12?

QUESTIONS CONCERNING MARK'S AND LUKE'S ACCOUNTS
1) Why doesn't Mark provide the "any cause" clause as in Matt. 19:3?

2) Why did Mark add the phrase, "adultery against her" in his account?

3) Why do Mark 10 and Luke 16 not have the exception clause of: *"whoever divorces his wife, except in the case of porneia"*?

Please note that the term "invalid divorce" refers to an unjust or treacherous divorce i.e., it is the grounds that are invalid, but divorce has happened and so is recognized by the relevant authorities.

As we attempt to answer all of the above questions point by point also, please note that progressive revelation is from partial to full—never from error to truth. So, what Jesus teaches is progressive from what is in the Mosaic Law but does not nullify it from a moral perspective. Also, we must exercise caution in our reading so that we do not invoke any wooden literalism. In fact, this is what has led in the past to the formulation of faulty teachings on this subject and which are contrary to the tone of God's love.

§

15

Understanding Jesus on Divorce
in Matthew 5:31-32

On the subject of divorce within his Sermon on the Mount, Jesus said that:

"It was said, 'Whoever divorces (Gk apoluo) his wife must give her a <u>certificate of divorce</u>' (Gk apostasion). ³²But I say to you that anyone divorcing his wife, **except for "a cause of sexual immorality"** *(Gk <u>porneia</u>), makes her a victim of [his] <u>adultery</u> (Gk moicheuo passive form). And whoever marries a woman <u>who has</u> (middle voice) divorced [in this way], commits <u>adultery</u> (active form)" (5:31-32 KGV).*

The above is a justified way of rendering the grammar here according to several Greek/English linguists. Please note that here Jesus references Deuteronomy 24:1 concerning the "certificate of divorce" and the phrase "a cause of sexual immorality" i.e., the Greek term *porneia*.

Correct Interpretation of the Law in
the Sermon on the Mount

The Hebrew word for "law" was *torah* which originally meant divine instruction and guidance with its principles and Jesus had no intention of destroying that, as he said at the beginning of his Sermon on the Mount:

"Don't think that I have come to destroy the Law or the Prophets. I haven't come to destroy, but to show them in their fullness (or "fulfil them"). ¹⁸I can assure you: until sky and land pass away, not one dot or one stroke of a letter will pass from the Law until everything has happened. ¹⁹So anyone who rejects one of the least of these commands, and teaches others to do the same will be called least in the Kingdom of Heaven. But anyone who practices them and teaches others to do so will be called great in the Kingdom of Heaven. ²⁰That's why I tell you: unless your covenant

faithfulness goes beyond that of the experts on Jewish teachings and the Pharisees, you will never get into the Kingdom of Heaven"
(Matt. 5:17-20).
Jesus followed this statement of his disciples needing "greater covenant faithfulness" than "that of the experts on Jewish teachings and the Pharisees" by giving correct interpretation of the law as recorded in Matthew 5:21 to 7:1-6. This instruction/guidance is more like the "wisdom sayings" with general principles and so these sayings must always be qualified. Indeed, they concern one's living to a high moral standard and according to a godly spirit in one's inner self—a spiritual standard that should come from the heart, rather than by regulations. In fact, Paul says that, when interpreted correctly, *"the Law is spiritual" (Rom. 7:14)* and *"the Law is holy and the commandment is holy and ethically right" (Rom. 7:12),* although Christians, *"serve in newness of spirit, and not in oldness of a written code" (Rom. 7:6).* So, part of Jesus' purpose was to show the Law at its intended level i.e., spiritualized—a word which means "elevated to the spiritual level" *(Oxford English Dictionary)* and the word "spiritual" = "relating to or affecting our human spirit."

THE SERMON ON THE MOUNT IS NOT A NEW SET OF REGULATIONS
In fact, as most theologians show, this cannot be a "new law" as regulations and requiring a judicial hearing if the rules are broken. Otherwise, such an idea would destroy the concept that ones' actions must come from the heart. Nevertheless, we may consider them to be a new *torah* according to the original meaning of that word as "instruction /guidance" and as part of the New Covenant (Jer. 31:31). Interestingly, Professor Robert Hach notes that:

> Jesus, while coming to bring an end to the legislative rule of the commandments of the Mosaic law over God's people, **did not come to abolish the Mosaic law in its instructional capacity as torah.** Instead, he came to fulfil it by bringing to pass its testimony about the Messianic fulfilment of God's promise to bless all nations...*The Passion and Persuasion* p. 43

Additionally, in his *Studies in the Sermon on the Mount* p.21, theologian D. Martyn Lloyd-Jones states that:

> What is of supreme importance is that we must always remember that the Sermon on the Mount is a description of character and **not a code of ethics** or of morals. It is **not to be**

90

regarded as law—a kind of new 'ten commandments' **or a set of rules and regulations** which are to be carried out by us—but rather as a description of what Christians ought to be, illustrated in certain particular respects...It is no mechanical rule...It is...a general principle and attitude.

Indeed, although Jesus said *"if you love me you would obey my commands" (John 14:15),* he did not mean that his "wisdom sayings" in the Sermon on the Mount are to be viewed as a set of regulations i.e. laws replacing the regulations in the Mosaic law, as just noted by Lloyd-Jones and other theologians to be not the case. Indeed, Jesus himself read the commands in the Mosaic law through the lens of love—he read it relationally. So, the Sermon on the Mount was not transformed into an even narrower, stricter, and more legalistic version of the Pentateuch which the Pharisees read legally. If the Sermon on the Mount is read this way it becomes an impossible-to-bear judgment—a series of mandates giving an impossible-to-attain standard. So, even when Paul uses the terms "the law of Christ" (Gal. 6:2) or "the law of faith" (Rom. 3:27) or "the law of the spirit" (Rom. 8:2) he does not mean that these are new regulations, even though they must be taken seriously. Also, please note when reading the Sermon on the Mount that there is a great deal of hyperbole used by Jesus, which should give us pause when trying to understand exactly what he meant on each facet of the Sermon on the Mount. So, from Jesus' approach to the Mosaic law in the Sermon on the Mount it is evident that the Christian should discern the moral principles which underlie each text of that law and then apply the relevant principle to the various situations in life and not be reading it like good Pharisees. So, Robert A, Guelich in his book *The Sermon on the Mount: A Foundation for Understanding* p.159 says:

> Contrary to the opinion of some, [Matt] 5:20 does not demand a more rigorous keeping of the Law or a more rigorous interpretation of the Law. Rather, Jesus demands *righteousness* congruent with his coming.

This same biblical approach helps Christians with their understanding of the subject of divorce and remarriage and which comes in the form of the principles drawn from the case law as presented primarily in Deuteronomy 24:1-4 and Exodus 21:10-11,

91

although there are other relevant passages on this subject. So, Christians are to discern the principles applicable to divorce and remarriage as much today as in Hebrew Scripture times just as Paul indicated in 2 Timothy 3:16.

1) What Is the Context of Jesus' Statements on Divorce in Matthew 5:31-32?

The context of Jesus' statements on divorce can be seen when all of his sayings in the Sermon on the Mount are examined, and they all concern things of the heart that are either inappropriate or are wrongly motivated concerning the following aspects of life: inappropriate anger (5:21-26), inappropriate sexual desire (5:27-30), divorce (5:31-32), failure to keep promises (5:33-37), the wrongness of retaliation (5:38-42), and the wrongness of hating one's enemies (5:43-48). Then Jesus spelled out factors concerning wrong motives concerning the giving to the needy (6:1-4), one's prayers, including failure to forgive (6:5-14), and one's fasting (6:16-18). Finally, he showed up wrong motives concerning wealth, clothing, and food (6:19-34), as well as that of judging others (7:1-6). All of this is summed up in his saying of, *"treat people the same way you want them to treat you. Indeed, this fulfils the Law and the Prophets"* (7:12). Clearly, in this context of things that are inappropriate and wrongly motivated, it is evident that "divorce," as noted here, must refer to wrongly motivated divorce involving a bad spirit. Furthermore, the full background that we have examined regarding divorce strongly indicates this. This background concerned God's own divorce, His sanctioning of Abraham's divorce from Hagar, and his purposely causing some divorces as punishment for wicked men. This all shows that, in the context of the Sermon on the Mount the divorce spoken of here must refer to treacherous invalid divorce as with the men in Malachi's time and the treacherous divorces perpetrated by Herod and Herodias as condemned by John the Baptist.

2) In the Exception Clause Presented in Both Matthew 5:32 and 19:9 What Does *"Porneia"* Mean?

The word *porneia* in the exception clause is recorded only in the two passages of Matthew i.e., 5:32 and 19:9. So, in 5:32 Jesus said:

"Anyone divorcing his wife, **except for** *"a* **cause of sexual immorality**, *makes her a victim of [his] adultery. And any man who marries a woman who has divorced [in this way] commits adultery"* and similarly in 19:9.

THE VALIDITY OF THE "EXCEPT FOR SEXUAL IMMORALITY" CLAUSE

Some commentators propose that Jesus himself never said the words "except for sexual immorality," but rather that Matthew added them. Even if this was the case that Matthew added the phrase back into his account, it is clear that the phrase is still part of the inspired text and was present and legitimate in the original debate. Indeed, Matthew adds other exceptions on other subjects that are only implied in the other Gospels—e.g., compare Matthew 12:39—"except the sign of Jonah"—but missing in Mark 8:11-12. Again, some who try to prove that Jesus did not allow divorce for any reason say that the Greek phrase *me epi porneia* in Matthew 19:9 does not mean "except for sexual immorality," but means "**not for** sexual immorality" as if there is no exception. This is incorrect because the United Bible Society's interlinear shows that *me epi* means "not based upon" and therefore meaning "except for." Indeed, all Bible translators render it as "except for." Also, in the parallel phrase of Matthew 5:32 the text directly uses the Greek word *parektos* which means "except for." So, it is clear that Jesus made an exception in Matthew 5 and therefore also in Matthew 19 in his condemnation of the "any cause" divorce policy of the Pharisees. Furthermore, because Matthew 19 is the fullest account of Jesus' words on this subject it should be viewed as taking precedence over the other less detailed accounts, these also implying the same as in Matthew 19.

"PORNEIA" IN THE SEPTUAGINT AS A TRANSLATION FROM THE HEBREW

The translators of the Greek Septuagint rendered the following Hebrew words using the *porne* word group: *taznut, zanah, zenut*, with a total of 49 occurrences and generally translated into English as a reference to **prostitution or unfaithfulness**, but with the meaning of **something shameful or indecent and applied to sexual matters** in Jesus' encounter with the Pharisees.

To What Does *Porneia* Not Refer

FORNICATION WITH ANOTHER PARTY DURING BETROTHAL

It has been proposed that, in the accounts of Jesus' teaching, the Greek word *porneia* refers to 'fornication' committed by a betrothed woman, so that she is dismissed before the actual wedding and therefore no certificate of divorce was required. This was because they were, supposedly, not actually married in the complete sense i.e. there was no binding marriage contract in the first place. However, this understanding does not fit for the following reasons: Firstly, the word "fornication" has changed meaning since it was used in the King James Version of the Bible, and secondly, although not an actual marriage, the Jewish betrothal was a verbal legal contract just as binding as marriage (Deut. 20:7; 22:24). In fact, legal action could be taken to divorce the sexually immoral party. Yet Jesus could not be referring to this situation because the Hillelite/Shammaite encounter between the Pharisees and himself concerned *marriage* in Deuteronomy 24 and not betrothal. So, Jesus would not have changed the commonly understood meaning of the terms under discussion, but only the faulty interpretation of the subject.

"THE FORBIDDEN SEXUAL RELATIONSHIPS"

Because Jesus was criticizing those who use the divorce certificate too freely, as in the Hillelite type of divorce, and therefore unjust, the definition of *porneia* as "incestuous marriages" does not fit. This is because a divorce certificate was not required in these cases—these being invalid as marriage from the start and not recognized as marriage by the rabbis. This fact seems to make the two Catholic renderings in the Gospel accounts of the exception clause of, "unless the marriage is unlawful" *(NAB)* and "except for the case of an illicit marriage" *(NJB)* incorrect. So, the definition of "the forbidden sexual relations," is too limited a definition to fit with the context of Jesus' teaching. Also please note that marriage is not a sacrament as in the Roman Catholic teaching. Furthermore, Professor of New Testament Craig Keener notes that: "there is nothing in the semantic range of "immorality" to limit the term to incestuous unions." ...*And Marries Another* p.29.

Porneia Refers to Sexual Immorality

What do Jesus' words "except for *porneia*" mean? The fact that the Hebrew term *erwat dabar* is rendered as "**some indecency**" in Deuteronomy 24:1 and that its definition is "nakedness of a thing" shows that there was a sexual component to it. So, it likely has the meaning of "some sexual indecency." This originally was taken to mean: **any sexual misconduct** on the part of a wife according to the accusation made by the husband in Deuteronomy 24:1. However, from the terms used by the Pharisees in their confrontation with Jesus, it is evident that Jesus used the term *porneia* in the way commonly accepted by both Hillel and Shammai, namely, as referring to sexual unfaithfulness or **sexual immorality,** just as most translations today render it. Such sexual immorality would include: **incest, prostitution (male or female), bestiality, and homosexual relations**—all of which are adulterous. However, sexual immorality in its older and broader sense likely would include: **rape of the wife or sexual deviations such as cross-dressing or other perversions.** On the other hand, Craig keener also proposes that:

> Matthew's point seems to be that sexual sin within marriage need not be limited to the wife's having intercourse with another man; what if she habitually pursues the other man, but he refuses to return her affections? She may not be technically guilty of adultery, but it is certainly sexual immorality in the broad sense. ...*And Marries Another* p. 32.

So even without committing actual adultery, any of these practices would break the marriage contract. Certainly, in Jesus' teaching, the above-mentioned types of sexual immorality by a husband or a wife would be grounds for divorce. Sadly, when Matthew 5:31-32 is read in a harsh literalistic way, by ignoring the obvious hyperbole, it would mean that Jesus abolished the protection for women created by the principles set out in Exodus 21:10-11 and Deuteronomy 24:1-4.

Now we will examine the lengthy statements made by Jesus as recorded in Matthew 19:1-12 on this subject?

§

16

Understanding Jesus on Divorce
in Matthew 19:1-6

Because Matthew 19:1-12 is by far the most detailed gospel passage on divorce, it is clear that the other divorce passages should all be read in the light of this passage. Also, as we have just noted in Jesus' statements on divorce in the Sermon on the Mount (Matt. 5:31, 32), he himself directly referenced two factors taken from Deuteronomy 24:1-4. Indeed, we must note that when, in Matthew 19:3-9, Jesus was confronted on the subject of divorce by the religious leaders they referenced one of those factors from Deuteronomy 24:1-4. This indicates that this entire passage has a strong bearing on his teaching on divorce. However, some modern-day Christians wrongly say that in Matthew 19:3-10 Jesus abolished all factors of the Law of Moses from the discussion on divorce or, at least, Jesus repealed part of the Mosaic Law of divorce. They say that, by appealing to Genesis 1:27 and 2:24 concerning God's original arrangement for marriage, Jesus was showing, in Matthew 19:4-6, 8, that divorce in any of the Mosaic law was only a temporary arrangement and was replaced by a "no-divorce" rule based on those two Genesis texts. This is clearly not so for all the reasons mentioned in the previous chapter and in Chapter 7 which showed that Jesus highly valued the Law. In fact, in Matthew 15:3-6 he quoted from the passages in Exodus 20:12 and 21:17 and stated that he was against nullifying any of God's word. Secondly, Jesus even told a certain Jew to "practice keeping the commandments" after which he listed several of these from the Ten Commandments (Matt.19:17-19). Thirdly, in Matthew 5:17-20, Jesus denied that he was abrogating the statements of the Mosaic law at that time. He simply corrected the Pharisees wrong interpretations of that law! Furthermore, both Jesus and Paul applied the spirit of the Law. This is why Paul later said that, *"all Scripture...is profitable for...training in moral uprightness..." (2 Tim. 3:16 KGV)*. This is a reference to the entire Hebrew Bible and is important because it means that we can learn something from every part of the Hebrew Bible, including every word Moses wrote! This alone shows that Jesus did not repeal the moral standard and principles described in the case law on divorce given by Moses and which show us God's way of thinking on various issues. Yet, what is said here is not a promotion of any keeping of the cancelled regulations of the Law since Jesus' crucifixion!

So now we will look at each of the questions posed at the end of Chapter 14 relating to Matthew 19:1-6.

1. Why and How Did the Pharisees Propose to Trap Jesus?

According to the statements made by Jesus, as recorded in Matthew 19:1 and Mark 10:2, the confrontation Jesus had with the Pharisees over the issue of divorce occurred in Perea—the territory governed by Herod Antipas. So, it is likely that the Pharisees hoped to trick Jesus into commenting negatively on the **divorce and marriage** of Herod Antipas who had dismissed his wife so that he could marry Herodias, the wife of his brother Philip. In fact, John the Baptizer had previously said to Herod, *"It is not lawful for you to be having her" (Matt. 14:4).* This was because of the Mosaic Law which said *"You shall not uncover the nakedness of your brother's wife; it is your brother's nakedness" (Lev. 18:16 and 20:21).* For this John was thrown into prison and later executed. So, to spring their trap upon Jesus the Pharisees used their interpretation of Deuteronomy 24:1 as well as aspects of the Hillelite/Shammaite debate to provoke Jesus into contradicting the Mosaic Law, so that he might be discredited in the eyes of the common people. However, Jesus did not fall into their trap, but made statements which showed the faultiness of the Pharisees' views and interpretations.

2. Evidence That the Pharisees' Question Concerned Deuteronomy 24:1 as Divorce for Men Only?

The Pharisees first question was, *"Is it **lawful** for <u>a man</u> to divorce a wife for "**any cause**"?"* Clearly, this concerned divorce for men only and their use of this phrase "for **any cause**," as connected to Deuteronomy 24:1, directly related to the Hillelite/Shammaite debate that was discussed in Chapter 13. The fact that the Pharisees raised the matter of "**the divorce certificate**" also makes it evident that this encounter concerned Deuteronomy 24:1, which was the only text referring to the divorce certificate, as well as involving the Hebrew phrase *erwat dabar*—"something indecent" or "nakedness of a thing." This was one of the very grounds that the Pharisees had determined for a man to divorce his wife." Professor James Dunn comments on this issue stating that:

> ...in Mark 10:2 the question reads simply, 'Can a man divorce his wife?'; but Matthew reformulates it, 'Can a man divorce his wife *for any cause?*' Thereby he transforms a general question and sets it within the rabbinic debate between the schools of Hillel and Shammai; the Matthean formulation in fact presupposes the then current practice of divorce and **asks Jesus for a verdict on the then dominant Hillelite position** (divorce permissible for any cause). With the same effect, the unconditional ruling of Jesus in Mark 10:11 is amended by Matthew to allow the possibility of divorce in cases of unchastity—the more rigorous position of Shammai (19:9; so 5:32). Jesus is thus shown as engaging in a current rabbinic debate and as favouring the stricter viewpoint of the Shammaites. *Unity and Diversity in the New Testament.* p. 247

Because of the terms and phrases used in this encounter between Jesus and the Pharisees, it is clear that it concerned the Pharisees' interpretation of Deuteronomy 24:1-4. In the question put to Jesus the Pharisees used the phrases: "**for any cause**" (or "any matter"), as part of the Hebrew phrase "erwat dabar," and "**certificate of divorce**" which are found only in Deuteronomy 24:1-4. So, Jesus' response concerned the interpretation of Deuteronomy 24:1-4 as the "any cause" position of these Pharisees.

3. Why the "Any Cause" Policy Promoted Scripturally Invalid Grounds for Divorce

In the context of Jesus' dealing primarily with the Hillelite Pharisees' position, such divorces were often treacherous and unjust, in spite of a certificate of divorce being provided. These divorces lacked genuine grounds based on Scripture and so they were not scriptural divorces—the grounds were invalid. Certainly, in the male dominated world of the time such a divorce was often unjust for the wives of treacherous husbands as in the time of Malachi, this resulting in God's condemnation of their cruelty. This kind of bad situation also seems to have existed in Jesus' time, because of the harsh advocating of treacherous and easy divorcing of wives i.e., with no substantial grounds for the divorcing and no repentance for it. So, the kind of divorce mentioned in all four accounts must concern the common "any cause" policy for divorce— this easy divorce being contrary to Jesus' biblical view obtained from the Mosaic law. Evidently, if all four of the texts concerning divorce were referring to a scripturally valid divorce, then the statements would be illogical. It would be comparable to saying: "Everyone who leaves the army and joins the navy commits an illegal act." But when the implied thought is added i.e., that they left the army **without a valid discharge** (the grounds), it makes sense. So, when we recognize that Jesus was referring to the popular, but **invalid, Hillelite type of easy divorcing of a wife** then his statements make sense. So, the man who simply divorced his wife or the woman who simply divorced her husband for the purpose of marrying another particular person, thereby having no legitimate grounds for divorce, would immediately be committing adultery at least in the metaphorical sense of "unfaithfulness" i.e., breach of the marriage contract (see Chapter 28) even though they may not have had actual sexual intercourse with that "other" person.

IT WAS ONLY TREACHEROUS DIVORCE THAT JESUS CONDEMNED

Furthermore, the fact that the Pharisees spoke of Moses as having given the law to provide "a certificate of divorce" shows that they thought that their "any cause" divorce procedure was legal simply because the divorcing man provided his wife with a "certificate of divorce." However, it appears that **Jesus did not agree that the providing of a certificate of divorce legitimized a divorce based on trivial grounds or with a treacherous motive**; so he really did not agree with any of the positions of the various groups of Pharisees in their interpretation of Deuteronomy 24, and so directed them to the earlier Genesis passages so that he might correct the Pharisees.

4. Jesus' Digression to Genesis 1:27 and 2:24

Jesus' quoting of the two Genesis texts and his other statements were absolutely not a discounting of the principles God established through Moses on this subject, but rather it was a digression to correct wrong thinking on the part of the Pharisees regarding their polygamy and the ideal of life-long marriage rather than the easy divorce that they espoused and which allowed for the practice of treacherous divorce for the men of the time. Jesus knew that all groups of Pharisees had down-played the application of these Genesis texts regarding faithfulness in marriage and now they were elevating their misinterpreted scenario from the passage in Deuteronomy 24. So now Jesus was correcting that misinterpreted teaching. The passage in Matthew 19:4-6 reads:

> "[Jesus] answered [the Pharisees], 'Have you not read that he who created them from the beginning made them **male and female** (Gen. 1:27), and said, "Therefore a man shall leave his father and his mother and <u>hold fast to</u> his wife, and they shall become one flesh" (Gen. 2:24)? So they are no longer <u>two</u> but **one flesh**. What therefore God has joined together **let not man separate**'" (ESV).

The use of Genesis 1:27 was part of the standard proof of monogamy. The use of Genesis 2:24 was the standard proof that marriage should be monogamous and lifelong. These two texts from Genesis are linked by Jesus into one thought in typical rabbinic fashion—a technique called *gezarah shavah*. In making his summary statement of: *"so they are no longer <u>two</u> but **one flesh**, and no one should break apart what God has joined together"* Jesus focused on the "sinless ideal" of life-long monogamous marriage i.e., when Adam and Eve were in their perfection. This is the absolute goal for every marriage—the ideal standard that Christians, even in their imperfection, should aim for! However, it may also be a reference to what marriage will once again be like in God's Kingdom. So, with the two Genesis texts Jesus was simply showing where he stood on this vital issue, namely: God's standard was of yoking *only two* people together in life-long marriage, so that there should never be easy divorce for trivial reasons or with a treacherous motive. **However, in no way was Jesus using these two verses from**

100

Genesis to repeal the principles contained in the case law on divorce given by Moses. This was not a way, given by Jesus, to demonstrate that Moses gave only **temporary permission for all divorce which must now be repealed because Genesis gives another law, an earlier so-called higher law.** Please note that neither the texts in Genesis 1:27 and 2:24 nor Jesus words in Matthew 19:1-9 use the words of later exegetes such as "permanent," "inviolable" or "sacred." Indeed, **the passage says nothing about repealing the God-given principles established in the Mosaic case law.** Otherwise, there would be no "exception clause." Also, we can see this by the fact that the "Pharisees approached in order to trap him" into contradicting the Mosaic Law—their reason being so that he might be discredited in the eyes of the common people. So, if Jesus had, at that time, repealed even *"one dot or one stroke of a letter" (Matt. 5:18)* of Moses' statements on divorce in front of these hypocrites he would have fallen into their trap—but he didn't! Indeed, these two quotations from Genesis were used by Jesus as a digression to correct their polygamy, their low view of marriage, and their acceptance of easy divorce. In particular, Jesus used these Genesis texts to show that these Pharisees were interpreting and applying Deuteronomy 24 incorrectly and so allowing for the easy divorcing of a woman for no good reason. In fact, the complete passage is really a condemnation of any hard-hearted man in his divorcing of his wife when he really has no legitimate grounds, but rather has concocted a lie about her. So here, Jesus was closing one of the loopholes in the Jewish case law used at the time. This had previously blocked women from divorcing such husbands for what was, in reality, the husband's faithless adultery.

NOTE: The term *"the two"* is not in the Masoretic text of Genesis 2:24, but only in a variant Hebrew text as well as in the Septuagint (LXX). Nevertheless, Jesus' phrase draws upon Genesis 1:27 ("male and female he created him") as well as the fact that even the animals were gathered "two by two (Gen. 7:9)."

DOES "CLEAVE UNTO" MEAN AN ABSOLUTELY UNBREAKABLE BOND?

It is sometimes taught that because a husband must "hold fast to" or "be joined to his wife" in Jesus' reference to Genesis 2:24 that it indicates an absolutely unbreakable and permanent bond. Is this true? On this the King James Version of Genesis 2:24 reads as: -

"Therefore shall a man leave his father and his mother, and shall **cleave unto** his wife: and they shall be one flesh." The argument that the term "cleave unto" refers to an absolutely unbreakable and permanent bond is supposedly further strengthened by the fact that Jesus quoted this passage in his debate with the Pharisees over the subject of divorce as recorded in Matthew 19:5. However, does the Hebrew term *dabag* rendered as "**cleave unto**" in Genesis 2:24 of the KJV really refer to such an absolutely unbreakable bond as if with super-glue and therefore permanent, no matter what? In spite of this definition of *dabag* being presented by certain writers on the subject of divorce, there is evidence to the contrary. This is because of the way the word is used in other passages of the Hebrew Scriptures. For example, *dabag* refers to the clumping together of soil after heavy rain (Job 38:38), and of a military alliance (Josh. 23:12), both of which were not permanent. For this reason, it is clear that the term *dabag* means a tight connection and **an intention of permanence**, but not necessarily absolute permanence. Therefore, the *God's Word Translation* renders Genesis 2:24 as: *"That is why a man will leave his father and mother and will **be united with** his wife, and they will become one flesh."* In fact, several other translations of Genesis 2:24 also use the term "united with" to show the tight connection and intention of permanence, but **not necessarily absolute permanence**. Furthermore, even though a different term is used, this is just as with Christians as being "united with Christ," but can fall away from him. So, clearly "cleave unto" does not mean that divorce can never happen! In fact, those who teach that *dabag* refers to absolute permanence of a marriage, but who then allow for Jesus' "except for sexual immorality" clause, are holding two contradictory thoughts and therefore a contradictory position. They must choose one or the other. If they choose the position of "permanence" then they must reject Jesus' exception. Clearly, the fact that Jesus' clause of "except for sexual immorality" shows that the bond may not necessarily be absolutely permanent. Similarly, the Greek word *proskallao,* used in Matthew 19:5 for Jesus' quotation from Genesis 2:24, also contains no sense of absolute permanence.

Because God uses "the authorities" to keep order in society (Rom. 13:1) a marriage service conducted by one of their representatives is just as valid as a "church wedding" and God has "joined together" this couple by being a witness to their marriage i.e., giving His approval. Additionally, the couple themselves *bind or join* themselves to each other by their making of contractual marriage vows. So, to summarize, God only *joins* the couple together because He is a witness (Mal. 2:14) to their marriage vows and gives them His approval.

NOTE: In Acts 5:36 Theudas' followers "joined up with him," but not permanently so.

ONE FLESH

Additionally, the term "one flesh" in Genesis 2:24 does not mean that the couple become one person, but that they become one family, one clan, one team, and a unit functioning in harmony, and so ending their right to make unilateral decisions. However, by New Testament times this term came to include the thought of a physical uniting i.e. the sexual relationship. Nevertheless, this does not mean that the "one flesh" union cannot be undone. For instance, Paul speaks of a man's "one flesh" union with a prostitute (1 Cor. 6:16), but in no way is such a union permanent. Indeed, the bond between a married couple is broken the moment he goes with a prostitute, so that "what God has joined" in his marriage gets broken by the man.

5. What Does "What God Has Joined Together Let No One Break Apart" Mean in 19:6b?

It is believed by many Christians that every marriage between a man and a woman is one which is "joined together" by God. However, in Chapter 12 we saw that this is not the case according to the situations described in Ezra chapters 9-10 and Nehemiah 13:23-27. Certainly, God would not be a "witness" to the marriage of a professing "Christian" couple who were living outside of His will, perhaps engaging in illegal activities. If, in Ephesians 5:11, God commands Christians to, *"keep away from the fruitless deeds of darkness,"* then God Himself is not going to look favourably upon a marrying couple who are engaging in those things. Furthermore, God is not going to approve of a union where one partner is a secretive practicing homosexual (see Appendix A). Such marriages will not be blessed by God, unless the guilty party in the couple repents and corrects all their wrong-doing.

"LET NO ONE BREAK APART"

The "no one" in this phrase obviously refers to the married couple themselves because no one outside of the marriage can make them divorce. Indeed, because the phrase, *"no one should break apart (Gk chorizo = divorce) what God has joined together"* is in the imperative, Jesus is really telling couples to keep their marriage vows and not to act in a way that would cause divorce. Unfortunately, there has been a misguided teaching within many denominations that there can never be any divorce. However, God does not approve of marriages where the marriage covenant has been broken by one or both partners by the persistent breaking of marriage vows. The fact is that God expects couples to live up to those vows and to continue living a holy life. If one or both partners fail in this then He no longer approves of their marriage.

WHAT ABOUT "TILL DEATH DO US PART"?

This church service wedding vow is one which is not found in the Bible. Although this is the goal of marriage it is an invalid vow and should not be made part of the responsibilities in a marriage. The appropriate vows are gleaned from and based upon the statements in 1 Corinthians 7:2-5 and Ephesians 5:21-33.

17

Understanding Jesus on Divorce in Matthew 19:7-9

One of the remaining questions on divorce in Matthew 19 posed at the end of Chapter 14 concerns a most vital subject on which we must get clarity. This is: "how should we understand what is commonly called the Mosaic Concession?" But before that we must deal with what appears to be an anomaly in 19:7-9a and Mark 10:4-5.

6. The Certificate of Divorce Was "Commanded" But Divorce Was Only "Allowed"

In the two parallel accounts of Matthew 19:7-8 and Mark 10:3-4 there is a reversal of the verbs "allowed" and "command." Why is this? The two accounts read:

> "[The Pharisees] said to him, "Why then did Moses <u>command</u> us to give a certificate of divorce **and to divorce her**? Jesus said to them, "Moses <u>allowed</u> you to divorce your wives because of your **hardness of heart**, but from the beginning it hasn't been this way" (Matt. 19:7, 8).
>
> "[Jesus] answered them, "What did Moses <u>command</u> you?" [The Pharisees] said, "Moses <u>allowed</u> a man to write a certificate of **divorce** and to divorce his wife. But Jesus said to them, "It was because of your hard heartedness that he wrote **this commandment** for you" (Mark 10:3-5).

A COMMAND FOR A DIVORCE CERTIFICATE-NOT A COMMAND TO DIVORCE
Because of the way the Pharisees used the two words "command" and "allowed" it appears that they were **trying to justify their teaching that divorce should be compulsory in cases of adultery.** This apparent discrepancy over the reversal of the verbs "allowed" and "command" in these parallel accounts is quickly resolved when one analyses them carefully to see that:

105

- In **Mark's account** Jesus showed that God, through Moses, gave the 'command' to give a *certificate of divorce* and an 'allowance' or tolerance of a husband's hard-hearted divorcing of a wife. Then Mark reveals that the **Pharisees weakened the "command" to give a certificate of divorce to being only an 'allowance.'** However, Jesus fully recognized that it was a "commandment" to give a certificate of divorce because of Jewish hard-heartedness toward their wives, but not a command to divorce her.

- In **Matthew's account** the Pharisees present the idea that God had made it compulsory to divorce an unfaithful wife; yet in Matthew the fact that they weakened the "command" to give a certificate of divorce to being only an 'allowance is not revealed.' However, **Jesus shows that it was only an allowance to divorce and therefore divorce was not compulsory.** Evidently, Jesus views the Jewish male hard-heartedness as God's toleration of their divorcing of a wife, resulting in the wife's release from a very bad situation. In fact, the phrase *"divorces his wife and he marries another"* shows that there was an improper motive for the divorcing of the wife, with no legitimate grounds. This was done so that the husband could marry someone for whom he already had feelings i.e., he divorces his wife so that he can marry another, as with Herod Antipas and Herodias.

Furthermore, in Deuteronomy 24:1 the Septuagint says *"he shall write,"* rather than "and he writes" which is in the Hebrew Masoretic Text. So, these rabbis misinterpreted Moses' command as if, in the case of *some indecency (erwat dabar)*, divorce of one's wife was to be **compulsory.** Therefore, both schools of the Pharisees, namely, Hillel and Shammai are saying that divorce is necessary because even Moses commands it for adultery and many other reasons, but Jesus says it was only allowed because of their hard-heartedness. The Pharisees introduced this thought of the "command...to give a certificate of divorce" into the confrontation with Jesus in order to counter Jesus' teaching on intended lifelong marriage, but Jesus responds that God, through Moses, did not command any divorce but only allowed it because of their hardheartedness toward a wife so that **she** could be free from any further abuse by the husband and by giving her the right to remarry. So, both Moses (in Deuteronomy 24) and Jesus were not condoning men's hard-heartedness, but were making and restating a caring provision for a mistreated wife.

7. How Should We Understand the **Mosaic Concession** in Matthew 19:8?

Jesus stated that: *"Moses <u>allowed you</u> to divorce your wives because of <u>your</u> hard-heartedness, but from the beginning it hasn't been this way."* Although there may have been many hard-hearted male Israelites from Moses' time right up to Jesus' time, here the hard-heartedness must be more specific because it is mentioned in the context of the debate on divorce based on Deuteronomy 24:1 where the wife "finds no favour in [her husband's] eyes." As we saw Chapter 9 this concerned any husband who had been hard-hearted toward a wife **by trivially or treacherously divorcing her** and likely had been neglecting her throughout the marriage. Such men showed significant disregard for their wives, their marriages, and their marriage vows. Furthermore, Jesus was very aware of the two more recent situations concerning treacherous divorce, namely, in Malachi's day and that of Herod/Herodius. Clearly, the Pharisees were no different than the hard-hearted men of earlier times. Indeed, one of the reasons they engaged with Jesus on this subject was so that they could legitimize the divorcing of a wife for no good reason by incorrectly interpreting Deuteronomy 24:1 in men's favour. In reality, this "any cause" divorce was trivial or treacherous divorce because of the hard-heartedness of these Pharisees toward their wives.

"BUT FROM THE BEGINNING IT HASN'T BEEN THIS WAY"
This phrase in Matthew 19:8 is connected to the Pharisees' assumed unilateral right to hard-heartedly divorce a wife for "any cause" (vs.3) i.e., trivial or treacherous divorce. This idea is what lay behind their question on this subject and this was how they interpreted Moses' words in Deuteronomy 24. So, it was the implication from the Pharisees' wrong interpretation that Jesus was referring to when he said, *"from the beginning it hasn't been this way."* Evidently, this phrase references Adam's marriage as an

archetype i.e., ideal model of what God intended marriage to be and was in the perfection of the Garden of Eden—prior to mankind's transgression/sin—hard-heartedness being an example of such sin. Indeed, when Jesus said, *"Moses allowed you to divorce your wives because of your hard-heartedness, but from the beginning it hasn't been this way"* we must ask ourselves what is the "it" that hasn't been from the beginning! Was it simply all divorce that was the concession? Or was it an allowance for "divorcing your wives because of your hard-heartedness, that is, **hard-hearted divorce**" Clearly, in Matthew 19:8 it is the latter as Jesus stated, namely, *"divorcing your wives because of your hard-heartedness"*—that is the "it" in this phrase rather than divorce per se! All of this is evident because Jesus then went on to show that divorce for a woman's "sexual immorality" would refer to a legitimate divorce in contrast to the dismissing of a wife for no good reason.

So, to reiterate: when Jesus says, *"Moses allowed you to divorce your wives because of your hard-heartedness, but from the beginning it hasn't been this way,"* it was **only allowed as a concession because of the "hard-heartedness" of husbands; and, in fact, was specifically to allow a wife to become free of a bad husband,** as well as to allow her to remarry—the certificate of divorce making this possible. So, researcher on the subject of biblical divorce, Barbara Roberts notes that:

> Jesus explained that Moses wrote these words not to command or authorize divorce but because of the hardness of heart of some husbands: they had a callous disregard for their marriage covenants and were divorcing their wives for no good reason. The so-called "Mosaic concession" was not an indulgent concession; Moses simply described the undesirable sin of hardhearted divorce in order to regulate the worst outcome which might eventuate after that kind of divorce—the abuse of divorce and remarriage so that they resembled pimping and adultery. In effect Jesus told the Pharisees: "Moses gave this passage in Deuteronomy 24 because of *your hardness of heart*. He did not license such divorce to indulge you in your selfishness and obstinacy. He did not give formal approval to men who wanted to divorce their wives treacherously. *From the beginning it was not so.* If you had interpreted Deuteronomy 24 in the light of Genesis 2, you would never have drawn the conclusions you have!" *Not Under Bondage* p.83

So, in Matthew 19:8, Jesus was not teaching that the principles gleaned from Deuteronomy 24:1 or any other part of the Law of Moses were now defunct or repealed, even though God's people were freed from the regulations of that law when Jesus died.

From his analysis of all the relevant Scriptures Craig keener notes concerning Jesus that: "His point is that Moses put up with their divorcing because the best he could get out of hard-hearted people was legal protection for the one divorced against her will." This is further indicated by Jesus when he says: "*don't think that I have come to destroy the Law or the Prophets. I haven't come to destroy, but to show them in their fullness (or "fulfil them")*" (*Matt. 5:17-19*). This is said not long before his statement on divorce in verses 31 and 32 which contextually concerns invalid divorce in the Sermon on the Mount, and so showing that we are not to think that Jesus would attempt to change God's moral standard. Since all morality is a reflection of God's character which cannot change, it is impossible for the moral standard for God's people to change. So, Jesus never changed any single moral factor in the Mosaic Law, but rather he corrected the things that had been obscured by rabbinic tradition. Indeed, he corrected the Pharisees who challenged him on this issue of divorce and this is just as he and Paul changed nothing regarding the view stated in the Hebrew Scriptures against homosexual conduct or other universal moral matters. We simply cannot pit Jesus against God in defining morality! However, nothing that Jesus said in Matthew 19:4-9 was said so as to disallow legitimate divorce, as for example the grounds of "sexual immorality." Certainly, it was only treacherous or trivial divorce using invalid grounds that was wrong according to Jesus. As shown earlier, God Himself was a divorcee, but for legitimate reasons.

Moving Away from the Misinterpretations of the Past

Those who teach that Moses gave only a **temporary permission for all divorce** and that God's original standard in the Garden of Eden is now absolutely binding on Christians as a law with no exceptions, so that divorce is always disallowed have sadly misread and misunderstood Jesus' intentions. This challenge to Jesus by the Pharisees as recorded in Matthew 19:1-9 did not happen in a theological or cultural vacuum and failure to realize this leads to the traditional misreading of Jesus' words. In fact, such a misreading contradicts Jesus' exception clause in both this passage and in Matthew 5:32 as well as Paul's exception in 1 Corinthians 7:15. Indeed, Jesus did not overturn this Mosaic concession to divorce because **it was not a concession to divorce**, but a concession for the benefit of a suffering wife.

MERCY IN CONTRAST TO HARD-HEARTEDNESS

In both Matthew 9:13 and 12:7 Jesus shows that the right way to interpret the Mosaic Law should be with mercy rather than with "hard-heartedness" as was the case with the Pharisees and earlier interpreters. In fact, Jesus said to these Pharisees: *"Go and learn what this saying means: 'I desire mercy, and not sacrifice' (Hos. 6:6); because I didn't come to call those [considered] faultless, but sinners"* (Matt. 9:13).

We now come to question #8, our final question listed at the end of Chapter 14. This was: "why were the grounds for divorce that are stated in Exodus 21:10, 11 not discussed in Jesus' debate with the Pharisees?"

18

Why Was Exodus 21:10-11
Not Discussed with the Pharisees?

The basic answer to this question is that Jesus' debate on divorce with the Pharisees was within the narrow confines of discussion on details from Deuteronomy 24. On this, Barbara Roberts explains that:

> Facing this kind of interrogation, it is unlikely that Jesus would have delivered a comprehensive teaching on *all* aspects of divorce and remarriage, or touched on all the Old Testament passages. Blomberg notes that "The specific historical background that informs this debate, the particular way in which the question is phrased, and the unscrupulous motives behind the Pharisees' approach all warn us against the notion that Jesus was comprehensively addressing all relevant questions about marriage and divorce. *Not Under Bondage* p. 86.

So, because this encounter significantly concerned the interpretation of Deuteronomy 24:1-4, as so-called grounds for divorce, the debate didn't deal with the known other valid reasons for a divorce that are detailed in Exodus 21:10, 11, namely, **material neglect** (concerning food and clothing) and **physical/emotional neglect** (concerning conjugal love). These grounds were accepted by all at the time, although none of the Gospel accounts directly inform us about Jesus' thoughts concerning those grounds for divorce.

Would Jesus Have Recognized the Statements in Exodus 21:10-11 as Grounds for Divorce?

Because Jesus named only the single exception of "sexual immorality" as grounds for divorce in the two accounts in Matthew and was silent on any grounds at all in Mark and Luke, it has been assumed that he did not recognize the grounds for divorce detailed in Exodus 21:10, 11. This, however, is a faulty assumption. Indeed, if we made the same assumption about the Shammaite Pharisees we would conclude that they thought that adultery was the only ground for divorce; whereas, in fact, they did actually recognize the three factors concerning neglect in the law of Exodus 21:10, 11 as grounds for divorce. However, because Jesus' focus had been narrowed by the Pharisees question to the issue in Deuteronomy 24:1-4 the most natural conclusion is that he certainly would also have respectfully acknowledged and agreed with the principles in the case law of Exodus 21:10-11. Indeed, for Jesus *"all scripture is...profitable for teaching" (2 Tim. 3:16).* In fact, if Jesus was teaching "no divorce for neglect or abuse" he would be contradicting the principles behind the Hebrew Scriptures on this issue, and he would have "nullified God's word" in the commandments that were still relevant at the time of the debate with the Pharisees (Matt. 15:3-6). He would even have invalidated the wording on the many marriage certificates of everyone listening to him at that time. If he had actually meant to do that, he would have **said something definite** about there being no divorce for neglect or abuse, but he didn't! In fact, it makes no sense to say Jesus was denying God's teaching in the Hebrew Scriptures merely because he did not actually say that he agreed with it! Even the marriage vows used by the churches of today include these necessary factors from Exodus 21 as vows (also taken from Ephesians 5:28-29). Indeed, these would serve as a basis for divorce if they were continually being broken.

Factors about the Strong Argument from Silence

When a silence concerns a significant belief or opinion or kind of conduct that is universally accepted at the time, and there is a suitable context, the silence most likely indicates agreement. Otherwise, silence can be misused, e.g., the Trinity doctrine which has no basis in the Hebrew Bible and which was never believed in during Jesus' time. So, the factors regarding Jesus' silence are:

a. **Jesus did not mention other grounds for divorce:** In this encounter with the Pharisees Jesus also spoke about matters that he was not asked about i.e., polygamy and lifelong marriage. This was because for him, these were vital issues. So, it would seem strange for him to raise these specific issues and yet fail to discuss the Exodus 21 biblical grounds **if he wanted to reject them** as grounds for divorce.

112

b. Everyone would assume that Jesus recognized that there were other grounds: No school of thought on divorce, of the time, rejected the Exodus 21 grounds for divorce of **material neglect** and **physical/ emotional neglect   or abuse**. If Jesus had wanted to teach a rejection of these grounds for divorce, he would have had **to say so very definitely**. Therefore, because he said nothing about this universally held belief of the Jews, it would certainly indicate his mental agreement with those grounds.

c. In the debate with the Pharisees, it was only necessary to mention points of disagreement in that particular discussion. These concerned the interpretation of Deuteronomy 24:1-4, but not that of Exodus 21:10-11. So, once again, this puts Jesus' silence on the issue into the strong silence category.

d. As an example of strong silence, it is commonly accepted that Jesus believed in remarriage after the death of a spouse—even though he was silent on the matter. Indeed, no one would assume that he forbade such an arrangement. In fact, it was the common practice. Certainly, either he or God guided Paul's later statement to that effect (1 Cor. 7:39). This puts Jesus' silence on that issue into the strong silence category. So, it is only logical that he believed in the biblical grounds for divorce that are stated in Exodus 21 in spite of his silence on the matter.

~

We now move on to answer each of the questions relating to Mark 10:2-12 and Luke 16:18 as posed at the end of Chapter 14.

19

Understanding Jesus on Divorce from Mark and Luke

1) Why Does Mark Not Provide the "Any Cause" Clause?

Matthew writes in 19:3: *"Then some Pharisees came and tried to trick him by asking, "Is it lawful for a man to divorce a wife for "any cause?""*" whereas, in the parallel account of Mark 10:2, the phrase **"any cause"** is omitted. Why is this? Actually, the phrase "for any cause" in Matthew is a reference to the earlier described teaching on divorce of the School of the Hillelites which said: "Even if she spoiled his dish, since it says: **[any] matter.**" This concerns the phrase from Deuteronomy 24:1-4 which the Hillelites had split into two. During this confrontation between the Pharisees and Jesus, the Jews would have mentally inserted the phrase **"for any cause"** because the question would have made no sense to them without it. To ask the question in the form that Mark gives it, and without any background understanding, could be answered only by a "yes, obviously"—because it says so in the Law and the Prophets and because there was no body of rabbis, scribes, Pharisees, Essenes, or anyone else who did not allow for divorce **under any circumstances. All groups taught that divorce was permissible** even though the grounds for it might vary. A modern-day example might be: If someone asked 'should women have equality?' it would not be necessary to add the phrase 'in the work-place' because that would be understood. However, Matthew inserts the phrase "for any cause" for later readers who would be unaware of the implied thought of invalid divorces. So, when we **insert the implied thought** into verses 2 and 10-12 of Mark's account, we get the understanding that:

> *"Some Pharisees approached in order to trap him. "Is it lawful for a man to divorce his wife [implied "for any cause"]?" they asked ... ¹⁰Then in the house, the disciples were again questioning him*

*about this. So he said to them, "Any man who divorces his wife [implied "for any cause"], and marries another woman, **commits adultery against her**. And if she divorces her husband [in this way] and marries another man, she commits adultery"*

(Mark 10:2-12 KGV).

In understanding this aspect of the situation, we have now removed one of the apparent contradictions noted earlier in Chapter 6.

2) "Commits Adultery against Her" Is Only in Mark 10:11

Because of Jesus' earlier focus from Genesis on monogamy as God's standard, he was now showing that polygamy was unacceptable and that adultery was no longer a crime against a husband only, but **also against a wife** as shown in his words: "**commits adultery against her**" (Mark 10:11). Nevertheless, the Mosaic Law clearly recognized that a man might commit adultery. Indeed, *"If a man commits adultery with the wife of his neighbour...both **the adulterer** and **the adulteress** shall surely be **put to death**" (Lev. 20:10 ESV)*. However, because of the general acceptance of polygamy a man was not treated as an adulterer toward his own wife if he had sexual relations with an unmarried woman who would then become a second wife. So, Jesus was now guiding the situation back to the biblical ideal, so that a wife could divorce her husband for his adultery. Also please note that although the Mosaic Law prescribed the death penalty for adultery, this was not applied in Jesus' time, especially under Roman rule from about 7 A.D. when the Jews were forbidden to apply capital punishment for any offence (John 18:31).

3) In Mark 10 and Luke 16 Jesus' statement of "Except for Sexual Immorality" Is Implied

The fact that Luke 16:18 and Mark 10:2-12 do not contain any mention of the exception clause does not nullify it because it is clearly stated in the two passages in Matthew. Also, exceptions are **not stated every time a general rule is mentioned** and, as shown above, it is only when these divorces are viewed as unjust and therefore unscriptural as divorce that Jesus' statements in Luke 16

115

and Mark 10 make logical sense. This then reveals the facts about any apparent contradictions. Secondly, it is because of **the exception clause** in both Matthew 5 and 19 that we can know that the accounts in Mark and Luke must have been abbreviated with the invalidity of such unjust divorce **as being implied** only, but readily understood by the Jewish Christian audience which made up the majority of Christians in the early days. An example of an implied thought would be: *"...everyone who looks at a woman with lustful intent has already committed adultery with her in his heart" (Matt. 5:28 ESV)*. It would be unnecessary to add the words 'except for his wife' because one cannot commit adultery with one's wife. Such a thought is implied and would be **mentally acknowledged** by the listeners. Indeed, many such general statements **must be qualified** according to varying circumstances. Many other examples could be given to show that there are many unsaid things in daily conversation that are understood by each one in a conversation in particular cultures.

JESUS' EXCEPTION WAS NOT THE ONLY EXCEPTION

Paul also refers to the different exception of **desertion by an unbeliever** in 1 Corinthians 7:15, yet, it is clear that he would not have felt free to do so if Jesus' exception was absolutely the only exception. This shows that Jesus' exception was only in the narrow context of his debate with the Pharisees on male divorcing of wives and therefore there could be other exceptions in other contexts.

A Different Conversation in Luke 16:8

This passage is not connected to the debate Jesus was involved in with the Pharisees in showing them that the "any cause" divorce teaching was wrong and could not be used to justify divorce. Indeed, Luke 16:18 is an isolated passage having its own context, namely, that of the poor stewardship of God's teachings by the Pharisees (verses 1-17). So, verse 18 then provides an example of this as given by Jesus when he highlight-ed and corrected that poor teaching telling them that:

> *"Anyone divorcing his wife for the purpose of* (Gk *kai* subjunctive mood. Usually rendered "and," but functions to introduce a result (see Bauer's Lexicon). In the flow of the discussion this presents us with a narrative explanation of why the first, unjustified divorce, occurred)

116

marrying another woman commits adultery; and anyone marrying a woman <u>who has</u> (middle voice) divorced from her husband [in this way], **commits adultery** *(active form)"*

(Luke 16:18 KGV).

Please note that, as with the other passages on divorce, Jesus gives the motive for the divorce, namely that this husband is treacherously divorcing his wife because he plans to marry another woman which is viewed as adulterous in the metaphorical sense. Clearly, his wife is the guiltless party. Furthermore, there is a similar bad motive on the part of any woman treacherously divorcing her husband so that she can marry someone else—the bad example of the day being Herodias.

The Key Factors Concerning the Background to Divorce

In restating the background to divorce from the Hebrew Scriptures we note that:

- The last recorded situation in the Hebrew Scriptures concerning divorce was that of the treacherous divorces that were happening in Malachi's day, as recorded in Malachi 2:14-16.
- God's metaphorical marriage to Israel (and Judah), His divorce from her (Isa. 50:1; Jer. 3:6-9; Hosea 2:16, 19-20), and His threatened divorce from Judah (Ezek. 16:8-20).
- The principles of Jewish case law for divorce as based on Exodus 21:10-11, Deuteronomy 21:10-14, and 24:1-4 were God's protection of any wrongly divorced or neglected or abused wife by providing her with a certificate of divorce so that she can remarry.

We must also note the background from recent first century events. These are:

- Herod Antipas' treacherous divorce of his innocent wife, so that he could marry Herodias.
- Herodias' unjust divorce of her husband Philip, so that she could marry Herod Antipas.
- The many shared assumptions or taken-for-granteds of a first-century listener. (Please see the earlier comments of James Dunn).

117

So clearly Jesus' focus was a condemnation of the easy and treacherous divorces of the day as well as in earlier times.

~

In the next chapter there are two lists summarizing the many factors concerning why certain approaches to this subject have been very misguided in the past and unfortunately are still so today.

§

20

Failure of Past Understanding of Jesus' Teaching on Divorce

The Teaching That All Divorce Is Disallowed Is Unscriptural

The general misunderstanding of the relevant passages on divorce has led some to the idea that all divorce is forbidden in the Bible. This has occurred because there has been a failure to recognize:

- That God, through **MOSES**, *regulated* divorce in the passages of Exodus 21, Deuteronomy 21, and 24, and one does not regulate something if it is forbidden. If it were forbidden then the biblical texts would say so clearly, but they do not.

- That the **PROPHETS** show *God as a divorcee* because of His "wife's" i.e., Israel's unfaithfulness leading Him to withdraw "food, clothing and love" from her. Certainly, God would not put Himself in the position of metaphorically being a divorcee if divorce were sinful.

- That in **MALACHI** there has been a translation error in Malachi 2:16, so that this passage does not nullify God's acceptance of legitimate divorce. Nevertheless, this concerned treacherous divorces.

- That **JESUS** condemned only the "any cause" "no fault" trivial or treacherous kind of divorce against a wife, but not divorce in general. He knew that God was a divorcee.

- That Jesus' exception clause concerning sexual immorality is part of inspired Scripture and is completely valid grounds for divorce.

- That Jesus, by giving his exception statement, showed that divorce is allowable in the case of a spouse's sexual immorality.

- The full context of Matthew 19:3-9, and in particular verse 8b *"from the beginning it hasn't been this way,"* which references only hard-hearted divorce.

119

In a later chapter we will see that Paul gave a further, and **different, exception** and so further regulating divorce—but in a Gentile world context. So, throughout the entire Bible there is God's hand regulating divorce to reduce the harm caused, primarily to vulnerable wives, by bad situations in marriage and that lead to divorce. Furthermore, there is also a certain general misunderstanding that has led many to the idea that biblically divorce can only be allowed if there has been sexual immorality by a marriage partner, and for no other reason.

The Teaching That Divorce Can Be <u>Only</u> for Sexual Immorality Is Also Unscriptural

This has been the case because there has been a failure:

- To reference the full range of the Scriptures which shows that there are other grounds for divorce—these concerning various forms of abuse and neglect.

- To realize that Jesus' debate with the Pharisees was in the narrow confines of male divorcing based on a wrong interpretation by the Pharisees of Deuteronomy 24:1-4, so that Jesus did not state all that there was to say about divorce.

- In understanding of the context of Matthew 19:3-9, concerning the Mosaic concession and in particular verse 8b *"from the beginning it hasn't been this way,"* which references only hard-hearted divorce.

- To recognize that Jesus' strong silence on the other passages in the Hebrew Scriptures in no way discounts them as showing a more complete picture of the subject of divorce and remarriage.

- Because of the exceptions by Jesus in Matthew 5:32 and 19:9 as well as Paul's exception in 1 Corinthians 7:15 there can be other exceptions.

- To examine the known background of the times in that particular Israelite culture with its **exceptions** to general rules. Examples are: Jesus statement in Matthew 5:22 that one should not call someone a fool and yet Jesus calls the scribes and pharisees "blind fools" in Matthew 23:17. He says that a man should not look lustfully upon a woman in Matthew 5:28 but this obviously does not refer to a man's wife (1 Cor. 7:2). Also, Jesus

120

and Paul recommend singleness (Matthew 19:11. 1 Cor. 7:7) even though marriage was the norm (1 Cor. 7:9).

The Revolutionary Implications of Jesus' Teaching

CORRECTING OF WRONG INTERPRETATION

Although Jesus did not contradict the principles in the Hebrew Scriptures regarding divorce, there was certainly a gulf between his biblical teachings and those of the Pharisees. Jesus differed with these people on their interpretation of Deuteronomy 24 inasmuch as he knew that it was not a text in favour of men for them to divorce their wives, but was a protective measure for wrongly divorced wives.

HILLELITE DIVORCE FOR "ANY CAUSE" IS UNSCRIPTURAL

The reaction of the disciples indirectly supports the fact that Jesus showed that the Hillelite position was invalid as divorce when they say: *"If this is the case of a husband with a wife, there's no advantage in getting married!" (Matt. 19:10).* In other words, **Jesus stopped the easy divorce situation** that they had all wrongly come to accept as normal.

MARRIAGE IS IDEALLY TO BE LIFELONG AND OF EQUALITY

This was God's original standard and so it was against God's will for either party *to break their marriage vows* and thus cause a divorce. Jesus' teaching would now **contribute toward saving many marriages.** Indeed, women could now divorce a husband if he was polygamous because Jesus reclassified it as adultery. Although polygamy was becoming rare it was still practiced by the rich and by the Pharisees. (*Note the earlier criticism of them by the Qumran Community*). The main consequence of Jesus' condemnation of polygamy was that **women gained the right to use a husband's sexual immorality as grounds for divorce.** As Andreas Köstenberger stated:

> Despite regulations in the Mosaic Law that stipulated equal testament of men and women with regard to divorce (Lev. 20:10-12), in Old Testament times a double standard prevailed according to which women were required to be faithful to their husbands (or punishment ensued) while the standards for men

121

were seen as considerably more lenient. In Jesus' teaching, however, conjugal rights were set on an equal footing.

DIVORCE IS ALLOWABLE BUT NOT COMPULSORY

However, divorce should be avoided unless the erring partner stubbornly refuses to repent or the innocent party refuses to forgive them. Yet divorce should be the course of last resort. So, the Pharisees' false teaching that a husband <u>must</u> divorce his wife was corrected by Jesus. This would also now **contribute toward saving many marriages.**

INFERTILITY WAS NO LONGER GROUNDS FOR DIVORCE

*"The disciples said to him [Jesus]: 'If such is the case of a man with his wife, it is better not to marry. But he said to them...there are eunuchs who have **made themselves eunuchs** for the sake of the kingdom of the heavens. Let the one who is able to receive this receive it'" (Matt. 19:10-12).*

This self-imposed state of making oneself a eunuch i.e., deciding to remain single, meant that marriage and therefore childbearing were no longer compulsory for those who accepted Jesus' teachings. So, this would take infertility in either partner out of the equation and remove it as grounds for divorce.

Forgiveness

The Christian path is always that of forgiveness <u>if the erring partner is genuinely repentant</u>. However, Jesus, in using hyperbole, has forgiveness as up to *"seventy times seven" (Matt. 18:22)* i.e., a significant number of times. However, there must come a time when any sexual immorality or persistent abuse or neglect goes past the point of any further forgiveness. So, it is wrong to say that forgiveness means that the offended party must always stay married to the guilty party. In fact, in cases of a single instance of severe abuse e.g., if it is life threatening and with on-going threats, one cannot tell the victim to be forgiving and that they must stay in that marriage. It would be like saying to parents who discover that a babysitter had molested their children: "Oh, but the babysitter said sorry and so you must forgive them and allow them to watch the kids again." Such foolishness would make a mockery of marriage!

Summary of Jesus' View of Marriage and Divorce

1. Marriage should be monogamous (Adultery against a wife was now to be grounds for divorce for her).
2. Marriage should be life-long.
3. Divorce is never compulsory.
4. Divorce should be avoided unless the erring partner stubbornly refuses to repent.
5. Forgiveness should be applied when the erring partner genuinely repents.
6. Marriage is optional (Matt. 19:11-12), but is the preferred option under normal circumstances.
7. Hillelite "any cause" divorce involves invalid grounds.
8. By his strong silence Jesus must have agreed with the principles contained in the laws on divorce as found in Exodus 21:10-11 and the Deuteronomy passages when correctly interpreted and applied.
9. There are limited exceptions to general rules.

JESUS' ISSUES WITH THE PHARISEES

Jesus' statements corrected the overly broad view that allowed for very easy divorce expressed by the school of **Hillel**. He showed them the necessity of returning to God's ideal standard of life-long monogamous marriage as set out in Genesis. That was the intention of the marriage vows. So, the invalidity of the "for any cause" divorce in the Pharisees question, "is it lawful to divorce one's wife "**for any cause**?" in Matthew 19:3 and the Pharisees' interpretation of Deuteronomy 24:1-4 were the prime issues in these accounts. However, Jesus was much more authoritative than even the school of **Shammai** on what constitutes invalid grounds for divorce. Jesus introduced further related factors into the debate so that all of his prime **condemnations of the religious views** of the day concerning marriage and divorce were expressed.

In addition to all these changes to the human thinking of the day concerning divorce, Jesus did not discount the legitimate grounds for divorce from the principles noted in Exodus 21:10-11, namely **material neglect** (food/clothing) and **physical or emotional neglect/abuse**. These were not part of the narrowly defined discussion with the Pharisees and Jesus said nothing that would indicate that he was removing them as grounds for divorce. However, unlike the Pharisees and other rabbis of the first and later centuries, Christians should not take a legalistic approach to these matters but should deal with them according to the spirit of the moral aspects of the Law. Indeed, the fact that, in the debate with the Pharisees, Jesus gave the exception of "sexual immorality," and did not mention the exception of "desertion/abandonment" as given later by Paul in 1 Corinthians 7, shows that this was a general rule of exceptions and that **there could be other exceptions.** Nevertheless, Jesus treated divorce very seriously. So, these grounds are only to be invoked as a last resort and every effort should be made by the two partners to avoid divorce and to bring about reconciliation. This means that the Christian spirit of forgiveness plays a major role in these matters.

Conclusion Regarding Jesus' Teaching on Divorce

Nowhere does Jesus do away with the moral standards of the Mosaic Law (Matt. 5:17-19). However, rather than following the letter of the law he correctly interprets it according to its principles. This is evident in the Sermon on the Mount, sometimes expressed with hyperbole, and in his many other teachings, as for example, when he corrects the Pharisees in their faulty interpretation of Deuteronomy 24:1 during the debate recorded in Matthew 19:3-9 and Mark 10:2-12. This narrowly defined debate does not deal with the other details of marriage and divorce, so there is no reason to imagine that Jesus excluded the biblical grounds for divorce of neglect or abuse shown in Exodus 21:10-11, and every reason to know that he supported God's moral standard in this regard.

PART FOUR

Paul on Divorce

21

Paul's Teachings on Marriage Obligations

Background Knowledge and Assumptions of a First-Century Reader

Just as it was necessary to be aware of the first-century reader's back-ground knowledge and assumptions concerning Jesus' statements on divorce, so too, is this the case in our attempts to understand the Apostle Paul's statements on this subject. Indeed, as Jesus' emissary Paul's teaching on divorce in no way conflicts with the position taken by Jesus. However, because Christianity had spread out into the Gentile world, Paul had to write concerning rather different circumstances than those that Jesus had dealt with. Nevertheless, Paul's basis for what he wrote is exactly the same as that which Jesus accepted and taught on this subject, but with additional factors.

Paul's Teachings Show the Same Marital Obligations for a Husband as Are Stated in Exodus 21:10, 11

As we shall see later, Paul allowed for divorce and remarriage on appropriate grounds. However, Paul's main comments on divorce identify the grounds for divorce by emphasizing the obligations within marriage according to biblically based vows. Most of what he has to say on this subject is found in 1 Corinthians 7 and Ephesians 5.

MATERIAL, PHYSICAL, AND EMOTIONAL OBLIGATIONS
Concerning these obligations Paul counselled the Ephesians:

> *"Husbands, love your wives as the Christ loved the Church and gave himself up for her...In the same way husbands should **love their wives** as their own bodies. He who loves his wife loves himself. For no man ever hated his own flesh, but **nourishes** it*

and **cherishes** it...let each one of you love his wife as he does himself and let the wife see that she respects her husband"
(Eph. 5:25-33 ESV).

As noted in the previous chapters, the principles taken from Exodus 21:10, 11 became the standard in the marriage contract of the husband's obligations. These stipulated that he was to provide his wife with **food, clothing** and **love**. Although the Hillelite and Shammaite Pharisees argued over the length of time before material or emotional neglect would become the basis for a divorce, they never disputed <u>the fact</u> of these failures as being the basis for divorce. So, Paul emphasizes these obligations showing that:

*"...the married man is anxious about **the worldly things**, how to <u>please his wife</u>...the married woman is anxious about the worldly things how to <u>please her husband</u>" (1 Cor. 7:33-35 ESV).*

Here, Paul highlights the material obligations—"the worldly things"—in a Christian marriage. So, the persistent failure to keep the marriage vows regarding these worldly things would eventually form the basis for divorce in harmony with Exodus 21:10, 11. Furthermore, when Paul responded to the letter from the Corinthians, he also dealt with the other major aspect of good marriage i.e., the rights of the partners regarding sexual intimacy in their marriage:

*"Now concerning the issues about which you wrote: "It is good for a man not to have sexual relations with a wife" (see NOTE). However, because there is so much sexual immorality, each man should have sexual relations with his own wife, and each woman with her own husband. The husband should give to his wife **her sexual rights**, and likewise the wife to her husband; because the wife isn't in charge of her own body; the husband is. Likewise the husband isn't in charge of his own body; the wife is. You must **stop defrauding each other**, except by mutual agreement for a specified time, so that you may devote yourselves to prayer; but then get back together again, in case the Satan might tempt you because of your lack of self-control. But I say this as a concession, not as a command. I wish that everyone was as I myself am*. But each has his own gift from God, one this gift, another that gift. To **the unmarried** and the widows I say that it's good for them to remain as I am. But if they cannot restrain their desire, they*

128

should marry, because it's <u>better to marry</u> than to burn with sexual desire!" (1 Cor. 7:1-9 KGV).

Paul's statement that "the husband should give to his wife **her sexual rights**" is based exactly on the principles taken from the case law described in Exodus 21:10 concerning the rights of a slave wife. So, a free wife would logically have, at least, the equivalent rights according to rabbinic analysis. Clearly, Paul was basing his teachings concerning Christian sexual behaviour on the morals and principles highlighted in the Mosaic Law just as Messiah Jesus had done. Furthermore, Paul shows that the husband also should not be emotionally deprived because, not only must *"the husband...give to his wife her sexual rights,"* but also *"the wife to her husband"* (1 Cor. 7:3) and again Professor of New Testament Craig Keener speaks of failure in these obligations based on Exodus 21:10-11 as being shown to be grounds for divorce. He says that:

> ...in contrast to Roman law, the wife had a right to maintenance of food, clothing, and other physical needs, according to the standard to which she had been accustomed growing up, as well as a weekly allowance. If her husband failed to fulfil his duties, she could at least in principle demand a divorce.

So, knowing the biblically-based marital obligations and vows in a marriage sets the scene for us to examine how the breaking of these can serve as the basis for divorce according to Paul's inspired statements in 1 Corinthians 7. We must also bear in mind that in this first letter to Corinthians Paul is giving pastoral counsel rather than a set of laws and so he does not envision the involvement of any ecclesial court regarding divorce.

NOTE: A few translations (CEV, GW, GNT, OGOMM) render 1 Corinthians 7:1 as, "It is good for a man not to marry." However, Professor Emeritus and Greek-English scholar Gordon Fee notes that translators can, "miss the meaning of the idiom, as can be seen in the original NIV...renderings of the first assertion addressed in 1 Corinthians 7:1 "It is good for a man not to marry," which unfortunately is both wrong and misleading. The idiom "to touch a woman" in every other case in antiquity means to have sexual intercourse with a woman, and never means anything close to "to marry"
How to Read the Bible for All Its Worth p.49.

§

129

22

Paul's Teachings on Divorce in Relation to the Gentile World

All that Moses and Jesus had said on the subject of divorce was within the confines of the nation of Israel in Galilee and Judea, that is, people who were supposedly following the Law regarding marital situations. However, with the commissioning of Jesus' disciples to proclaim the message of *"the good news about the kingdom and everything about Jesus the Messiah" (Acts 8:12)* to people of the nations (Matt. 28:19), a new situation arose concerning those Gentiles who became believers, but who were already married to someone who was still an unbeliever. Additionally, it appears that Jewish people in the Greco-Roman world adopted Greco-Roman customs with regard to divorce. So, this new situation is the reason for the Apostle Paul's counsel recorded in 1 Corinthians 7:10-16; 25-28 regarding what to do in certain marital situations.

With Jesus, Paul Upheld God's Moral Standard Contained in the Hebrew Scriptures

In 1 Corinthians 7 Paul is working toward Jesus' statement of the divine ideal for marriage, but he acknowledges that that the ideal will not always be achieved, so he doesn't give any inflexible rules. Indeed, Paul followed Jesus in not creating any new legislation regarding divorce and remarriage. His thoughts on it did not vary from the principles set down in the Hebrew Scriptures on God's moral standards and principles based on the Mosaic law (Ex. 21:7-11) which allowed for divorce and remarriage. This is just as Jesus and Paul changed nothing regarding the stated view in the Hebrew Scriptures against homosexual conduct or other moral matters. It was only treacherous or trivial easy divorce which was invalid (Mal. 2:4-16)—this is the only kind of divorce that God is against and was also the kind of divorce that Jesus spoke about. Even a male or female **slave** could go totally free from a master who beats them (Ex. 21:26-27), and so if they ran into further financial trouble, they could become the slave of a new owner. How much more would this apply to an abused wife who later seeks remarriage as shown in the passages from Deuteronomy and Exodus! So, why would God, through Jesus or Paul, now change His earlier stated moral principles which protected innocent parties in cases of very damaging abusive marriages and treacherous divorce? Why would God deny the wonders of good marriage for the divorced when, in fact, He advocated marriage in the first place? In fact, he condemned those who denied marriage (1 Tim. 4:1-3) even of a previous divorcee.

The Greek Word *Chorizo* Means Divorce in Divorce Contexts

In Paul's statements on the subject of divorce he uses two Greek words: *chorizo* = to separate, and *aphiemi* = to dismiss. A typical rendering of 1 Corinthians 7:10-11 is: *"the wife should not **separate** (Gk chorizo) from her husband...and the husband should not **divorce** (Gk aphiemi i.e., dismiss) his wife" (ESV)*. However, it is very well documented that this Greco-Roman separation or dismissal was a legal divorce in that world. In fact, there were more than fifty words for divorce in Greek marriage and divorce contracts. Also, in Greco-Roman society the Greek word *chorizo* was the most common of the words used for divorce. So, whoever owned the home "dismissed" the other party and whoever did not own the home "separated themselves" from the other party. Usually Paul spoke of *"separation"* as the wife's action—"**divorce-by-separating**," but *'dismissal'* as that of the husband's action (unless the wife owned the home)—"**divorce-by-dismissing**." Certainly, *chorizo* means "divorce" in divorce contexts according to major authoritative sources such as: *The Theological Dictionary of the New Testament, Bauer's Greek-English Lexicon, Mounce's Expository Dictionary of Old and New Testament Words,* and *Thayer's Greek-English Lexicon.* These all show that ***chorizo*** (for "separation" means "divorce" in divorce contexts. Concerning *chorizo* Moulton and Milligan write: "The word has almost become a technical term in connection with divorce." So, David Instone Brewer explains that:

> The word "separate" (a standard term meaning "to divorce," with almost exactly the same semantic field as the word "to

131

divorce" (literally "to release"), which was used in the Pharisees' question to Jesus...In fact, if [Paul] was referring to simple separation, as in a Jewish context, the woman would not have the right to remarry, and neither of them could be called "unmarried." *Divorce and Remarriage in the Bible* pp.140, 200.

These facts are confirmed by all the Greek background information revealed from archaeologically discovered documents showing that the word *chorizo* regularly appears in bills of divorce more than any other term for divorce. So, it is obvious that *chorizo* means divorce in the context of 1 Corinthians 7:11, where the husband also should not dismiss/divorce *(Gk aphiemi)* his wife. And indeed, most translations render *aphiemi* in verse 11 correctly as "divorce," but sadly fail to render *chorizo* as "divorce," possibly because of holding to some traditional view of "separation" in modern-day terms.

CHORIZO DOES NOT MEAN "SEPARATION" IN THE MODERN-DAY SENSE

Because the Greek term *chorizo* used by Paul means divorce in divorce contexts, it does not mean the same as the modern-day sense of separation where individuals remain married, but live separately. Such modern-day "separation" contravenes the biblical basis of marriage as primarily that of companionship as well as diminishing the chances of "reconciliation" by inhibiting attempts to face the issues the couple must attempt to deal with. Additionally, it violates Paul's command in 1 Corinthians 7:1-5 which says that each married man and woman should have sexual relations with their marriage partner, (not an ex-wife i.e., one who is now "unmarried). Furthermore, although Paul is not in favour of it (1 Cor. 7:1-5), he makes the concession of a married couple's agreeing to a period of abstinence from sexual relations for prayer purposes. But then they should *"get back together again, in case the Satan should tempt you because of your lack of self-control" (1 Cor. 7:5)*. However, the modern-day concept of "separation" but still married, sets up the husband or wife for unnecessary sexual temptation.

GRAMMAR ISSUE

The word *chorizo*, meaning "divorce" in verse 10, is in the **reflexive mood**, i.e., "separate herself from," even though it is exactly like the passive mood in the Greek which means "be separated." However, in 7:15 Paul uses the same word, with exactly the same form, in a context where it cannot possibly be passive and so must be reflexive. So, for verse 10 the Revised English Version reads, "a wife must not **separate herself from** ..." Also, many other translations read, "she must not separate from" and so showing that it is the wife's action. Therefore, here Paul instructs that neither believer should desert the other by using the unscriptural Greco-Roman 'separation/dismissal' type of divorce i.e., leaving for no good reason.

Did Paul Omit to Mention Jesus' Teaching on Divorce?

For whatever reason, in Paul's explanation concerning "the married" in 1 Corinthians 7: 10, he does not directly mention Jesus' statement concerning the no-divorce teaching "except for sexual immorality" (Matt. 5:32, 19:9), although, in verses 2-5, he does try to prevent any possible sexual immorality. So, does this mean that Paul excluded Jesus' "exception" from reasons why a person might decide to divorce? Obviously not! Since Christians were to, "be teaching [new disciples] everything I [Jesus] have commanded you" (Matt. 28:19) they would have known this exception in divorce mentioned in the Sermon on the Mount (Matt. 5:32) as well as knowing about Jesus' debate with the Pharisees, but in its context (Matt. 19:9). So, we can confidently say that it was implied that the Corinthians would already have known of the "exception" clause! Furthermore, and again for whatever reason, just like Jesus, Paul does not directly mention the principles from Moses' case law in Exodus 21:10-11 as grounds for divorce for the severe mistreatment of a slave wife even though adultery by a wife and severe mistreatment of a wife were universally recognized as grounds for divorce in Paul's time.

So, in analysing Paul's words on divorce, one must keep in mind the entire biblical picture involving Jesus' exception clause in Matthew 5:31-32; 19:3-9, the principles in Moses' case law of Exodus 21:10-11 along with the points made in Deuteronomy, as well as Paul's own comments in 1 Corinthians 7:1-5, 33-35 on how a wife should be treated and his later comments in Ephesians 5:25-33 on this. It is likely that Paul omitted these factors because his readers would already be knowledge-able about them and so implied in Paul's writings as the taken-for-granteds.

133

The Basics of Paul's Pastoral Counsel on Divorce

The Corinthians had written to Paul presenting the idea that, "*it is good for a man to have no sexual relations with a woman (specifically his wife)*" *(1 Cor. 7:1).* They had decided that sex was unspiritual and so they should abstain from it. This was all part of their attitude toward asceticism added to which was the fact that many had unbelieving partners who they may have wished to separate from. However, Paul's answer to this in 1 Corinthians 7:1-5 showed that he was against such an idea and that, where possible, there should be a regular loving sexual relationship in a marriage, so that neither partner is tempted toward sexual immorality. This applied even if the partner was an unbeliever. However, this background does show that when we begin to analyse Paul's following statements in vs. 10ff they are in a context of proposed divorce for ascetic reasons and with a wish to separate from a partner who is an unbeliever.

After Paul's statements in 7:1-9 he goes on to discuss three hypothetical situations to help "the married" to stay together. These are:

1. A believer shouldn't divorce their believing marriage partner by using the Greco-Roman manner of easy divorce (vss. 10- 11).

2. A believer shouldn't divorce an unbelieving marriage partner if the unbeliever **is content in the marriage** (vss. 12-14) and behaving well as a marriage partner.

3. However, if an unbeliever does divorce a believer this will count as legitimate divorce for the believer because "they are "no longer bound" (vs. 15) and so are free to remarry.

With the above facts in mind, we can now proceed to examine the first of the three hypothetical situations regarding the maintaining of a marriage in the Greco-Roman world with its particular type of easy divorce. We begin with the very big question of: Can two believers ever divorce?

§

23

Can Two Believers Ever Divorce?

A Believer Should Not Divorce their Believing Marriage Partner – *1 Corinthians 7:10-11*

Here Paul firstly addresses the situation for two married believers in the Gentile culture of the day when he says:

> *"To the married I give this instruction (not I, but the Lord): a wife shouldn't divorce [by-separating] (Gk chorizo) herself from her husband; (**if she does**, she should **remain unmarried** or **be reconciled** to that man (Gk andros)), and the husband shouldn't "divorce [by-dismissing] (Gk aphiemi) his wife"* (KGV).

"NOT I, BUT THE LORD," REFERS TO ONE OF JESUS' SAYINGS

In verse 10 Paul directs us to one of Jesus' sayings, even though not yet written down. Most likely this was the saying that was later recorded in Mark 10:11 of: *"Whoever divorces his wife and marries another woman commits adultery against her."* But here we must take into account the 'taken for granted" statement by Jesus of "except for sexual immorality" later presented in Matthew 19:9. So, from a biblical perspective, this husband, noted by Paul, may have dismissed his wife for no good reason as with the Jewish male usage of the "any cause" divorces of Jesus' day. In other words, his wife did not commit any form of sexual immorality or persistently seriously fail in other wifely duties.

NOTE: Paul wrote 1 Corinthians before the Gospels were written.

"A WIFE SHOULDN'T DIVORCE HERSELF FROM HER HUSBAND"

Similarly, from a biblical perspective, this wife could have walked out for no good reason. In other words, her husband had provided her with food, clothing, and a loving relationship as well as his never having committed any form of sexual immorality. Certainly, this statement by Paul says that two believers should not divorce. However, because of Jesus' exception clause stated in Matthew 5 and 19, it is evident that what Paul says here is also a general principle, as with Mark 10:11, so that there may be other exceptions. After all, in his debate with the Pharisees, Jesus was dealing only with the interpretation of Deuteronomy 24:1-4 and did not nullify the principles embodied in other case law statements such as in Exodus 21:10-11. Furthermore, principles taken from Paul's own statements regarding marriage obligations—the breaking of which can be the basis for divorce—should be taken into account in seeing the other allowable exceptions. These factors imply that divorce of two believers for legitimate reasons can take place. But some might say, 'surely the couple described in verses 10 and 11 are still to be viewed as married!' Actually, this is not so!

The Woman Is Now "Unmarried" - Divorced

First of all, please note that the woman is "**unmarried**" (vs. 11)— she is divorced by separation from her husband under Greco-Roman law. She is not in some half-way stage such as married but separated. This hypothetical woman "separates herself" and is "**unmarried.**" So, Bible educator Rick Walston states that:

> In verses 10 and 11 the context is set, and it is clearly about divorce....—unmarried in this context is clearly "divorced." It is simple logic that a woman cannot be married to a man and unmarried at the same time.
> *Something Happened on the Way to "Happily Ever After"* p.31.

This point is important in practical cases because here it would be a serious mistake for anyone to say that the couple "are still married in God's sight" when, in fact, they are legitimately and legally divorced i.e., she is "unmarried." Furthermore, a counsellor may inadvertently lead a couple into sin by stating that they are still married, and so implying that they may still engage in sexual relations when, in fact, this would be fornication.

Likely Reason for Such a Divorce in 7:10-12

This kind of separating divorce initiated by a wife, as noted in verse 10, may have been because she had involved herself with another man, perhaps seeking to marry him. Indeed, most divorce at that time seems to have followed the pattern of treacherous divorce in Malachi's day and that of Herod/Herodias. Certainly, she is the one at fault here! However, a woman may legitimately divorce her husband because he was at fault for any of the following reasons:

- His interest in another woman perhaps leading to actual adultery. Or,
- His persistent serious negligence in doing his husbandly duties. Or,
- His persistent serious abuse of her.

Now when we consider verse 11b where Paul's counsel is that, "the husband shouldn't divorce-by-dismissing *(Gk aphiemi)* his wife," the husband's reason for divorce by dismissing his wife may have been because he had treacherously involved himself with another woman, perhaps seeking to marry her and so making this a case of hard-hearted divorce. Certainly, he is the one at fault here! However, a husband may divorce his wife because she was at fault for any of the following reasons:

- Her interest in another man perhaps leading to actual adultery (Matt. 5:31-32; 19:9). Or
- Her persistent serious negligence in doing all the duties of a wife, including the prevalent idea that any Christian wife may now abstain from the sexual relationship. However, Paul corrected this idea in 7:1-5.
- Her persistent serious abuse of him.

"Worse Than an Unbeliever" – 1 Timothy 5:8

Nevertheless, if the reason for either Christian spouse's divorcing of their partner was hard-hearted and simply to marry another person, then they have sinned. Also, if they have no just cause against their marriage partner then, again, they have sinned. However, if this divorcing is **caused by** one partner because of persistent significant mistreatment of the other, then how is he or she to be viewed if they do not repent of these things? Paul informs us that:

> "If anyone _does not provide for_ his relatives, and especially for members of his own household, he has denied the faith and is **worse than an unbeliever**" (1 Tim. 5:8).

137

Although this text is in the context of looking after widows the principle here applies equally to those who are divorced. In fact, there is a strong biblical connection between divorcees and widows that we will note later. So, by extension this statement applies just as much to a wife who fails to keep her marriage vows. Indeed, Paul would have assumed that a Christian who persistently mistreated their spouse or who committed adultery would respond to the admonition from Jesus via Paul in 1 Corinthians 7:10-11 and that he or she would now treat the spouse properly and that they would stop the adultery or other persistent failures. However, such a person may refuse to do so, even after being counselled by the mature <u>Christians in a congregation which properly</u> <u>understands</u> <u>biblical divorce</u> and as acting on behalf of the primarily innocent partner. In this case the mainly guilty party has put themselves in the position of being a Gentile or tax collector i.e., a non-Christian (Matt. 18:15-17) and as an unbeliever (1 Tim. 5:8). Indeed, with the earlier clarification as to how Jesus likely viewed divorce, one can understand that a believing husband who mistreats his wife has, in fact, deserted her even though she has been pushed to divorce him. He is certainly, "worse than an unbeliever" because, by dismissing her, he no longer provides materially or emotionally for her. Furthermore, Paul's statement in 1 Timothy 5:8 that, *"If anyone <u>does</u>* *<u>not provide for</u> ...members of his own household he has denied the* *faith and is* **worse than an unbeliever***"* is remarkably similar to what is stated by Moses in Exodus 21:10-11 where a husband who, *"does not provide [his wife] with these three things, she is to go free"* i.e., divorce him, and the three things to be provided were, *"food,* *clothing and marital rights."* To Paul this failure would have been a legitimate reason for a wife to have divorced her husband. This is especially true because of his statements on how a husband should nourish and cherish his wife (Eph. 5:25-33), as well as not defrauding her of her sexual rights (1 Cor. 7:1-5). Indeed, a husband was to provide his wife with the necessaries of life to please her (1 Cor.7:33-35).

PERSISTENT VIOLATIONS OF THE COVENANT OF LOVE

Both partners in a marriage have vowed to love one another (Ex. 21:11, Eph. 5:21-32), and by extension to love any children brought into the family. However, if either one of the partners, or both of them, continually sins against their spouse it constitutes a repudiation of that marriage. Such actions as persistent serious abuse or adultery or desertion all result in emotional damage. In reality the aspect of persistent abuse may concern physical, verbal, emotional, sexual, financial, or social abuse, including any illicit or illegal actions that threaten the safety of the family. None of such actions fit with the biblical definition of love (1 Cor. 13:4-7) or of one's claim to be a Christian. Any of these bad actions means that the marriage vows have been repudiated and so unofficially bringing marriage to an end.

A PARTNER MAY LEAVE THE FAMILY HOME IN CASES OF DANGER

Nevertheless, there may be cases where a spouse (and/or the children) must leave the family home for their own safety and well-being because of a significantly abusive partner. However, this separation should be only short-term so that any abuse is minimized and in anticipation of a better situation without any abuse in the future. Yet, this should not be viewed as a way to resolve the marital issues. On this Bible commentator Barbara Roberts notes that:

> Some Christian advice has been more responsible, teaching that abuse victims have the right to separate, or the right to divorce. This idea is argued from the scriptures by extending general principles of Christian conduct. For example, the sixth commandment *You shall not murder* implies you should not remain in a position where you might be killed or hurt by another. *Not Under Bondage* p.17.

Although most cases concern abuse of a wife, there are numerous cases where raging wives have seriously physically damaged their husbands, and in some cases even breaking their bones. Indeed, many men were raised to never hit a woman and therefore do not retaliate, especially so in line with Jesus' counsel in the Sermon on the Mount. However, far more often it is the husband who becomes a wife-beater or child-molester and so making it necessary for them to leave the family home.

"Remain Unmarried or Be Reconciled" - *7:11b*

Certainly, Paul's concern is that of putting any broken marriage back together if possible. This means that the couple should seek reconciliation and hopefully it will result in remarriage to that now ex-husband. This is why Paul says she should *"remain unmarried or be reconciled"* to her husband (really "ex-husband at this point because the Greek word *andros* can refer to him as "a man" i.e., an ex-husband). But some commentators say that "she should remain unmarried" <u>forever</u>. However, this is actually ungrammatical, unreasonable, and unloving. So, Professor of Bible and theology William Luck explains that Paul:

> ...does not say, as we might have expected, "Be reconciled or remain unmarried"; he says it the other way around, *"Remain unmarried or be reconciled."* I see in this the advice applying as long as reconciliation is a reasonable option. It deals with the immediate, not the long-range. *Divorce and Remarriage* p.189.

So, the mistreated wife should "remain unmarried" i.e., not marry another man during the necessary time for the process to attempt reconciliation. But please note that nowhere does the Bible state that there <u>must</u> be reconciliation between the couple regarding the marriage, even though that is hoped for. However, **such numerous attempts at reconciliation could go on for only a reasonable time and not indefinitely.** If reconciliation is accomplished, which is what Paul wants, then the couple would remarry, i.e., she or he would return permanently to the family home. If she is the guilty party this would include her repentance and his forgiveness if she has committed adultery or persistently failed badly in other ways. If he is the guilty party this would include his repentance for his mistreatment of her and her acceptance of his promise to now treat her properly. On the other hand, if, after the many attempts at reconciliation have failed, then the couple would be able to seek new partners because she is already "unmarried" and therefore implying that he is also unmarried. Certainly, after all attempts at reconciliation have failed, the guilty and unrepentant partner would now be classified as an "unbeliever." So "the Christian" is now viewed as an unbeliever. This means that the solution for the innocent party is the same as in the third category situation that Paul speaks of in verse 15 where he says of a believer with an unbeliever, *"let it [the divorce] take place. In such cases the brother or sister is **no longer bound** (lit. enslaved) to the marriage. God has called you to peace."* So, the believer remains divorced and is free of all responsibilities and privileges in that marriage and therefore entitled to marry someone else.

If on the other hand no attempt is made at reconciliation by the "separating" or "dismissing" party, then the party who was **divorced against their will** is free to remarry. Furthermore, although the context here concerns two believers, it is evident that the attempt to reconcile should also be made with an unbelieving partner. Indeed, God would recognize such divorce as legitimate because the ancient worldly authorities (Rom. 13:1-2) have <u>acknowledged</u> it or in the modern-day case the authorities have <u>granted</u> it. So, yes! Two believers can divorce, but only if one of them is unrepentantly behaving as an unbeliever.

NOTE: Since Paul has specific terms for the widowed (*chera* v. 8) and the never-married (*parthenos* vs. 25,28, 34, 36, 37, 38), *agamos* is best understood as including the divorced (vs, 8,11, 32, 34) as well as the widowed and the never-married.

24

Two Situations for
a Believer Married to an Unbeliever

 # 1. A Believer Should Not Divorce an Unbeliever If the
Unbeliever Is Content in the Marriage - *7:12-14*

> *"Concerning other things, I say (I, not the Lord) that if any*
> *brother has an unbelieving wife, and **she is content to live with***
> ***him**, he shouldn't divorce [by dismissing] her. And if a woman*
> *has an unbelieving husband, and **he is content** to live with her,*
> *she shouldn't divorce [by-dismissing] him. Actually, the*
> *unbelieving husband is set aside for God by virtue of his union*
> *with his wife, and the unbelieving wife is set aside for God by*
> *virtue of her union with the brother..." (KGV).*

"I, Not the Lord" – *7:12a*

What is said by Paul is fully the inspired word of God; the
statements in verses 10 and 11 are from "the Lord" and inspired, and
what is said by Paul in verse 12 onward is equally under inspiration
from God. So, from verse 12 onward Paul is simply adding to the
teachings of Jesus because there is an additional issue that neither
Moses nor Jesus had to deal with. The issue is that now, with the
world-wide preaching of the Good News, God's people are being
drawn from the Gentile world of "unbelievers," so that some who
have become Christians are already married to those who remain
"unbelievers." However, we should not, as some have done,
legalistically make any artificial distinction in Paul's rules
concerning the three issues described by him. So, what is said
concerning the two issues for a believer married to an unbeliever
may apply in the case of married believers where one divorces the
other, perhaps leading a sinning partner to be viewed as worse than
an unbeliever.

The Unbeliever's Contentment in the Marriage – *7:12b*

Mixed marriage in religious terms only stays intact if, "the unbelieving wife or husband is **content** to live with" their believing partner and lovingly also seeks success in the marriage. However, the phrases *"he shouldn't divorce [by dismissing] her"* and *"she shouldn't divorce [by-dismissing] him"* do not mean that divorce might never take place. What if the unbeliever is regularly breaking the marriage vows, but wishes to stay married? There is the possibility that such a husband is "content to live with" their believing partner, but only because he is dominating the marriage and mistreating his wife, even in subtle ways. What if that unbelieving partner is committing adultery or is significantly neglecting or significantly abusing the believer? Indeed, Paul's phrases here would then be qualified as with Jesus' statement on adultery (Matt. 5:31-32 and 19:9) and the principles within Moses' case law on abuse and neglect in Exodus 21:10-11, along with Jesus' evident acceptance of them. This would mean that a wife would no longer be obliged to stay married to a man who persistently failed in his material or physical/emotional obligations, and no husband would be obliged to stay married to a wife who persistently failed in her similar obligations. Of course, it is also possible that the believing partner is the cause of the divorce or contributes to it. If unrepentant, then that person may be treated as an unbeliever. Clearly, Paul wants all marriage to work and so he strongly encourages the believer to try his or her hardest to make it work, but evidently not at any cost.

The Unbelieving Partner Is "Set Aside for God" - *7:14*

This means that the unbelieving husband or wife and the children are in the unique position of being in an environment of exposure to the message of the Good News—even though it may only be *"without a word" (1 Pet. 3:1-2).* This is a very strong reason for the believer to stay with, "an unbelieving husband" if *"he is content to live with her."* This is the same for a believing husband with an unbelieving wife. Certainly, the Christian influence of the believing partner upon the unbelieving "content" partner and their children should be maintained and may, in time, lead to their becoming Christians.

✦

2. When the "Unbeliever Divorces by Separating Himself or Herself from the Believer" - 7:15a

Paul would not feel free to introduce a new "exception" to the one that Jesus had already stated (albeit in a narrow context) unless he realized that Jesus' exception was not the only possible exception. So too, Jesus' clear statement that sexual immorality is grounds for divorce, Paul adds the further grounds **of desertion/abandonment by an unbelieving marriage partner** when he says:

> *"But **if the unbelieving partner divorces [by separating]**"* (Gk *chorizo̱*) **himself or herself** *let it take place. In such cases the brother or sister is **no longer bound** [to the partner]. God has called you to peace" (KGV).*

This situation concerns the unbelieving partner as having already initiated the divorce i.e., "divorced-by-separating" (Gk *cho̱rizo̱*) from the innocent believer for no good reason, even though the believer has not been the cause of the abandonment/divorce. Therefore, the phrase *"let it take place"* is simply a direction for the believer to accept the situation that the marriage has ended, both in reality and officially.

CONSTRUCTIVE DESERTION/ABANDONMENT
Sometimes an innocent marriage partner may feel compelled to leave an abusive non-Christian spouse. This is called Constructive Desertion and was part of English law as far back as the 1500s. It was recognized by both Reforming and Puritan Bible scholars of the time and meant that the abusing spouse's behaviour is the cause of the innocent spouse being forced to leave the family home. It amounted to the guilty partner's repudiation of their marriage vows and so making a justified divorce likely, unless they repented and were forgiven by the damaged spouse.

The Believer "Is No Longer Bound"- 7:15b

Several different meanings to this phrase have been presented by certain Bible commentators. However, the reality of this phrase is that it means that the remaining partner, who is a believer and has done everything possible to reconcile, may treat this as a completed divorce, so that they may get remarried if they wish to. This will be further explained later in this book.

God Has Called You to Peace"- 7:15c

Professor Gordon Fee explains that the phrase "for the sake of peace" occurs in early rabbinic writings and was used to indicate that a pragmatic solution was necessary, even if it was not legalistically correct; and so common sense must prevail so that peace is brought to a situation. This is true of the situations some couples get themselves into so that a divorce may be the only way to bring peace to the couple, even though it does not exactly fit any of the biblical grounds stated in the Mosaic law. So, Paul uses this phrase of *"God has called you to peace"* so that, for instance, if an unbelieving Jewish husband refused to give his wife the required certificate of divorce, she would simply be treated as if she had been given it and that it was a valid divorce and so allowing her to remarry if she chose to do so. Additionally, because there would have been significant strife between the married couple during their failing marriage leading toward divorce, their divorce itself may eventually bring peace for one or both of the parties to the divorce. Indeed, Jesus said, *"my peace I am giving you; I don't give it to you as the world gives it. So, stop letting your hearts be so distressed or intimidated"* (John 14:27). In time there may even be peace between the parties to the divorce with a reduction in any strife between them and possibly along with forgiveness.

25

What Constitutes Abuse and Neglect?

In the following descriptions of abuse and neglect these details are NOT to be used as any flimsy excuse to gain an easy divorce from a partner. In all cases these various forms of abuse and neglect concern what is very serious and goes on for a considerably long period of time. Furthermore, many appeals to the abuser and much hard work should be put in by the abused partner to help the abuser to change.

What Is Abuse?

Abuse comes in different forms as listed below and is a very powerful weapon used against another person. Its purpose is that of controlling the other partner in the marriage and to distort their view of reality. Certainly, all Christians fail at times in their conduct and speech i.e., they sin on occasion; perhaps it is in being careless or selfish or inconsiderate or neglectful of their partner. However, this does not mean that a marriage partner can cry "abuse" on the rare occasions when these things happen or claim that the partners are incompatible. Nevertheless, when abuse or neglect becomes **very serious and persistent** then there is a major problem in the marriage and counselling should be sought with the goal of saving the marriage. However, if there is no progress in the elimination of the abuse or neglect, then the injured partner may feel pushed to break from the marriage.

Clearly, the Scriptures do not cover every finely detailed aspect of the valid grounds for divorce, but rather they give guidance through principles and case law from which principles can be discerned and applied. So, when Paul says, *"God has called you to peace"* (1 Cor. 7:15b) he is showing that one must not be legalistic in these issues, but that there would be many practical applications of the basic principles. Indeed, in situations where there is on-going serious abuse or neglect over some reasonable period of time then such abuse could form the basis for divorce should the injured party wish for this resolution to the problem. Of course, this would take into account whether or not the guilty party remains unrepentant! The following are the various forms of abuse:

Physical Abuse

This is when either partner persistently abuses the other partner by:

- Hitting or beating them and so creating a violent home environment.
- Behaving violently as a result of addiction to drugs or alcohol.

Note: If a slave can go free because of his master's physical abuse of him (Ex. 21:26), then certainly a wife or husband can become free of a physically abusive spouse.

Sexual Abuse

This is when the abuse is because:
- There is not a mutual consent to all the couple's sexual activities. Perhaps the husband has tried to force his wife to do something that is morally objectionable to her or physically painful. This amounts to rape. There is no requirement for a wife to submit to her husband in these ways. In fact, her first priority is her submission to God.
- A husband becomes addicted to pornography/masturbation and so continually deprives his wife of the sexual relationship.
- A wife often uses sex as a negotiating tool to get something she wants.

All of this is abusive because sex should be that of loving generosity and sensitivity on the part of both partners (1 Cor. 7:3-5). There is here a degree of crossover with some aspects of emotional neglect.

Verbal Abuse

This is when either partner persistently abuses the other partner by:

- Often lying to them.
- Using biblical truths to justify a lie.
- Twisting the true intent of biblical statements to satisfy his/her own selfish motive.

147

All of this is designed to distort the truth a person holds about something or someone, including themselves. Such deception is done in order to gain control over the victim's mind. Because of this distortion there is an initial confusion in the victim' mind so that they no longer know what is true and what is false until they finally embrace what is false and have no idea that they have been deceived.

Emotional Abuse

This is when either partner persistently abuses the other partner by:
- Being dismissive of them or their views or belittling them in private or (worse still) in public.
- Playing cruel mind-games on them.
- Being continually bitter, unforgiving, or holding a grudge concerning them.

Emotional Neglect

This is when either partner persistently neglects the other partner by:
- Not caring about their general emotional needs.
- Never showing interest in them and the things they do.
- Not caring about their partner's legitimate sexual needs (1 Cor. 7:2, 5). This refers to a failure in all the verbal, physical, and sexual expressions of love. This is a necessary significant component of any marriage and follows the pattern shown in the Song of Solomon and later emphasized by the Apostle Paul in 1 Corinthians 7:2-5. Failure in this may lead to adultery by the deprived partner. However, there may be **mitigating circumstances** in all of this as follows:

1. Are life's demands on a partner such that they have little energy for the love-making relationship.
2. Is either one of the partners suffering chronic illness and so diminishing their ability in the love-making relationship.
3. For wives who have gone through the menopause their sexual desire likely will have diminished and caring husbands must take account of this. Nevertheless, there can still be a loving relationship between the two.

4. It is likely that old age will reduce both the husband's and the wife's abilities in the love-making relationship.
5. Has either one of the partners become physically or mentally limited or incapable of engaging in the sexual expressions in a loving marriage?

Material Neglect/Financial Abuse

This is when either of the partners (an unbeliever or a Christian who is reclassified as and unbeliever) purposely or lazily fails to provide for the material needs of his wife and the children (if any). Or the wife is continually extremely lazy in doing the necessary domestic things in providing for her husband's material needs and those of the children (if any). None of this concerns the partner's "wants" but only their "needs." **Furthermore, if one partner abandons** the other partner for no good reason (1 Cor. 7:15) and does not return or repent, this would result in neglect in many of the ways described above. It is also likely that **abandonment** by one partner will also cause **material** and/or **physical/emotional neglect** and may actually end in divorce. So those who say that that there is only one ground for a Christian to divorce because Jesus only mentioned one, are missing this other ground, namely, desertion (1 Cor.7:15) given by Paul and so showing that Jesus' exception principle was simply one exception and that **there could be other exceptions** as, for example, those based on the moral standard expressed in Exodus 21:10-11.

MITIGATING CIRCUMSTANCES
Of course, some of the above issues depend on the circumstances in the marriage and life's demands. For instance:
- Is it difficult to find work or is available work very low paid?
- Do both partners need to go out to work?
- Are there any children in the family?
- Does a child need special care?

No doubt there could be other mitigating circumstances that reduce the abilities of either one of the partners in their marital role. Even so, the loyal love that was expressed in the marriage vow of, "for better or worse" should always be exercised. However, this should not be used as an excuse by an abusive partner to continue their abusive behaviour and to say, "you cannot divorce me anyway because our marriage is for better or worse" and "until death do us part!"

Social Abuse

This is when either partner persistently abuses the other partner by:

- Often stopping the other from going out—virtually holding them prisoner in their own home.
- Often stopping the other from visiting any member of their family.
- Often stopping any member of the other partner's family from visiting them. Although there may be a good reason to restrict this.

Note: Proverbs 18:4: "who can bear a crushed spirit."

Spiritual Abuse

This is when either partner persistently spiritually damages the other partner by, for example:

- Manipulating to persuade a partner to serve a false god.
- Engaging in occult demonic practices.
- Misusing the Scriptures to promote their excessive control or domination in the family.
- Stopping or inhibiting their spouse in regard to their Bible reading/study, attending Christian meetings, or other spiritual practices.

ABUSED CHILDREN

This is when either partner persistently physically, emotionally, or sexually abuses their children. Even if the children are not permanently damaged physically, they will certainly be damaged emotionally.

Love is Not Abusive or Carelessly Neglectful

Nevertheless, if either partner persistently failed to be concerned as to how they "may please" the other (1 Cor. 7:34) in all the above areas of life this would be part of the downward spiral of the

150

marriage, so that eventually it is no longer a marriage. So, in reading 1 Corinthians 13:4-7, which details the way love is shown, it is evident that all the above situations will break a marriage because there is no real love. Indeed, Paul shows just the way that love actually is and is not:

> "Love is patient; love is kind. Love isn't envious or boastful or arrogant; it doesn't behave shamefully or insist on its own way. It is never easily provoked to anger and it **never bears a grudge**. Love doesn't take pleasure in injustice, but is thrilled with the truth. It bears everything, believes everything, hopes everything —endures everything."

Later Paul added that Christians should:

> "...serve each other through love; because the entire law can be summed up in a single statement, namely, "You must love your neighbour as yourself" (Lev. 19:18). But if you continue to bite and devour each other, watch out that you're not annihilated by each other"...¹⁹Now the actions of the old unspiritual inclinations are quite evident: sexual immorality, moral corruption, promiscuity, idolatry, occultism, hatred, quarrelling, jealousy, outbursts of rage, selfish rivalries, dissensions, party intrigues, malice, drunkenness, wild parties, and similar things. I am warning you, as I had warned you before: those who practice such things will not inherit God's Kingdom! But the fruit of the spirit is love: [encompassing] joy, peace, patience, kindness, goodness, faithfulness, meekness, and self-control. Against such things there is no law" (Gal. 5:13-15, 19-23).

However, the refraining from all of the above noted abuses or neglect does not mean that there will be perfection in all or any of the various aspects of marriage. This is simply because during this age prior to the coming of the Kingdom of God human imperfection will cause some problems in a marriage—even the simple factor of misunderstandings or the little niggles about one's partner. Nevertheless, the daily application of Paul's words in 1 Corinthians 13:4-7 and Galatians 5:13-15, 19-23 by both marriage partners will produce a very good and happy marriage.

151

Further Principles Which Apply to the Issues of Abuse and Neglect

Keeping in mind that "God is love" it is evident that He does not want to keep His own people in permanently difficult situations—even though He may discipline them at times for their actual sins (Heb. 12:5-11); and of course, they expect persecution from outsiders. Evidently, from this it would appear that God would not make rules that create long-term damaging situations for any of His people. Indeed, any persistent seriously neglectful or abusive conduct by a spouse means that the perpetrator has repudiated his or her vows in the marriage contract—this leaves the spouse who is the victim of this conduct in a position whereby they may consider divorce. So, the following are some basic principles concerning abuse and neglect that can be seen from the Scriptures:

1. If a slave was allowed to depart free from a master who physically abused him or her (Ex. 21:26-27), then how much more a wife who suffers either physical or emotional abuse from her husband. But please note that, although it is generally women who suffer domestic abuse, it is estimated that 1 in 6 men in the UK also suffer domestic abuse.

2. If an animal is to be well-fed how much more a human—a spouse in a marriage (Deut. 25:4, 1 Cor. 9:8-11).

3. Because life is precious the sixth of the Ten Commandments, namely, *"you must not murder" (Ex. 20:13)* implies that any person should not stay in a position whereby they could be killed by their spouse. Therefore, any spouse who feels threatened by their marriage partner should physically get out of that environment. If the threat is ongoing this may finally lead to divorce.

4. The eighth law concerning stealing (Ex. 20:15) applies when a spouse squanders the assets of the family. Again, if this is persistent then the marriage vows have been persistently broken and this, too, may end in divorce. The penalty for the breaking of numerous of the Mosaic laws was death and so the innocent spouse ended up without her or his partner. So too,

today, when a marriage partner involves themselves in such things as rape within the marriage, homosexuality, or the occult then the innocent spouse may, according to the Scriptures, seek divorce from that person because the marriage has already died. The penalty for the breaking of numerous of the Mosaic laws was death and so the innocent spouse ended up without her or his marriage partner. So too, today, when a marriage partner involves themselves in such things as rape within the marriage, homosexuality, or the occult then the innocent spouse may seek divorce from that person.

With all of this information available I find it incredible that anyone would consider long-term persistent abuse or neglect of a spouse as not being grounds for divorce. Clearly, God regulated divorce so that treacherous divorce should never happen, but as a God of love He surely would not make a rule for His own people that those who are being damaged in their marriage could not find a happier marriage—"in the Lord" of course!

A Reasonable Position to Take Regarding Divorce

For the Apostle Paul to say to the Philippians, *"Let your reasonableness be obvious to everyone" (Phil. 4:7)* means that Paul himself must have been a reasonable person and so implying that Jesus was the same. So, it is clearly <u>unreasonable</u> (Jas. 3:17) to tell a physically battered or psychologically abused wife or husband that she or he must stay in such an unchanging abusive situation or to remain in that marital union. The idea that a wife is sinning if she divorces a husband who beats her as long as he has not slept with someone else is outrageous!!

MISAPPLICATION OF THE APOSTLE PETER'S COMMENTS
Some Christians speak of what a person in a bad marriage may have to tolerate and tell them that there is nothing they can do about it. Such Christians use Peter's words when he said, *"But even if you people should suffer for doing what is right, you will be blessed for it" (1 Pet. 3:14, 17)*. However, this is a misapplication because these words concern persecution in general for doing God's will. Certainly, it is <u>unmerciful</u> (Matt. 12:7) to tell a physically battered

153

or psychologically abused wife or husband that she or he must stay married in such an abusive situation. Although, in Peter's time, some wives might not be able to get out of their bad situation and so must endure it there may have been others who were in a better economic situation and therefore be able to follow the principle in Paul's advice to bond-servants, when he says: *"if indeed you are able to become free, make use of the opportunity..."* (1 Cor. 7:21). Nevertheless, things are very different in our day, so that a wife is very likely able to become free of any terrible situation.

Recovering from an Abusive Relationship

Deep emotional scars can be left from suffering years of any and all of the types of abuse. However, Jesus came to heal the broken-hearted and can bring about full restoration, even though the process may be painful. Jesus is a Christian's "helper" and reaches out to those who have been abused if they *"listen to him"* (Matt. 17:5). This means reading his words and those of his representatives —the apostles. In this way one receives holy spirit and one's life can be turned around into happiness and blessedness once again. Furthermore, in prayer to him and to his heavenly Father an abused person can share their pain and finally reach a place of peace and happiness, certainly other Christians can do their part to help. Indeed, *"the words of the wise brings healing"* (Prov. 12:18).

26

Final Thoughts on Bible-Based Divorce

The Effects of Divorce upon Children in the Family

The Bible says very little about children in a divorce situation. It is only the Apostle Paul who has something to say on this; which is that if the believing parent stays in the marriage there will be a reduction of the contamination of the world upon their children (1 Cor. 7:14b).

Certainly, psychological research shows that the divorce of parents has significantly negative effects on the children in the family. These are generally because of the change in the family structure. However, research also shows that children who grow up in a family where the parents stay together, but are often in significant conflict, because at least one parent is persistently abusive, generally have more psychological problems and a distorted view of marriage than children in similar families whose parents get divorced. So, it is really a no-win situation for children although they may be less scarred by the divorce of their parents because they are no longer put under the stresses of hearing and seeing all of the abusive or out of control conflict of the parents.

Conclusions Concerning Valid Grounds for Divorce

Most importantly it must be re-emphasized that divorce is the absolutely last resort in a failing marriage and a very great amount of time and effort should be spent on trying to save the marriage. Nevertheless, it is clear from this examination of the Scriptures in a culturally sensitive way that legitimate divorce is not a sin. In fact, it is the persistent breaking of one's marriage vows that is the real sin. However, Roman Catholicism allows for no divorce because it wrongly treats marriage as a sacrament which therefore, cannot be changed. Instead, it operates a system of annulment which is based on the view that the marriage was never valid. This is certainly unsatisfactory to many separating Catholics because it means that any children of the marriage would be wrongly viewed as illigiti-

-mate so that their names would be besmirched. However, neither Jesus nor Paul ever presented an annulment situation or required those in second marriages to separate or to get a divorce. Anglicanism allows divorce for adultery and for desertion, yet remarriage after the desertion is not allowed. Many other churches allow divorce only for sexual immorality after which remarriage may take place. Indeed, all these positions are based on a reading of the texts without taking into account the relevant principles contained in the Hebrew Scriptures, along with an understanding of the essential first century Jewish background which was only just beginning to be known in the mid-1800s, but not fully comprehended until the latter part of the twentieth century. So, these positions, based on faulty teachings regarding divorce have led to absolutely intolerable situations for some wives and husbands. Yet is it really likely that Jesus, as a reflection of our loving heavenly Father, would make rules requiring a person to stay married to a spouse who is physically, emotionally, or sexually abusing them or persistently seriously neglecting them? None of this fits Paul's description of how a wife should be highly valued, loved and cherished by her husband (Eph. 5:28-29).

It may be impossible for innocent victims to tolerate the adultery of a partner or to tolerate that partner's desertion or continuing negligence or abuse. The innocent spouse may even be forced to leave the family home and then seek a divorce from the guilty spouse. Additionally, based on the definition of literal adultery, any sexual abuse of the children by a parent is valid grounds for divorce. So, would Jesus or Paul really have made a rule that meant that a marriage must continue in spite of the fact that the husband consistently abuses family members or fails to provide the necessaries of life for his family? Such a person is worse than an unbeliever. Furthermore, the above denominational positions based on faulty teachings regarding divorce have led to situations, for some husbands, which are also absolutely intolerable. Perhaps a wife has persistently misused or failed to use what the husband has provided for the family or has persistently denied her husband dignified marital intimacy. Yet, in context, the understanding of Jesus' words shows that he never established the basis for the occurrence of any such appalling situations to be created for his own followers.

§

PART FIVE

Jesus and Paul on Remarriage

27

Background to Remarriage
for Christians

Erasmus, one of the clearest thinkers among the Reformation scholars in the 1500s, broke with Roman Catholic teaching on divorce and showed that remarriage would be legitimate after any valid divorce. However, the New Testament teaching on remarriage is not so specifically clear. Indeed, it is only once one realizes that remarriage in biblical times had been a fundamental right and even an obligation upon divorcees that one begins to gain some clarity on this issue. The scriptural practice of providing a wife with a certificate of divorce also makes this certain (Deut. 24:1, 3; Matt. 19:7). Furthermore, the Roman Emperor Augustus made it law within the Roman Empire that any divorcee must get remarried within eighteen months of their divorce. So, although Paul advocated the single life during critical times, he did not speak against that Roman law.

In all Jewish and biblical terms marriage is a contract (covenant) between a man and a woman, but with God as a witness. However, once that contract is broken or is persistently broken by one or both parties, the marriage is over—the person is free from that marriage (Deut. 24:2; Ex. 21:11). This is just as when death leaves someone as a widow or widower (1 Cor. 7:39). So, if a marriage no longer exists it is normal and logical to view the parties to that former marriage as single, and, therefore free to remarry. But what of Romans 7:1-4 doesn't that indicate that divorcees should not remarry?

Romans 7:1-4 Does Not Exclude Remarriage

At the outset of our discussion on remarriage we must realize that the passage in Romans 7:1-4 has been very much misunderstood and misused by those who wish to deny that a divorced Christian can remarry. We need to understand the meaning of Paul's words in this passage when he says:

> "Don't you realize brothers and sisters—I speak **to those who know the law**—that the law is master over a person only for such time as he lives? Certainly, the married woman is **legally bound to** her husband while he lives; but if her husband dies, she is released from the law [of marriage]. So then, she will be called an **adulteress if, while her husband lives, she becomes another man's**. But if her husband dies, she is free from that law, so that she is no adulteress if she becomes another man's. Similarly, my brothers and sisters, you also were put to death in relation to the law through the body of the Messiah, so that you could become another's—the one who was raised from among the dead... (KGV).

Firstly, this passage is directed to **"those who know the law"** and therefore already know that the law regulated divorce, but did not forbid it. Nevertheless, this passage is often misapplied to the subject of divorce and remarriage, but as we shall see it is not actually about divorce and remarriage i.e., **Paul was not teaching about those subjects.** In fact, the subject in this passage is that of Christians who are no longer under the regulations of the Mosaic Law because they are now united with Christ. So, Paul is here using Jewish marriage only as an illustration, and no **illustration of itself** can be taken as a proof text for any particular doctrine. In fact, writers rarely draw upon all of the detailed complexities of the subject that they choose to use as an illustration; and this is also the case with this illustration as used by Paul, just as many commentators have shown. In this case, Paul is illustrating the Christian's death to the Law with the subject of a marriage that runs its full course and ends with the death of the husband. So, this illustration is of a **normal successful marriage** (until she commits adultery) and is **not about divorce** or remarriage **per se** because under Jewish law a woman had no right to directly divorce her husband, but had to request it from a court with evidence of his neglect. Yet in verse three Paul posits a situation, as part of the illustration, where a woman *"would be **committing adultery if she married another man"...** "while her husband is alive."* Nothing is said about him being her ex-husband. In other words, she would be an adulteress and a bigamist by marrying another man while still married to her existing husband or simply an adulteress if it concerned only an affair. So, although this shows Paul's view of normal marriage as a lifetime union he is, nevertheless, not here teaching that a wife cannot, under any circumstances, remarry after divorce until the man who was her husband dies. He certainly is not saying that *only* death dissolves the marriage bond. He simply is not drawing upon all the many factors that can be involved in marriage, including divorce.

Now that we have some clarification on these words from Paul in Romans 7, we can begin to examine what would have been Jesus' understanding of the rights of his followers in regard to remarriage.

28

Did Jesus Forbid Remarriage?

It is usually assumed that Jesus forbade remarriage in the four accounts in which he comments on the subject of adultery *(Gk moichia)*. So exactly how does Jesus use the phrase, "commits adultery"?

Although many have tried to prove that later remarriage after any divorce is the adultery that Jesus spoke about, this is not the case. Firstly, the subject scripturally is treacherous divorce i.e., without proper grounds and secondly the grammar of Matthew 5:32, shows that it is the divorcing husband who is guilty of adulterizing his wife. So, Craig Keener, in referencing the work of William Luck, explains that:

> ...the verb is passive, and there are very few examples where the passive form has an active meaning. In other words, Matthew could be claiming that the divorcing husband is the one guilty of adultery, against Jewish custom: he "adulterizes" her, treats her unfaithfully, by divorcing her without adequate cause. This would fit the context: the innocent wife of 5:32 is no more guilty than the lusted-after woman of 5:28 or the brother hated without cause in 5:23. *...And Marries Another* p. 36.

Furthermore, the actual adultery in the other three of the four accounts seems to occur at the same time as the divorce according to the syntax. If so, then it cannot mean that it occurs when a person remarries. In fact, remarriage is not the issue and is never a sin provided that the divorce is on valid grounds. So, when a woman is guilty of sexual immorality, divorcing her does not make her commit adultery—she has already committed adultery. Therefore, the sin here is that of the husband's unjust treacherous divorce (Mal. 2:14-16) and viewed by Jesus as the committing of adultery metaphorically.

In his *The Unvarnished New Testament* translator Andy Gaus notes in the glossary: "**Adultery** *(moicheia)*. The word appears to be fairly specific: marriage breaking, not just illicit sexual activity, which would be *porneia*." So, it is the man's breaking of his marriage vows to his wife by his divorcing of her without proper grounds. However, the man is not necessarily committing a literal sexual sin, so how should we understand this kind of adultery?

Metaphorical Use of the Word "Adultery"

Many words in the New Testament have both a literal and a metaphorical usage and meaning breaking faith with a partner i.e., violating one's pledge as for example when a partner abuses or neglects their spouse or in treacherous divorce which causes a person to be adulterated.

So clearly, in reflecting Jesus' teaching in these relevant passages the term *moichia* used by the Gospel writers has this metaphorical and hyperbolic meaning i.e., that of **non-sexual adultery**. This simply refers to the man's unfaithfulness or breach of their marriage covenant because his motive was to dismiss his wife with no substantial justification—it is non-sexual unfaithfulness. So, the "adultery" occurs possibly because the man, prior to the divorce, is already focused on another particular woman (Matt. 5:28) and desires to marry her as with the Herod/Herodias case and therefore has planned to get rid of his first wife. Such metaphorical "adultery" concerned the actions of ancient Israel as recorded in the Hebrew Scriptures (Jer. 9:2; 23:10). It referred to Israel's **breach of covenant** with God because of her idolatry and habit of lying. There are also examples of this non-sexual adultery in the New Testament as in Matthew 12:39 where Jesus declares the people to be, *"an evil and **adulterous** generation [that] seeks for a sign."* Jesus also says: *"whoever is ashamed of me and of my words in this **adulterous** and sinful generation..."* (Mark 8:38). Furthermore, James calls some Christians an *"**adulterous** people! Do you not know that friendship with the world is enmity with God?"* (Jas 4:4). Evidently such adultery concerns the breaking of faith with God—it is all non-sexual adultery. It is also apparent that only women in Israel could commit literal sexual adultery because a husband was allowed to be polygamous. So, it appears that here Jesus is using the term "adultery" in a metaphorical and likely hyperbolic sense when he applies this to any man who breaches the covenant with his wife by divorcing her without valid grounds because he is already focused on another particular woman to marry. Additionally, in Mark 10:12, Jesus gives the reverse picture where a wife's adultery is because she unjustly/ groundlessly divorces her husband. Again, the adultery mentioned here is not literally sexual, but is that of breaking faith with her husband by divorcing him for no justifiable reason and likely desiring to be with another particular man whether or not she has already committed any literal sexual sin with that man. So, the claim by some that later remarriage after any divorce is the "adultery" Jesus spoke about is only an assumption. It is also a very forced explanation because Jesus did not say, "the man will later commit adultery <u>when he remarries</u>." It was the "any cause" divorcing i.e., divorce for no good reason that was wrong, rather than remarriage.

WHAT IF THE "ADULTERY" DOES NOT OCCUR AT THE SAME TIME"?

However, if it can be shown that syntactically the adultery mentioned in these three passages concerning divorce does not occur at the same time as the divorce and therefore is not metaphorical **non-sexual adultery,** then a literal reading would be correct. Yet, because the divorce here was for "any cause" including unjust, even treacherous reasons, such divorces would still have invalid grounds in Jesus' view. Therefore, the first marriage is not over and any subsequent marriage would simply involve a committing of literal sexual sin—which then, of course, breaks the first marriage anyway. However, because of the above factors concerning "non-sexual adultery" this may not have been what Jesus meant when he made his statement of: "commits adultery." So, whether the term adultery is used in a metaphorical or a literal way it does not mean that someone who has a valid divorce "commits adultery" when they remarry.

Jesus' Attitude toward
Those Who Remarry After Divorcing

Only relatively few leading scholars and commentators today would say that Jesus never allowed remarriage for Christians. Those noted for saying this are, Gordon Wenham, Charles Ryrie, and Lesley McFall. In fact, this is a relatively new approach based upon the misunderstandings of some of the early church fathers. However, William Heth, who previously agreed with these other scholars, has repudiated that view because, as he says, there is no credible biblical evidence for it. In fact, it is just as sinful to make a rule where God has not done so, as it is to ignore God's proven view of matters. All the biblical evidence and all background knowledge of the times show that remarriage was the norm for those who are legitimately divorced. Indeed, Jesus' statements in Matthew's gospel allowed for that. So, Craig keener comments on Matthew 19:3-9 that:

> ...this passage clearly permits the innocent party in a divorce to remarry. In the Old Testament, of course, the adulterous spouse was executed, so the remaining partner would have been permitted to remarry as a widower, even if Moses had not allowed circumstances for divorce in Deuteronomy 24:1. Our contention is that Jesus' teaching does not impose a greater hardship on the innocent party whose spouse has continued in adultery...If the divorce is valid, so is the remarriage; Jesus calls remarriage after an invalid divorce adulterous only because the divorce was invalid, due to insufficient grounds.
>
> *...And Marries Another* pp.33 and 44.

NO CLEAR STATEMENT BY JESUS AGAINST REMARRIAGE

The strong argument from silence applies here because remarriage was universally accepted as the norm at that time. Indeed, this was the purpose of God's law regarding the **certificate of divorce** (Deut. 24:1, 3) and Jesus did not contradict God's law on this matter (Matt. 19:7, 8). This makes it fairly certain that Jesus also accepted remarriage as the norm, even though he did not make any direct statement about it. A further indication of his likely acceptance of remarriage was the fact that he made **no clear statement that any person must not remarry**.

Validly Divorced People Who Remarry Are Not Adulterers

Some Bible teachers propose that the passages concerning the divorcing of a wife refer to a scripturally valid divorce and so prove that any remarriage after divorce is adultery. Contrary to that view, Jesus classifies such divorces as having invalid grounds because he shows that "any cause" means that valid grounds were completely missing. What Jesus spoke against was a man's divorcing of his wife **for no good reason**, usually so that he could marry a woman he currently desired, as with Herod Antipas' desiring of Herodius. These ones committed adultery metaphorically by breach of contract (non-sexually) at the very point of treacherously divorcing their respective spouses and possibly literally during the time of their previous marriages. They did not become adulterers simply by remarrying and then having a sexual relationship with the new marriage partner. In fact, as with many other statements Jesus made, he used **preacher's non-literal rhetoric concerning remarriage as adultery** in these accounts. In other words, it is his use of hyperbole to exaggerate the situation and make his point forcefully, as Craig Keener shows in *The IVP Bible Background Commentary* p.59. Under the heading **Remarriage as Adultery** Keener states regarding Matthew 5:32: "This seems, however, to be hyperbole (as in 5:29-30), a graphic way of forbidding divorce except when the other partner has irreparably broken the marriage covenant" (also see pp. 97, 161). This detail fits with the metaphorical usage of the word "adultery" as referring to a **breach of contract** or covenant. So, whether or not a person had been divorced or their spouse has deceased, the result is the same—they are without a partner. It is illogical to say that a divorcee is still married to their first spouse. Certainly, Jesus was never illogical! If the grounds for divorce are legitimate in God's sight, then a second marriage cannot be "adultery." So, it seems evident that Jesus was using the term "adultery' with regard to those who had divorced for no good biblical reason and in a way that is rhetorical so that he emphasizes the wrongness of the interpretation and position of the Pharisees of his day. So, it is evident that his statements on "adultery" do not apply to those who have a valid divorce.

Remarriage for the Innocent Partner

Once the marriage contract is broken by one or both parties the marriage is over unless there is genuine repentance by the guilty partner followed by forgiveness by the hurt partner. If not, then the innocent person is free of that marriage (Deut. 24:2; Ex. 21:11). This is just as when death leaves someone widowed—they are fully free to remarry (1 Cor. 7:39). Also please note that the <u>divorced and the widowed</u> are often classified together in the Hebrew Scriptures (See next chapter), and so indicating the full right of a divorced person to remarry. Indeed, why would God, through Jesus, now change His

166

earlier stated moral laws which protected innocent parties in cases of very damaging abusive marriages and treacherous divorce? Why would He deny the wonders of good marriage for the hurting innocent divorced person, but grant it to widows? Indeed, it is God who promoted marriage in the first place by saying that, *"it is not good for the man to be alone" (Gen. 2:18)*. In fact, God, through Paul, condemned those who denied marriage (1 Tim. 4:1-3), including remarriage after a legitimate divorce.

Furthermore, Jesus was a person who showed **mercy** to those who were in difficult situations. So, Craig keener makes the point that:

> ...forever disallowing the remarriage of the innocent party seems to annul Jesus' law of mercy (9:13; 12:7): If Jesus' emphasis in this passage is the sanctity of marriage, then penalizing rather than defending an innocent partner appears more like the sort of interpretation the "hard-hearted" foes of Jesus (19:8) would offer than the kind that Jesus would offer. *...And Marries Another* p. 35.

The two texts that Keener cites are quoted by Jesus from Hosea 6:6. So he says in Matthew 12:7, *"If you had known what this means: 'I desire mercy and not sacrifice'* (Hosea 6:6), *you wouldn't have condemned innocent people."*

THE WOMAN AT THE WELL

The concept that Jesus did not allow for divorce and remarriage is completely contradicted by the event concerning the woman from the town of Sychar, Samaria (John 4:16-18). Jesus stated that she had had five "husbands." If the no-divorce and no-remarriage view were correct Jesus should have said to her: "you have had only one husband and the other four relationships as well as the man you are now living with have all been adulterous relationships. So, you need to go back to your first husband." But Jesus made no such comment and so recognized the legality of those divorces and remarriages. If Jesus had required her to return to a first husband, and then had made a comment to that effect, then she would have had to break the law forbidding remarriage to a previous, but bad, husband (Deut. 24:4). Because of the law for the provision of a certificate of divorce in first century Israel remarriage was a fundamental right of a divorcee and Jesus did not change that.

Must an Invalidly Divorced and Remarried Person Return to Their First Spouse?

There is nothing in Jesus' teachings to suggest that he expected anyone to separate from their second wife or husband and return to the first spouse. In fact, this would be wrong biblically (Deut. 24:3-4) and would be an advocating of divorce for totally unjustifiable reasons. This would then result in an actual remarriage to the first wife—the very thing the anti-divorce/remarriage party denounce. Sadly, these people have misunderstood Jesus' statements and this has led them to this wrong conclusion concerning divorce of the second spouse. In fact, reconciliation with the ex-spouse is likely to be impossible; and although technically the original invalid divorce likely involved a metaphorical form of adultery—a breach of the marriage contract—it would cause chaos in families if Jesus had taught that there must be a return to ones' first spouse. Indeed, Jesus' use of the word "adultery" is most likely to be a rhetorical hyperbolic statement of exaggeration which was said so as to hammer home his point just as in Matthew 5:32 which he presented in a context of numerous hyperbolic statements. Just as a brother hater cannot be charged with actual murder, so too, no remarried person is to be charged with actual adultery. So, this point follows through to apply to Matthew 19, Mark 10, and Luke 16. Indeed, literal adultery is an act and no act of adultery can be considered a state of adultery i.e., remarried Christians are not "living in a state of adultery, even when the grounds for their respective divorces were unjustified."

Remarriage for the Guilty Partner

God understands the human need to be with a spouse (Gen. 2:18). So, He does not hold sin against even the guilty partner <u>forever</u>, provided he or she is repentant for their part in all that led to the divorce. It is not *"the unforgivable sin" (Matt. 12:31).* Certainly, those who are redeemed Christians are not meant to live in permanent penance, but rather our loving heavenly Father gives the repentant Christian a new beginning, having learned from his/her past mistakes. If others do not forgive, then they are the ones who have a problem (Matt. 6:15). Certainly, marriages subsequent to a divorce are real marriages because a civil divorce terminates a marriage. In fact, there is no biblical precedent for breaking up a second marriage.

~

We will now examine all that Paul had to say under inspiration of God's spirit on the subject of remarriage.

§

29

Paul's Teachings on Remarriage

Under What Circumstances Did Paul Discourage Marriage or Remarriage?

Paul's motive for discouraging marriage or remarriage at that time <u>in Corinth</u> as stated in 1 Corinthians 7:26, 28 was: *"in view of the **present crisis"*** and *"those who marry **will face a difficult time**, and I am trying to spare you that."* This crisis and the personally difficult times were probably caused by the famines that were being experienced in Corinth at the time and which made it very difficult for a man to provide for a wife and family. Also, for a Christian man, there was the ever-present threat of imprisonment or even execution for preaching the Christian message, and so leaving his family destitute. For these reasons it was not a good time to get married. So, Paul is not saying that marriage is incompatible with Christian service in general and under normal circumstances, but rather he was sparing those in Corinth from a worse situation of even greater difficulties at that particular time by encouraging them to remain unmarried if they were able to—if they had "the gift" for it (vs. 7). In fact, with no criticism, Paul recognized that Peter and the other apostles were married men.

Remarriage for the Widowed

This is a closely connected subject to that of divorce. On this Paul says:

> *"A wife is bound to her husband as long as he lives. But if her husband dies, she is free to be married to whom she wishes, only in the Lord"* (1 Cor. 7:39 ESV).

This statement was unlikely to have been said for the purpose of negating the principles in the Mosaic Law on Levirate marriage, as some have thought. This is because such a thing is unlikely to have been practiced in Corinth. However, because this is addressed to widows it does not concern the four Jewish scriptural grounds for divorce. It is speaking of the situation of a marriage that runs right through to the death of the husband and that neither of the partners has had any significant problems causing a divorce, or that if there were any such difficulties they were resolved. Therefore, one cannot say that the only time a woman may remarry is if her husband dies. To do so would contradict Jesus' exception on legitimate divorce (Matt. 5:32, 19:9) as well as Paul's exception stated in 1 Corinthians 7:15. In fact, a few verses earlier, he also said that those divorcees who marry "have not sinned"—verses 27 and 28.

The Divorced and the Widowed Are to Be Treated the Same Way

One major reason why many denominations reject divorcees is that they have placed them in the wrong category. This is rectified when one understands a certain factor in the Hebrew Scriptures, which is that those who are widowed and those who are divorced are often classified together in terms of how they are to be treated (Lev. 21:14, 22:13, Num. 30:9, Ezek. 44:22). In fact, the terms "widow" and "widowhood" come from the root Hebrew word, *alman*, which means "discarded" or "forsaken," which is exactly what happens to a divorcee as well as to a widow. So, the method by which the spouse is left without a husband is rather immaterial. Indeed, a woman had to be very specific when describing her circumstances. For instance, when a certain woman addressed the king, she said, *"I'm a widow; my husband is dead" (2 Sam. 14:5)*. This shows that she had to state specifically <u>how</u> she became "a widow" i.e., "without a husband" which was, in this case, because her husband had died. If she had not said "my husband is dead," but simply said 'I'm a widow' there would have been uncertainty concerning whether or not her husband had died or had deserted her, or had divorced her. However, from a different angle, after King David had escaped from Jerusalem, his **wives** and concubines who were left behind i.e., separated from him, were said to be *"living in **widowhood**" (2 Sam. 20:3)*, and yet their husband, David, was clearly still alive. Similarly, the Greek word *chera* meaning "widow" has some overlap with the term "unmarried" (Gk *agamos*) which includes those who are divorced (1 Cor. 7:8). This term *chera* can mean "a woman lacking a husband" and so equally applies to any divorced woman as much as to any widow. Furthermore, Paul

171

speaks of, *"...the unmarried ...the widows ...[and] the married..." (1 Cor. 7:8-10)*. Here, the "unmarried" (as a general term) are those who are not married, i.e., those who were never married, and those who were divorced and had never remarried. So, the term "widow" refers to someone who had been married but now does not have a husband because of either death or divorce. Evidently, any breaking of the sexual union has the same effect whether it is by death or by divorce. In fact, divorce may be viewed as the result of the death of a marriage—the same effect as the literal death of one's spouse. So, when Paul says that a widow is *"free to be married to whom she wishes..." (1 Cor. 7:39)* it is evident that a divorced woman would also have this same right, so that she also would not risk poverty. It is illogical and unjust to treat a person who is the victim in a bad marriage resulting in divorce any differently to a widow.

HOW ARE WIDOWS TO BE TREATED?

Paul writes that Christians should, *"Support widows who are genuinely widows. But if any widow has children or grand-children they should learn to practice their religion toward their own family first and to repay their parents, for this is pleasing to God. The genuine widow, left all alone, has put her hope in God and continues night and day in petitions and prayers; however the one who is self-indulgent is dead even while she lives. Insist on all this with authority so that widows will not be blamed. Now if a person does not provide for his own relatives, especially for his household, he has denied the faith and is worse than an unbeliever" (1 Tim. 5:3-8 OGOMT)*. Then James states that, *"Pure, uncontaminated religion consists in this: to look after...widows in their distress" (Jas. 1:27 OGOMT)*. So, on the basis that divorcees are to be treated the same way as those who have lost a husband in death, this is how such divorcees should be treated rather than shunning them or denigrating them if they should later remarry.

Remarriage for the Divorced Because They Are "No Longer Bound"

In 1 Corinthians 7:15b Paul states that:

> *"...if the unbelieving partner "divorces-by-separating" himself or herself let it take place. In such cases the brother or sister is **no longer bound** [to the partner]."*

Some Catholic and a few Protestant scholars present a twisted meaning to the term "bound" as meaning 'free to remain single' or 'free to separate but not to remarry.' However, the phrase "no longer bound" (1 Cor. 7:15) means free from their marriage—the term "bound" being defined as "married" in 1 Corinthians 7:27 in contrast to "released" as meaning "divorced." Paul also made a distinction between "the virgins" (those who had never married) and those who were divorced. Neither group would be sinning if they married (1 Cor. 7:27-28). Although Paul encouraged those at that critical time to be single, he certainly recognized marriage, and therefore remarriage, as being the right thing to do under normal circumstances. Further confirmation of this is found in Paul's use of the term "bound" in 1 Corinthians 7:39 so that a husband's death releases a wife from the marriage bond leaving her free to remarry because: *"A wife is **bound** to her husband as long as he lives. But if her husband dies, **she is free to be married** to whom she wishes, only in the Lord"* (1 Cor. 7:39). In both instances, the marriage has ended because of the permanent departure of the partner. In one sense it really doesn't matter whether it was by physical death or by death of the marriage leading to divorce—the result is the same— the marriage ends! Also, if "not bound" merely meant permission to live as a single person, Paul would not need to give such permission, because the divorcee had no choice in the matter. So the phrase "no longer bound" is taken by most scholars to mean that the divorced person is free to remarry, but as in the case for widows—"only in the Lord." i.e., they should marry a Christian. So, in this case the believer is free from all marital obligations to the ex-partner because he or she is "no longer bound to that partner." This is because the unbelieving partner has already separated himself or herself—it is a final and unconditional divorce, at least after attempts to reconcile have failed.

Some have proposed that, although a believing wife or husband *"is no longer bound"* to the unbelieving partner, this did not apply to two believers as mentioned in verses 10-11. However, Paul's later statement in verses 27 and 28 of 1 Corinthians 7 shows this to be incorrect, because that statement concerns any of those Christian men who *"have been released from a wife"* i.e., divorced. Also, because a Christian couple marries "in the Lord" they have accepted all the responsibilities that go with such a marriage and to live up to the vows set out in the Scriptures. If one partner persistently breaks

173

these vows, then it seems wrong for the innocent partner to be penalized by not being allowed to divorce and to remarry at a later date. Such an arrangement would be unjust.

Sadly, Christians who remarry while their ex-partner is still alive have been wrongly labelled as being in adultery and therefore, should not remarry. Concerning this lie and restriction one internet commentator proposed the following questions to see how much one has been conditioned by such denominational distortion. He asks:

> If you were divorced or your spouse was deceased, would you still have a mate? Of course not! Let me ask the same question a different way. If you are a woman and your husband was divorced from you or deceased, would you have a husband? And if you are a man and your wife was divorced from you or deceased, would you have a wife? To seek answers to these simple questions may seem silly, but if we have answered them as "Yes", that's what we've been taught.

So, a validly divorced person is in the same position as someone who has lost their partner in death. So, the "no remarriage" restriction on the divorcee unless or until their ex-spouse should later die is simply illogical and with no biblical support (see comments on Romans 7:1-4 in Chapter 27). In this case, for a woman it is clearly not true that her **husband** is alive—it is her **ex- or former-husband** who is alive. Indeed, the faulty thinking in this misuse of Romans 7 might promote a wishing for the death for the ex-partner or gladness if they should happen to die. Only after that sad event do they feel that they can remarry in good conscience and then be in good standing with their denomination, in spite of such an awful and unchristian wish.

"God Has Called You to Peace"
- 1 Corinthians 7:15c

This statement by Paul implies that there are exceptions beyond straight abandonment by a partner as grounds for divorce. Rather than making rules, Paul is showing that this principle can be applied to the many **practical situations** that are mentioned earlier because all these wrongs make a travesty of marriage. Certainly, if a deserting spouse (for no good reason), or an abusing spouse, or an adulterous spouse refuses all attempts at reconciliation (and repentance) he or she has placed themselves in the position of an unbeliever. Indeed, Paul's principle may be applied to even new situations which occur in the modern-day world.

This principle of "peace" within a marriage was viewed by Paul as more important than narrowly defined legalistic prohibitions. So, in Romans 12:18 Paul said, *"If possible, so far as it depends on you, live at peace with everyone."* However, not everyone in a marriage wants to live at peace. Yet Paul recognized that: "God has called you to peace." This phrase is reminiscent of the pre-A.D. 70 rabbinic phrase **"for the sake of peace"** and was used to indicate that **a pragmatic solution** to something that had been sought for the sake of peace, rather than following a strict law. So, it seems that Paul cut through any legalism and presented a pragmatic solution for believers who had been divorced for a less than biblical reason and/or against their will. Furthermore, any attempts to persuade a couple to stay together long after their relationship has become nothing more than a "legal shell" with no commitment will simply drain the couple of all their spirituality. Whatever the situation, we must remember that the fault lies with the person who was the cause of the divorce by their failure to keep their marriage vows.

THE VIRGINS AND THE DIVORCED MAY MARRY...1 CORINTHIANS 7:25-28

> *"Now concerning those who have never married (lit. virgins), I have no command from the Lord, but I give my opinion as one shown mercy by the Lord to be trustworthy. I think that **in view of the present crisis** it is good for a man to **remain as he is**. ²⁷If you've been **bound to a wife**, stop seeking to be released. If you've been **released from a wife**, stop seeking a wife. **But if you marry** (in context—after a divorce)**, you haven't sinned.** And if a virgin woman marries, she hasn't sinned. Yet those who marry **will face a difficult time**, and I am trying to spare you that"*
>
> *(KGV).*

The term "released" here means "divorced" as shown in the NET Bible's rendering of: *"The one bound to a wife should not seek divorce. The one released from a wife should not seek marriage. But if you marry (i.e., after your divorce), you have not sinned."* This does not seem also to apply to those who have become widowed because the term "released" does not seem appropriate to the situation of the loss of a person's spouse through death. It seems only to apply to those who are divorced.

The phrase *"but if you marry"* in verse 28a refers directly to those who have been *"released from a wife"* i.e., having divorced her or been divorced by her. Paul treats these ones separately from the "virgin women" i.e., those who have never married. This shows that in neither case would marriage be a sin for them. So, if one disallowed marriage for male divorcees one must also disallow it for female virgins. But, of course, Paul never says that, but simply says that those who marry do not sin in the case of divorcees and separately in the case of those who have never married. Indeed, if there is a divorce for any valid reason, even by separation or dismissal in the Greco-Roman style according to Paul's pragmatic approach, remarriage would be allowed because the divorcee "is not bound" (NAB) i.e., no longer married according to verse 15 as meaning that he or she was free to remarry.

Mistranslation of 1 Corinthians 7:27b as "Free from a Wife"

Certain translations of verse 27b have wrongly expressed this verse in the present tense i.e., *"free* from a wife" *(ESV)*, as if to include those who have never been married, rather than in the past tense as shown in the Greek as meaning *freed*. However, here the contrast is between the married state i.e.: *"Are you bound to a wife?"* (Gk *dedesai gunaiki*) and the divorced state: *"Are you freed from a wife?"* (Gk *lelusai apo gunaikos*). So grammatically and in context the phrase *"freed from **a wife**"* does not mean that a man was never married, but rather that he is now divorced from a wife as shown word for word as: "If you **have been freed** *(Gk lelusai)* from a wife" (UBS Interlinear). However, the rendering in the NIV and a few other translations of: "Are you unmarried?" does not fit the Greek grammar as shown by many scholars. Other translations render verse 27b according to the grammar as:

- "Are you released from a wife?" (NASB)
- "Has your marriage been dissolved?" (NEB, REB, N. T. Wright, and Barclay).
- "If you are divorced, don't try to find a spouse" (CEB).
- "Are you divorced from your wife? Don't look for another one" (GW).

- "The one released from a wife should not seek marriage" (NET).
- "Are you loosed from a wife? Do not seek a wife" (NKJV and HCSB).
- *"If you have been released (or "freed") from a wife, stop seeking a wife"* (KGV). This last rendering of verse 27b is even more literal than in the above versions.

With reference to verses 27 and 28 Craig Keener comments that:

> Paul does not say "free," but "freed." The person who is "freed" can therefore only be a person who was previously bound. In its context this can only mean that the person was previously married. Given the fact that "freed" in the first line refers to divorce, we must take it as referring to divorce in the second line as well; if Paul did not mean us to take the word the same way, he could have indicated this easily enough by using a different word ... The references to virgins in 7:28 and, indeed, in 7:36-38, show that Paul's discouragement of remarriage for those once married is only on the same level as his discouragement of marriage for virgins. Those who disallow remarriage for divorcees under all circumstances must also prohibit marriage for virgins. ...*And Marries Another* p.63.

Indeed, verse 34 contrasts "the woman who is **unmarried**, and the **virgin**" showing that "unmarried" here means 'no longer married,' i.e., divorced. This term could include the "widowed" (verse 9), but they are likely to be in a separate category here in this context.

~

However, some have said that rather than applying to those who had been married, the above passages apply only to the betrothed. Is this true?

30

Don't Paul's Words on Marriage Apply Only to the Betrothed?

Gordon Wenham, whose entire set of comments are against any remarriage, has proposed that 1 Corinthians 7:27-28 applies only to those who are betrothed and not to those who have divorced after marriage. So, let us examine these verses again, but now from the perspective that Paul may have been referring to <u>only</u> the previously "betrothed" rather than the previously "married":

> *"Now concerning those who have never married* (lit. **virgins**, *but the ESV renders it as "betrothed"*) *... I think that* **in view of the present crisis** *it is good for a man to* **remain as he is.** *²⁷If you've been* **bound** *(in betrothal)* **to a wife,** *stop seeking to be released. If you've been* **released from a wife,** *stop seeking a wife.* **But if you marry, you haven't sinned.** *And if a virgin woman (but the ESV renders it as "betrothed woman"), marries, she hasn't sinned...."*

The term "virgins" in verse 25 refers specifically to **all those who have never married** i.e., single people, (although in certain contexts in the Scriptures this term does refer specifically to "the betrothed"). So, the ESV rendering of 1 Corinthians 7:27-28 is far too limiting. Furthermore, unlike the modern-day view of an engagement, the Jewish view of "betrothal" was effectively a marriage with a legal contract just as binding as marriage (Deut. 20:7; 22:24) and requiring divorce to end it. This means that one cannot easily distinguish between "betrothal" and a completed marriage in some texts. However, what helps us to see the distinction in 1 Corinthians 7 is that the betrothed would mostly be virgins. Indeed, the previously "married man" of verses 27 and 28a is distinguished from "the virgin woman" in verse 28b, and so showing that verse 28 is focused upon remarriage for that previously married man. Also, although the term "wife" is applied to a betrothed woman on rare occasions in the Scriptures, it primarily and obviously referred mostly to a married woman, and this is what we find in verse 27 containing the word "wife." So, the phrases "bound to a wife" and "released from a wife" apply at least as much, if not more, to those who were married and then divorced as they might to the betrothed and then divorced. Also, just as Jesus digressed in his debate with the Pharisees on this subject, so too, Paul digresses from the subject of the "virgins," in verses 25 and 26, to the subject of those who are married or divorced as noted in verse 27—possibly even including "the betrothed." So, Wenham's view that the passage could refer **only** to "the betrothed" is certainly wrong as other scholars show, although some of "the betrothed" could certainly be included in the group along with the married ones.

This Is Not a Case of Special Pleading

In no way is any of the reasoning on the above recent chapters or understanding of individual texts a case of special pleading as some have proposed. If special pleading were the case, then language starts to have no meaning and Christians would have trouble defending their understanding of several subjects in Jesus' belief system, because he never made a comment on them. Clearly, he never commented on these subjects because such issues would never have arisen in Jewish minds. So, too, with the subject of divorce! It never was an issue about whether a person could divorce or remarry. All sectors of the community believed in the possibility of divorce and followed by remarriage.

~

Indeed, the Bible nowhere presumes that remarriage is sinful. The right of remarriage is explicitly granted by the Apostle Paul as Jesus' representative.

One final aspect to this subject of marriage after divorce needs to be studied so that we can see what the implications are for the entire subject of divorce and remarriage.

31

"The Unmarried" with Strong Sexual Desire Should Marry – 1 Cor. 7:9

In 1 Corinthians 7:8 Paul speaks of "the unmarried." Unlike verses 27b and 34, the use of this term in verse 8 encompasses both "the virgins," "the widowed," and "the divorced"—all of whom are unmarried (Gk *agamos*). So, for any individuals in this group who have strong sexual desire **Paul recommends**, in verse 9, **that they marry**. He says: *"But if they cannot restrain their desire, they should marry, because it's better to marry than to burn with sexual desire!"* Paul later recommends the same for the younger widows (1 Tim. 5:14). Certainly, it would make no sense to say that the younger widows can remarry and yet to deny this opportunity to the younger divorcees.

Additionally, the grouping of **the divorced and the widowed together** in the Hebrew Scriptures (Lev. 21:14, 22:13, Ezek. 44:22), on the basis of their freedom from former husbands (Num. 30:9), leads to the conclusion that the New Testament permission for widows to remarry would also apply to divorced women (Rom. 7:2). So, if remarriage of legitimate divorcees were viewed negatively by some Christians, and counsel against remarriage was given, then those so counselling would be guilty of perpetrating an injustice against divorcees.

Indeed, when a marriage becomes sick and is followed by its death, the divorce is simply the burial of the figurative body after the death of the marriage. Therefore, in a certain sense, there is not a great deal of difference between the death of a marriage and the literal death of one's spouse—it results in the tragic loss of a partner. This leaves those who are divorced free to remarry, just as much as those who are widowed (1 Cor. 7:39). In fact, marriage generally comes to an end when the wronged partner is forced to decide that it has ended. This will occur after all attempts at reconciliation have failed and forgiveness can no longer be offered to the primarily guilty party.

Paul, as Jesus' representative, having received information on this subject from Jesus, also allowed for remarriage of a believer after being divorced by an unbelieving partner. As with Jesus, Paul did not need to say much about remarriage because it was the generally accepted thing to do at that time in Israel as well as among the Gentiles. Indeed, there are strong indicators that Paul would have agreed that anyone could get remarried under normal circumstances, especially when applying God's universal moral laws to the allowing of remarriage. Also, as with Jesus, Paul says nothing to the effect that anyone must remain <u>permanently</u> unmarried as shown earlier in this book. So, reconciliation obviously takes time and if, after several attempts have been made and those attempts have failed, then the primarily innocent partner would be able to seek a new partner. This is the reasonable, logical, and grammatical approach to Paul's statement rather than the cruel and unwarranted approach advocated by harsh-minded people.

32

Putting the Record Straight on Remarriage

The Teaching That All Remarriage Is Disallowed in the New Testament Is Unscriptural

For all of the following reasons those who condemn remarriage are operating under misguided thinking. This is because they may be unaware of or choose to ignore the following facts:

1. Remarriage after divorce was encouraged in Israel and in the Greco-Roman world as law.

2. No teachers in Israel taught against remarriage and neither did Jesus or Paul.

3. Although Jesus said little about remarriage, he never said that remarriage was wrong (Please note comments in Chapter 28).

4. Both Jesus and Paul followed God's moral laws and did not say that He (through Moses) was wrong on the principles related to divorce and remarriage.

5. Jesus only spoke against a man's divorcing of his wife for no good reason (Deut. 24:1), and likely so that he could marry a woman he currently desired—as with Herod. A divorce on valid grounds always allows for remarriage.

6. In his statements on divorce, Jesus most likely applied the term "adultery" in a metaphorical and rhetorical way and as occurring when the man treacherously divorced his wife, not at a later time when he or his ex-wife should marry someone new.

7. If taken literally the term "adultery" would apply to those who treacherously divorce a partner. So, Jesus was not calling those with a valid divorce "adulterers."

8. Jesus acknowledged the certificate of divorce as permitting remarriage.

9. Jesus' teaching on mercy does not impose a hardship on the innocent marriage partner or on a repentant guilty partner by denying them remarriage.

10. Jesus never condemned the woman at the well for all her remarriages or made her return to her first husband.

11. Never does Jesus contradict God's original statement that, "it is not good for the man to be alone. I will make a helper suitable for him" (Gen. 2:18). This applies equally to Christian men who are left on their own after a divorce, so that they may have the opportunity to enjoy a happy marriage. By extension this also applies to women.

12. Even after Jesus' statements on the single life the general rule among Christians was that of marriage and re-marriage.

13. If the widowed can remarry, then, in fairness and mercy, why not those who are the innocent party in a divorce?

14. In 1 Corinthians 7:1-5 Paul encourages "the married" to engage in their legitimate sexual relations so that they are not tempted into sexual immorality. He is hardly likely to forbid remarriage for those who have been divorced and thereby put them into unnecessary temptation of falling into sexual immorality.

15. In 1 Corinthians 7:8-9 Paul encourages "the unmarried" who have strong sexual desire to marry. This must include those who have been divorced for the same above reason.

16. Paul shows, in 1 Corinthians 7:15b, that a Christian who has been divorced by an unbeliever "is **no longer bound.**" This means that they are free to remarry.

17. Paul shows in 1 Corinthians 7:27 that a Christian who was "married" and is **now "released" does not sin if he or she marries again.**

18. Paul taught, in 1 Timothy 4:1-3, that those who "forbid marriage" are promoting "the teachings of demons" and "deceiving spiritual thoughts." This must include the forbidding of remarriage for some of the reasons stated above.

Conclusions Concerning Remarriage

Certainly, Paul, in dealing with the situation for Christians in the Gentile world, did not contradict Jesus' position on these matters, so this leaves us with several situations which allow for remarriage:

A. Having a scripturally valid divorce because of an adulterous or abusive or neglecting or deserting partner.
B. Having been divorced as the guilty partner, but now repentant, yet that guilty partner has not been forgiven and received back by the innocent partner. It is not the unforgivable sin.
C. Having lost one's spouse in death.

Because legitimate divorce is not a sin, clearly neither is remarriage. Certainly, the doctrinal posture that does not allow for remarriage is oppressive to those whom God is trying to redeem. However, the persistent breaking of one's marriage vows is a sin. Nevertheless, even after reading all the above information in these studies there will be those Christians who will view divorce and/or remarriage as sinful for their own reasons. However, Rick Walston observes that desire-beliefs are by definition wrong beliefs. Then he goes on to say:

> Humans are interesting and curious beings. One of the many curious things that we have the ability to do is believe something because *we want it to be true.* We have the ability to do the opposite as well. We can choose not to believe something because *we do not want it to be true.* ... There is a persistent desire-belief with regard to Jesus and divorce. Some people see divorce as so sinful (due to faulty information and bad research) that they cannot fathom the idea that Jesus would ever allow it in any way, shape, or form. Thus, they desire that Jesus always denounce divorce in every situation.

Something Happened on the Way to "Happily Ever After" pp. 82, 83.

It is a fact that the human mind holds tenaciously to traditional patterns of belief, even in the face of overwhelming evidence to the contrary. Indeed, the above clear evidence shows that divorce for a Christian is allowed for valid grounds and those valid grounds include persistent serious abuse or neglect. It also shows that a divorcee with valid grounds can happily get remarried. Yet for all

184

that evidence I understand that many will still stick to their traditional beliefs on this subject by their application of single phrases taken from Jesus' or Paul's words without taking account of their full context and background. This approach keeps one in his or her comfort zone, but is really a spiritually dangerous place in which to stay. This is because our loving heavenly Father and His exalted Son, Jesus the Messiah require that we seek what is true of them and their views on matters. Certainly, our faith and our maintaining of God's favour depend on our being biblical truth seekers.

33

Anomalies and Injustices in Current General Church Policy

From the Scriptures it is clear that marriage is part of God's design for humans and is a basic and God-given human right and privilege which is promoted by Him. However:

* If no divorce is allowed for any reason, then clearly those divorced against their will can never remarry. To deny remarriage to such divorcees is a lifetime injustice perpetrated upon them. Such a policy is on a par with that of the pagan nations in Moses' time because they did not provide a certificate of divorce for a divorced woman, and therefore made remarriage very difficult for her.

* Allowing divorce for sexual immorality, but not for things that are much worse physically makes no sense e.g., beating a partner, beating the children, or even attempted murder.

* Allowing for "separation" in modern-day terms rather than divorce forces a person to live as a single person without the choice to remarry and may pressure them toward sexual immorality (1 Cor. 7:2). This is directly contrary to Paul's teaching (1 Cor. 7:3-5, 25-28, 33-34).

* Denying remarriage to those who have been divorced against their will or those who have repented of their wrongs in the marriage and yet have not been able to reconcile with their ex-spouse is a further injustice which may condemn them to a life of loneliness in contradiction of God's design for humans (Gen. 2:18).

* Allowing remarriage for widows, but not for divorcees is another anomaly and an injustice.

* To teach against remarriage of those who are legitimately divorced is classified as a deceiving spiritual thought—a teaching of demons (1 Tim. 4:1-3).

186

There are also a number of lesser anomalies and injustices in the various policies of the different denominations. However, the Scriptures never show that either God or Jesus would purposely make rules that cause long-term suffering or hardship to those who love them. So, in terms of church attitudes Professor Craig Keener comments that:

> If the wronged partner is seeking reconciliation, the wronged partner is not to be interrogated concerning where on the range between a "perfect" and a "mediocre" spouse he or she may have fallen. God who knows the hearts of us all will ultimately vindicate or condemn; but his church, if it errs, must err on the side of mercy rather than judgment. Paul allows for the existence and remarriage of an innocent party, and it is time that many Christians today learn to do the same. ... The legalists who oppress divorced believers in this way, believers who may have already been crushed by their spouses' abandonment, may be among those who cause Jesus' little ones to stumble (Matt. 18:6-7)—placing their own position before God in serious question. ...*And Marries Another* pp. 66 and 82.

Nevertheless, there seems to be a steady change of viewpoint on this subject taking place among individual Christians who are studious of this subject. However, there is as yet only very limited change among denominations. Hopefully, as the kind of information from the best of investigators on this subject filters down to the individual pastors and others involved in God's work, there will be a notable change and so giving hurting Christians the freedom that they need to extract themselves from some of the lonely and even horrendous situations that they have found themselves in. This would then be followed by a far more empathetic and sympathetic attitude from other church members.

34

Concluding Comments

What Jesus Accomplished in Regard to Divorce

Jesus' great accomplishments in the area concerned with marriage were that he brought God's ways, according to the Scriptures, back into godly life. By doing this he removed the inequalities for women by speaking out against polygamy, so that a wife could get a divorce from her unrepentant husband because of his sexual immorality. Jesus also showed that the "any cause" divorce, which was very popular because the men could get a divorce on a whim, was in fact a breach of contract by those men. This may all have seemed new to the disciples, but Jesus was simply directing the people to return to God's original standard as laid out in all of the Hebrew Scriptures.

A High View of Marriage Includes Divorce for Abuse and Neglect

Although Christian leaders strive to maintain a high view of marriage, they fail when they allow persistent severe abuse to continue in a marriage by denying the victim the opportunity to get out of that marriage by means of divorce. In fact, they are presenting an unbiblical view of the subject. Even though a victim may forgive that doesn't mean that they have to live with the guilty party. It may be that the relationship simply cannot be continued in the way that it was before the marriage contract was broken. Initiating legitimate divorce is simply done by the victim to show that he/she has been violated and that the marriage contract was broken by the guilty party.

Since the Bible presents divorce as an option in certain circumstances, it may, in fact, be the Christian thing to do and so maintaining the high view of marriage, rather than a low view which considers it to be acceptable for a marriage to be abusive and the guilty party absolved from their wrong-doing. Does God hate divorce more than He hates abuse and sexual sin against a victim?

Hardly! He Himself had to initiate divorce from Israel. Even the biblical picture of Messiah's relationship his people shows that he died to deal with "Sin" in all its forms including abuse and neglect. Certainly, this understanding protects marriage by refusing to allow sinners to abuse the institution of marriage with impunity.

Forbidding of Remarriage for Those Who Are Free to Remarry Is a Deception

If anyone forbids marriage after a divorce for an individual whose marriage has truly scripturally ended then such a forbidder puts themselves in a similar position to those who are condemned by Paul's words to Timothy:

> *"Now the spirit explicitly says that in later times some will abandon the faith, by continually paying attention to <u>deceiving spiritual thoughts</u> and teachings of demons, through the hypocrisy of liars whose consciences are permanently damaged. They will* **forbid marriage***..." (1 Tim. 4:1-3).*

Because of all that Paul had said to the Corinthians, this phrase does not refer only to first marriages. Indeed, there is no exception clause in 1 Timothy 4:1-3, such as, "except for those who are divorced." If there had been any exception it would contradict all that Paul has already said in 1 Corinthians 7. So, under normal circumstances, any forbidding of remarriage after a valid divorce should never happen. Furthermore, neither valid divorce nor remarriage are **included in any list of sins that will keep a Christian out of God's Kingdom** (1 Cor. 6:9-11; Gal. 5:19-21) because these persons have not been guilty of adultery (see Chapter 27). Additionally, Paul stated that, *"because there is* **so much sexual immorality***, each man should have sexual relations with his own wife, and each woman with her own husband" (1 Cor. 7:2).* It would seem strange for Paul to say this, but to exclude divorcees from marriage and so to put them into the very danger he was seeking to avoid for other Christians. Furthermore, it is likely that Paul's encouraging of *"the younger widows to marry" (1 Tim. 5:14)* was a way to counter the false teaching of forbidding remarriage. This would especially be important to a woman in Bible times. She would want to remarry as quickly as possible because her financial situation would otherwise become very difficult or dire.

Preconceived Ideas and Closed Mindedness

Nevertheless, even after reading all the above information in this book there will be those Christians who will view divorce and/or remarriage as sinful for their own reasons. There appear to be several possible reasons why some will reject this biblical view of divorce. These are that:

1. Some simply do not like change.

2. Some may be so used to reading Jesus' words without its context or background that they just cannot adjust their thinking.

3. Perhaps some victims of abuse have put up with the abuse for a very long time because they were required to according to church teaching. So now they don't want to learn that it was all for nothing and that God had made the way out of such abuse all along.

4. They just do not grasp this more loving understanding of the grounds for divorce, even when reading all that is written about it.

5. Some may fear that their marriage partner may misuse these grounds for divorce as an excuse to wrongly initiate a divorce.

6. They were or are the abuser in a marital relationship.

7. They are such a harsh minded person so that they will not allow for any other view but their own. For them God's words apply when He says, *"I will give you a new heart, and a new spirit I will put within you. And I will remove the heart of stone from your flesh and give you a heart of flesh" (Ezek. 11:19; 36:26).*

All that can be said to such Christians is for them to read the scholarly investigative works of the many others who have written on this subject. These are listed in the back of this book. Obviously, this is also a matter that should be prayerfully thought about regarding God's love and mercy. Certainly, traditional patterns of belief play a powerful part in people's lives, so much so that even very powerful evidence for something different can fail to change people's minds on various subjects. But please remember the

190

confusion that exists in the various denominations on the subject of divorce and remarriage as shown in chapter 7 of this book. So here I have endeavoured, with the helpful investigative works of the many scholars, to get some clarity on these issues. But mostly, I hope that this presentation will bring some reassurance to those who are suffering in one way or another in a constant really bad marriage. I also hope this gives some reassurance to those who have been divorced and are wondering if they have acted against God's will, when in fact, they probably have not.

I also certainly hope that, rather than having to face the prospect of divorce, those who have read this book continue to have sound, happy, and loving marriages by continuing to follow the Bible's counsel on marriage. Helpfully Deitrich Bonhoeffer wrote in his *Letters and Papers from Prison:*

> In a word, live together in the forgiveness of your sins, for without it no human fellowship, least of all a marriage, can survive. Don't insist on your rights, don't blame each other, don't judge or condemn each other, don't find fault with each other, but accept each other as you are, and forgive each other every day from the bottom of your hearts..."

A Merciful Attitude toward the Divorced

Clearly those who are forced to divorce because of the persistent wrongs committed by their spouse should not be forced to live a life of loneliness because others say that they should not remarry. Such a condemnation is not in the nature of God who "is love" or of Jesus who is the perfect reflection of God. Such stigmatizing of those who have opted to remarry contradicts what the spirit-guided Bible writers have affirmed and then make spiritual orphans of those whose marriages have failed. Rather the loving attitude of onlookers would be to:

> *"Defend the defenseless, the fatherless and the forgotten. the disenfranchised and the destitute. Your duty is to deliver the poor and the powerless; liberate them from the grasp of the wicked"*
>
> *(Ps. 82:3-4).*

So, there should never be a mean spirit toward divorced persons, but one of care and concern for them.

§

Appendices

A

Homosexuality as Grounds for Divorce

This subject applies just as much to those who claim to be bi-sexual.

THE BIBLICAL DEFINITION OF MARRIAGE

Clearly, in the Bible every marriage is heterosexual—there is no occurrence of a same-sex marriage. Marriage is defined in the Bible as being of one man and one woman with a desire for each other. (Please note that King David and Jonathan were not in a homosexual relationship as wrongly proposed by some).

HOMOSEXUAL PREDISPOSITION AND ORIENTATION

Of the many medical research studies to date on the causes of a homosexual predisposition or orientation it would seem that the causal factors are a mix of several, including minimal genetic factors, hormonal events in the womb, environmental factors, and early life experiences and influences related to sex, including sexual abuse. In fact, although the Bible does condemn homosexual practice it does not condemn a person for having a homosexual orientation, because it is really a malfunction caused by these many factors, but not the way God designed humans to be in their sexual life.

HOMOSEXUAL PRACTICES

Nevertheless, God disapproves of engaging in homosexual acts, either male with male or female with female and so is contrary to nature as God set it out as shown by a number of scriptures, including those in the Hebrew Scriptures.

Now although Christians are **not under the works or regulations of the Mosaic Law**, they are obliged to live by the very spirit of that law (Rom. 3:31; 7:14; 8:4) and follow its universal moral code. So, it is vital that they apply the following text where God's command for men is that:

> "You must not have **sexual intercourse with a man** as you would with a woman; it is a detestable practice"
>
> (Lev. 18:22 CEB. Also Lev. 20:13).

195

Jesus respected the Mosaic Law and would have been fully cognizant with the statements in this Holiness Code of Leviticus 18 and 20 which show that God detests homosexual acts—they are an abomination to Him. So, Jesus' silence on this speaks volumes. In fact, he was silent on such behaviour as "incest" and "bestiality" and other wrong behaviour in the Holiness Code, yet we can hardly think that he thought differently to what was said in that code concerning those behaviours. Such silence on the subject could only have been understood by the disciples as acceptance of the basic position on homosexual acts embraced by all Jews of the time. This strongly indicates that Jesus was opposed to all homosexual activity. Nevertheless, Jesus did make known his view on this subject through his emissary, the Apostle Paul, in the following passages: Romans 1:26-27; 1 Corinthians 6:9b; 1 Timothy 1:10. For example, in Romans 1:26-27 Paul states that the Gentiles had suppressed the truth about the proper use of sexual organs and so:

> "For this reason **God abandoned them to** degraded passions. Indeed, even their **females <u>exchanged</u> their natural sexual function for what is <u>contrary to nature</u>.** [27]In the same way the males **abandoned** their natural sexual function with females and were inflamed with their uncontrolled passion for each other, males acting indecently with males, and receiving back in themselves the inevitable penalty for their having gone astray."

Indeed, pagan Gentiles had developed their culture in such a way that they had exchanged what is normal heterosexual functioning from birth for engaging in homosexual intercourse—something completely unnatural and which God had "given them over to" i.e., allowed to continue. This was "contrary to nature" i.e., contrary to the fittedness of the male and female sexual organs. Certainly, Paul's words here encompass all situations involving same-sex intercourse as well as directly concerning females as a condemnation of lesbianism. However, the condemnation of male homosexuality in other texts applies by extension just as much to lesbianism. This is because laws that say: "If a man ..." must also mean that a woman should not perform similar wrong acts. (Please see my book *Living the Christian Life According to Jesus* pp.173-213).

CHANGE IS POSSIBLE

In spite of the factors leading to a homosexual orientation, there are some well documented success stories of those who have broken away from the homosexual lifestyle. However, even if a person with a homosexual orientation does not engage in homosexual activity (which would constitute adultery), but has married someone of the opposite sex, there almost certainly will be major problems because of the orientation toward homosexuality. Such a marriage is not a normal heterosexual marriage and so cannot be considered as marriage in the full biblical sense. The Song of Solomon demonstrates the sexual desire that a husband and wife should have for each other and the apostle Paul encouraged married couples to engage in their personal sexual activity with each other so that sexual immorality may be avoided (1 Cor. 7:2-5).

HELP AND FORGIVENESS

If one's marriage partner is fighting against his or her homosexual orientation then one should show love to them and offer support as they fight their way away from their predisposition to homosexual thoughts, feelings, and actions. However, forgiveness by the "normal" partner can only extend so far and must not be presumed upon by the homosexually oriented partner. So, if the homosexually oriented partner rejects any help regarding his or her sexual thoughts or has received much good help, but still has made no progress in changing their thinking so that they may please God and their spouse, that spouse may consider divorcing them so that they could seek to have the opportunity for a normal marriage.

———— ❑ ————

197

B

Can Divorced Men Serve as Overseers or as Fellowship Servants (Deacons)?

Paul wrote in 1 Timothy 3:1-2 and 12 that, *"If someone aspires to guardianship, he desires a good work...The overseer, therefore, must be above reproach. He must be* **a husband of one wife**.*...¹²Fellowship servants must each be a husband of one wife..."*

Does this mean, then, that divorced men cannot serve in these positions? The Greek phrase is *mias gynaikos andra* and means "a one-woman man." And so, the NRSV is incorrect when it renders this phrase as "married only once." Nevertheless, this phrase is a little difficult to interpret and so must be interpreted in the light of all that Paul teaches on divorce and remarriage. Some have proposed various answers, such as that the man must:

1. Be married, or
2. Not marry another woman after his wife has died, or
3. Not marry another woman **after his divorce** from a first wife, or
4. Not be polygamous i.e., not have two or more wives at the same time, or
5. Be fully faithful to his wife.

#1. The phrase "a husband of one wife" has led some to teach that no person living the single life can be an overseer. However, this would contradict all of Paul's encouragement that those who have the gift for singleness remain so (1 Cor. 7:32-35), as well as Jesus' statement that there are eunuchs for the sake of the kingdom" i.e., those who have chosen singleness (Matt. 19:12). It would also contradict the fact that some in the early Church were single and did serve in those capacities.

#2. To deny a man this office because his wife has died would contradict Paul's words that any widow can remarry, and so implying the same for any widower (1 Cor. 7:39).

#3. To say that a man cannot be appointed as an overseer because he has married another woman **after divorce** from a first wife cannot be correct because of all that has been shown in this book regarding remarriage as the norm in Jewish society of the first century and not contradicted by Jesus or by Paul. If such a rejection of a divorced man were the case it would be a further form of discrimination against these ones, as if there were not enough discrimination against them already in the modern-day churches.

#4. To say that this refers only to a man's not being polygamous is refuted by the fact of the related phrase "wife of one man" (1 Tim. 5:9) i.e., a "one-woman man." This is because women were never polygamous in that society. In fact, polygamy by men was against the Roman law in the Greek areas to which Paul's letter would have gone, and so it is very unlikely to have been his primary meaning in the phrase "a one-woman man." Even the Jews outside of Palestine followed the regular Greek practice of avoiding polygamy. Clearly, Christian men of the time would not have been polygamous anyway, especially in view of Jesus' correction of this practice as recorded in Matthew 19.

#5. The most likely meaning of the phrase "one-woman man" is: **a man who is fully faithful to his wife** in a monogamous marriage. He is true to the one woman who is his wife. If on the other hand she is not faithful to him at some point in time and it results in divorce or she dies, there is no issue concerning his remarrying and then being fully faithful to his new wife.

In summary, there is no biblical reason to deny an upright qualified man who has remarried, either before or during his time as a Christian, the right to be considered as an overseer or as a fellowship servant.

———— ❏ ————

C

Summary of Biblical Teaching on Divorce

God Does Not Forbid All Divorce

CORRECT RENDERING OF MALACHI 2:16

"'If he **hates and divorces** [his wife],' says the LORD God of Israel, 'he covers his garment with injustice,' says the LORD of Hosts. Therefore, watch yourselves carefully, and do not act treacherously" (Mal. 2:16 CSB).

It is the husband who hates and divorces his wife, that is, it is a treacherous divorce. This rendering is according to the Hebrew text and the Septuagint. Other similar translations are: ESV, NIV, Smith and Goodspeed, NEB, and REB.

DIVORCES APPROVED OF BY GOD

- Abraham's divorce from Hagar (Gen. 21:12).

- Joseph's planned betrothal divorce from Mary (Matt. 1:19).

- God's divorce from Israel and giving her a certificate of divorce (Jer. 3:6, 8, Hos. 2:8, 9; Ezek. 16:16, 19, 20; Isa. 50:1).

Regulating Divorce So That a Wife Is Not Mistreated

The Hebrew exegetical rule *qol vahomer*—"if this is true, then surely this is also true" was applied by the Apostle Paul in 1 Corinthians 9:8-11 showing that if God cares for animals He cares at least as much for humans, including slaves and therefore he cares at least as much for free persons so that they have rights no less than a slave has and are not to be neglected or abused (Ex. 21:26).

EXODUS 21:10-11

"If a man who has **married a slave wife** takes **another wife** for himself, he must not neglect the rights of the first wife to **food**, **clothing** and **sexual intimacy**. If he fails in any of these three obligations, she may leave as a free woman without making any payment" (NLT).

200

So, a free wife has these same rights in marriage and if these are not provided, she may consider divorcing her husband.

DEUTERONOMY 21:10-14

> *"When you go out for battle against your enemies ...and you see among the captives a woman beautiful in appearance...and you may* **marry her**, *and she may* **become your wife**. *And then if you do not take delight in her, then* **you shall let her go** *to do whatever she wants, but you shall* <u>not treat her as a slave</u>, *since you have dishonored her" (LEB).*

So, this wife also is divorced, but is treated as if she were a free wife with the same rights.

DEUTERONOMY 24:1-4

> *"When a man takes a wife and he marries her and then she does not please him, because he found something objectionable (**some indecency** ESV. Heb. erwat dabar) and writes her* **a letter of divorce** *and puts it in her hand and sends her away from his house, and she goes from his house, and she goes out and* **becomes a wife for another man**, *and then the* **second man dislikes her** *and he writes her* **a letter of divorce** *and places it into her hand and sends her from his house, or if the second man dies who took her to himself as a wife, her* **first husband who sent her away is not allowed to take her again** *to become a wife to him after she has been defiled, for that is* **a detestable thing** *before Yahweh, and so you shall not mislead into sin the land that Yahweh your God is giving to you as an inheritance" (LEB).*

This is a case where the first husband has perpetrated a treacherous divorce upon his wife by attributing to her something viewed as seriously bad, but which she did not do. The evidence for this view is as follows:

- The penalty for adulterous actions was death (Lev. 20:10, Deut. 22:22-24), rather than divorce as was the case for "**some indecency.**" So, this term must refer to something less than adultery.

  The husband's double standard here is seen inasmuch as the wife cannot be accused by the first husband of being "unclean" enough to be divorced (vs. 1) and then "clean" enough to be married again by him (vs. 4). This indicates that the real reason for the divorce was not actually a very serious one, although portrayed as such.

- The passage is in a context, from Deuteronomy 23:15 to 24:7, of protection of individuals, so that they are not viewed as a mere chattel. Certainly, **the certificate of divorce** in verse one was for the woman's protection. This concept makes more sense if she were unjustly divorced rather than guilty of any unfaithful sexual behaviour.

- When Jesus speaks of men's "hardheartedness" it is most likely a reference to Deuteronomy 24:1. This is because that was the original subject of discussion raised by the Pharisees in their debate with Jesus (Matthew 19). This is indicated by the use of the terms "any cause" and "certificate of divorce." Indeed, these terms were mentioned only in Deuteronomy 24:1 and therefore concerned a man's hard-hearted and unjust divorcing of his wife.

- Because God legitimately divorced Israel and with a purpose of remarrying her after her repentance, it seems clear that the restriction of remarriage on the first husband in Deuteronomy 24 indicates that this was his trivial or treacherous divorcing of his wife.

Neither Jesus nor Paul Contradicted God's Universal Moral Standard in the Hebrew Scriptures

Paul followed Jesus in not creating any new legislation regarding divorce and remarriage. Jesus corrected wrong interpretation, but neither his nor Paul's thoughts on it varied from what was set down in the Hebrew Scriptures on God's moral standards and developed as workable principles (Ex. 21:7-11). This allowed for divorce and remarriage. It was only treacherous divorce which was invalid (Mal. 2:4-16).

Jesus' Position Within Israel

Jesus did not create new law concerning divorce. He did not overturn the principles contained in the laws in the Hebrew Scriptures (The Old Testament) whereby a victim should be allowed to bring his or her suffering to an end. His view was in the same spirit as expressed in the Hebrew Scriptures. He was also aware that, at least in a metaphorical sense, God was a divorcee for fully legitimate reasons; and yet, if divorce were a sin, God would never have put Himself in the position of being viewed as a sinner—a blasphemous thought! In fact, He even sanctioned Abraham's divorcing of Hagar. Indeed, the corrections on this subject that Jesus made were only to the faulty thinking of the religious leaders of his time, so that:

1. Marriage should be taken more seriously than it was taken in his time, and should be for life as God's ideal.
2. Polygamy was wrong and so now a wife could divorce her husband for "a cause of sexual immorality."
3. The "any cause" rule of the Pharisees for divorce was confirmed as invalid, that is, it is not grounds for a legitimate divorce.
4. Sexual immorality—as detailed by Jesus in Matthew 5:32 and 19:11 is grounds for divorce.
5. Jesus did not discount the Mosaic case law principles on divorce.

Paul's Position in the Wider Gentile World

Certainly, as Jesus' emissary Paul held to the same view on divorce as did Jesus, although Paul's comments relate to the Greco-Roman situation existing in Corinth and the Gentile world in general. So, Paul gave two further sets of counsel on how a believer should react to an unbelieving marriage partner. The first was that if the unbeliever was "content" in the marriage then the believer should not divorce, However, this is qualified by Jesus' teaching on sexual immorality and by Moses' Exodus 21:10-11 teaching as restated by Paul in Ephesians 5:25-33 and 1 Corinthians 7:1-5, 33-34. The second was that if the unbeliever divorced the believer, then the believer should let that divorce stand.

The Basic Grounds for Christian Divorce

The overall biblical picture whereby a Christian may initiate a divorce gives the following reasons:

- **Unrepentance for Sexual immorality**—Matthew 5:32 and 19:11. This may include, bestiality, certain forms of incest, prostitution (male or female), or homosexual relations. Furthermore, because of the wide range of meaning to the Hebrew phrase *erwat dabar* this may involve a partner's persistent attempts to form a sexual relationship with a person outside of the marriage.

- **Persistent and significant material neglect** (concerning food and clothing)—Exodus 21:10-11; 1 Corinthians 7:33-34.

- **Persistent and significant physical/emotional/sexual neglect or abuse** (failure to love, including sexual love)— Exodus 21:10-11; Ephesians. 5:28-29, 33; 1 Corinthians 7:2-5. Please note the principle concerning the mistreatment of a slave who can then depart (Ex. 21:26-27).

- Abandonment by an unbeliever or a Christian who is re-classified as "worse than an unbeliever" for the above reasons (1 Cor. 7:15).

- For anything worse than these three grounds e.g., attempted or actual murder of a family member (Ex. 20:13) or abuse of the children.

Yet within the categories of grounds for divorce it is evident from the Scriptures concerning marital relationships that both of the marriage partners should show genuine **love and care for one another** (Eph. 5:21-32) and seek "to please" (1 Cor. 7:33-34) their partner. However, where there is on-going serious abuse or neglect over some reasonable period of time, such situations would form the basis for divorce.

EXCEPTIONS TO THE GENERAL RULE OF NO DIVORCE

Because both Jesus and Paul gave exceptions to the general rule against divorce it seems obvious that there could be other except

-ions. However, these must be from within the framework of the Scriptures and its principles. So, it is evident that key principles taken from Exodus 21:10-11; Deuteronomy 21:10-14; and 24:1-4 can be brought to bear on broken marital relationships so that a spouse can stop being abused or neglected. Furthermore, other principles can be drawn from the Scriptures by noting the way other classes of individuals must be treated e.g., slaves (Ex. 21:26-27) and animals (Deut. 25:4, 1 Cor. 9:8-11). From these it is evident that a wife or husband must not be physically neglected or abused because if a lower order of individual must be well-treated, even more so must a wife or husband be well-treated. So, Craig keener asks:

> Can we honestly maintain that a valid marriage exists when one spouse is treated only as an object for venting the other's repressed, violent rage? Is this not infidelity in some sense? And does not Paul's ad hoc exception, addressing a specific situation, point us to the kind of exceptions we must make in analogous situations? ...*And Marries Another p.106.*

Jesus Did Not Limit the Grounds of Divorce to Only Sexual Immorality

Matthew 5:31-32; 19:9; Mark 10:11-12; and Luke 16:18.

The basis for divorce in Jesus' time was almost entirely for *"any cause,"* and which Jesus showed to involve some scripturally unjust divorce. Case law principles, based on Exodus 21:10-11 and Deuteronomy 21:10-14, speak of valid divorce, after which remarriage can take place. The "any cause" divorce debate with the Pharisees concerned only their misinterpretation of Deuteronomy 24:1 containing the phrase: "some indecency." In opposition to the Shammaite Pharisees, the Hillelite Pharisees had split this phrase into two to make two legal terms: 1) divorce for "any cause" and 2) divorce for "sexual immorality;" this latter phrase becoming redundant. So, the following was Jesus' teaching, saying:

> *"Anyone divorcing his wife for the purpose of* (Gk *kai* subjunctive mood. Usually rendered "and," but functions to introduce a result (see Bauer's Lexicon). In the flow of the discussion this presents us with a narrative explanation of why the first, unjustified divorce, occurred) *marrying another woman commits adultery; and anyone marry*

205

-ing a woman _who has_ (middle voice) divorced from her husband [in this way], **commits adultery** (active form)" (Luke 16:18).

"Then some Pharisees came and tried to trick him by asking "Is it lawful for a man to divorce a wife **for "any cause"**? (Deut 24:1).

"....whoever divorces his wife, **except for "sexual immorality"** (Gk _porneia_), and (Gk kai – also implying purpose i.e., "so that he") marries another woman, commits adultery (Gk moicheuo)"

(Matt. 19:3, 9).

"...because of your hard-heartedness {**stubbornly unrepentant after persistent breaking of marriage vows and/or divorcing a wife for no justifiable reason**}" (Matt. 19:8b).

"Whoever (treacherously) divorces his wife _and_ (Gk kai – also implying purpose i.e., "so that he") marries another woman commits adultery **against her** [his first wife]. And if she divorces her husband _and_ (as above) marries another man, she commits adultery" (Mark 10:11, 12).

"It was said, 'Whoever divorces (Gk apoluo) his wife must give her a _certificate of divorce_' (Gk apostasion). ³²But I [Jesus] say to you that anyone divorcing his wife, **except for "a cause of sexual immorality"** (Gk _porneia_), makes her a victim of [his] _adultery_ (Gk moicheuo passive form). And whoever marries a woman _who has_ (middle voice) divorced [in this way], commits _adultery_ (active form)" (Matt. 5:31-32).

So, Jesus' issue with the Pharisees on the subject of divorce is most likely based on the treacherous divorces detailed in Malachi 2:10-17, as well as those of Herod Antipas and Herodias in their divorcing of their spouses, so that they could marry each other. So, the use of the term "divorce" in the above passages refers to scripturally, "_unjust, treacherous divorce_." Indeed, Jesus' statements concerning grounds for divorce must be seen in the light of the phrases: "_any cause_" and "_a cause of sexual immorality_" cited from Deuteronomy 24:1 only. These therefore, do not concern the _Exodus 21:10-11_ requirements for a husband to provide his wife with "food, clothing, and conjugal love" (see Eph. 5:25-31, 1 Cor. 7:2-4). Failure to provide these was also the basis for legitimate divorce (Ex. 21:11) in Jewish case law.

So, Jesus' silence on Exodus 21 in these accounts does not mean that he discounted these three failures of a husband as grounds for divorce or of the failure of a wife to keep her marriage vows. Indeed, all these details would simply be assumed by Matthew, Mark, and Luke, and their original listeners. Jesus even gave a Deuteronomy 24 context to his statement in Luke 16:18 in verse 17 where he references the Law. Clearly, Jesus' view was against the view of the Shammaite School, but even more so against the view of the Hillelite school's *"any cause"* teaching and so showing it to give too wide a grounds for divorce and so creating easy divorce. Therefore, Jesus' statements in these accounts do not deny valid divorce that is caused by the persistent breaking of the marriage vows. Furthermore, the phrase "commits adultery" in these texts most likely refers to "a breach of covenant," i.e., non-sexual rather that sexual adultery. Jesus certainly did not expect a person to divorce their new marriage partner and return to the first (Deut. 24:4). Indeed, without the context of the Hebrew Scriptures and the first century background, Jesus' statements would all seem quite contradictory.

Paul Did Not Forbid Divorce

Paul begins in 1 Corinthians 7:10, 11 by speaking of "separation" *(Gk chorizo)*. However, this is not in the modern-day sense, but as being a legal divorce in the Greco-Roman world—a very well documented fact.

> *"...a wife should not "divorce by separating" herself {a legal Greco-Roman divorce = the Jewish "any cause" divorce} from her husband; (if she does she should remain unmarried {only while attempting to reconcile} or be reconciled to that man (Gk. andros), and the husband should not "divorce-by-dismissing his wife."*

Indeed, the Greek-English lexicons show that, in the context of the subject of marriage, *chorizo* means divorce by separation. Also, *apoluo* and *apheimi* mean divorce by dismissal. It was divorce that included biblically invalid grounds just as was the Jewish Hillelite divorce for "any cause." Nevertheless, Paul allowed for divorce on the grounds of desertion by an unbeliever (1 Cor. 7:15). This would also apply to unwarranted desertion by a believer who leaves a partner, but refuses to return in compliance with verse 11 and so becomes "worse than an unbeliever" (1 Tim. 5:8).

In following Jesus, Paul also recognized the requirements of a husband to nourish and cherish his wife (Eph. 5:29, 1 Cor. 7:2-4) as detailed in Exodus 21:10-11. Significant neglect or abuse in marriage would be legitimate grounds for divorce. God cares that marriage is based on love!

———— ❑ ————

D

Summary of Biblical Teaching on Remarriage

Jesus Did Not Condemn Those Who Remarry

When Jesus used the word "adultery" *(GK moichia)* in the relevant passages on divorce he used it in its metaphorical sense i.e., that of **non-sexual adultery** concerning unfaithfulness or breach of the marriage contract committed by the divorcing man. This was similar to the cases of Herod and Herodias. Examples of **non-sexual adultery** in the New Testament are to be found in Matthew 12:39—***"adulterous** generation,"* Mark 8:38—***"adulterous and sinful generation...,"*** and James 4:4—***"adulterous** people."* So, the claim by some that later remarriage after any divorce is the "adultery" Jesus spoke about is only an assumption. It is also a very forced explanation because Jesus did not say, "the man will later commit adultery <u>when he remarries</u>." It was the "any cause" divorcing i.e., divorce for no good reason that was wrong, rather than remarriage.

MERCIFUL TREATMENT OF THE WOMAN AT THE WELL—John 4:16ff
Jesus did not condemn this woman for remarrying a number of husbands. Jesus was a person who advocated the showing of **mercy** (Matt. 9:13; 12:7) to others. If Jesus had required this woman to return to a first husband he would have had to say so, but he didn't.

Summary of Paul's Teachings on Remarriage

ROMANS 7:1-4 DOES NOT EXCLUDE REMARRIAGE
*"So then, she will be called an **adulteress if, while her husband lives, she becomes another man's**. But if her husband dies, she is free from that law..." (KGV).*

This is an illustration, but not about divorce and remarriage. The wife "would be **committing adultery if she married another man**"..."while <u>her husband</u> is <u>alive</u>." Nothing is said about him being her ex-husband. It is this action that makes her an adulteress and a bigamist.

209

"THE UNMARRIED" WITH STRONG SEXUAL DESIRE SHOULD MARRY

"The unmarried" (Gk *agamos*) in this verse encompasses "the virgins," "the widowed," and "the divorced"—all of whom are unmarried. So, for any individuals in this group who have strong sexual desire **Paul recommends, in verse 9, that they marry.** Paul later recommends the same for the younger widows (1 Tim. 5:14). It would make no sense to say that the younger widows can remarry and yet to deny this opportunity to the younger divorcees. So, 1 Corinthians 7:15b says:

> "...if the unbelieving partner "divorces-by-separating" himself or herself let it take place. In such cases the brother or sister is **no longer bound** [to the partner]. God has called you to peace"

The term "bound" is defined by verse 27 as meaning "married" in contrast to "released" as meaning "divorced." Further confirmation of this is found in Paul's use of the term "bound" in verse 39, so that a husband's death releases a wife from the marriage bond leaving her free to remarry. So, the phrase **"no longer bound"** means that the divorced person is free to remarry. **If this is true for a spouse who is deserted by an unbeliever, it is just as true if the divorce happened between two believers for biblically valid grounds.**

The principle of being "called to peace" within a marriage was viewed by Paul as more important than narrowly defined legalistic prohibitions (Rom. 12:18) and was used to indicate that **a pragmatic solution** to a problem was sought for the sake of peace.

1 Corinthians 7:25-28

THE VIRGINS AND THE DIVORCED MAY MARRY

> "Now concerning those who have never married (lit. virgins), I have no command from the Lord, but I give my opinion as one shown mercy by the Lord to be trustworthy. I think that **in view of the present crisis** it is good for a man to **remain as he is.** ²⁷If you've been **bound to a wife,** stop seeking to be released. If you've been **released from a wife,** stop seeking a wife. **But if you marry, you haven't sinned.** And if a virgin woman marries, she hasn't sinned. Yet those who marry **will face a difficult time,** and I am trying to spare you that."

The term "released" here means "divorced" (See the NET Bible). So, the phrase *"but if you marry"* in verse 28a refers directly to those

210

who have been "released from a wife" i.e., having divorced her or been divorced by her. Paul treats these ones separately from the "virgin women" i.e., those who have never married. This shows that in neither case would marriage be a sin for them. So, if one disallowed marriage for male divorcees one must also disallow it for female virgins. But, of course, Paul never says that, but simply says that those who marry do not sin in both the cases of divorcees and of those who have never married. Furthermore, this passage does not refer only to the betrothed, but may include them. Indeed, why would God, through Jesus or Paul, now change His earlier stated moral laws which protected innocent parties in cases of very damaging abusive marriages and treacherous divorce? Why would God deny the wonders of good marriage for the divorced when, in fact, He advocated marriage in the first place? In fact, he condemned those who denied marriage (1 Tim. 4:1-3) including remarriage.

———— ❑ ————

E

Will the Institution of Marriage Exist in God's Kingdom?

This question has usually elicited the answer that marriage as an institution will permanently cease for Christians from the time of the first resurrection. This response is based on Jesus' statements as recorded in the parallel accounts in the synoptic gospels when Jesus said:

> "At the resurrection they neither marry nor are given in marriage, but are like angels in heaven"" (Matt. 22:30).

> "...when they rise from among the dead, they neither marry nor are given in marriage, but are like angels in heaven"
>
> (Mark 12:24).

> "...Those who are considered worthy to share in that age and in the resurrection from among the dead neither marry nor are given in marriage" (Luke 20:35).

However, this general response that marriage will permanently cease for Christians from the time of the first resurrection is really based more on a very limited and surface reading of Jesus' words, whereby neither the context nor the background have been taken account of. These factors must always be brought to bear on any particular subject in one's attempt to understand a biblical subject or issue. In this particular case of Jesus' words that, "they neither marry nor are given in marriage," the background and context concern the mindset of the Jewish religious leaders called Sadducees; and this mindset concerned their acceptance of only the five books of Moses. Because of this they rejected the concept of resurrection, mistakenly believing that these books did not teach that resurrection was a future reality. They were in conflict with the Pharisees over this issue of the resurrection.

The Argument from the Levirate Marriage Law

When confronting Jesus over the issue of resurrection the Sadducees used a very clever argument based on the Mosaic Law and taken from the book of Deuteronomy. This law stated that:

*"When brothers dwell together and one of them dies and has no son, the wife of the deceased shall not become the wife of a man of another family; her brother-in-law shall have sex with her, and he shall take her to himself as a wife, and he shall perform his duty as a brother-in-law with respect to her. And then the firstborn that she bears shall represent his dead brother, **so that his name is not blotted out from Israel.** But if the man does not want to take his sister-in-law, then his sister-in-law shall go up to the gate, to the elders, and she shall say, 'My brother-in-law refused to perpetuate his brother's name in Israel, for he is not willing to marry me.' Then the elders of his town shall summon him and speak to him, and if he persists and says, 'I do not desire to marry her' then his sister-in-law shall go near him before the eyes of the elders, and she shall pull off his sandal from his foot, and she shall spit in his face, and she shall declare and she shall say, 'This is how it is done to the man who does not build the house of his brother.' And his family shall be called in Israel, 'The house where the sandal was pulled off'" (Deut. 25:5-10 LEB).*

So, this law concerned, not only marriage simply for the purpose of procreation, which is not the only reason for marriage (Please see NOTE at the end of this chapter), but a specific kind of marriage arrangement so that the "brother's name is not blotted out from Israel." This is called Levirate marriage. Now, the Sadducees argument was given authority by their stating that "Moses said" and then quoting his teachings on this law so that they built their clever argument against the idea of resurrection. And so, on the particular occasion that they approached Jesus on this issue they said to him:

"Teacher, Moses said that if a man dies without having children, his brother must marry the widow and father children for his brother. Now there were seven brothers among us. The first one married and died, and since he had no children he left his wife to his brother. The second did the same, and the third, down to the seventh. Last of all, the woman died. So, in the resurrection, out of the seven, whose wife will she be, because they all had her?"
(Matt. 22:24-28).

As was often the case, the various groups of religious leaders tried to trap Jesus by his responses to their trick questions. This was one such situation here when the Sadducees used, as a basis for their argument, the Levirate law requiring the brother of a deceased man whose widow was left childless, to marry the woman to try to produce offspring for the family line and to ensure that the land owned by the family would remain as belonging to the family.

Jesus' Answer Concerns Immortality Rather Than Marital Status

However, Jesus was always aware of these attempts to trap him in his words and so his response, as usual, was based on the Scriptures and his superior logic:

> *"But Jesus answered them, "You are wrong, because you know neither the Scriptures nor the power of God. For in the resurrection **they** neither marry [third person plural] nor are given in marriage, but are like angels in heaven" (Matt. 22:29-30 ESV).*

So, Jesus' answer concerns the "**they**" that the Sadducees had described i.e., any Jewish man who would normally be required to "marry" his deceased brother's childless widow, as well as the particular widow herself who would normally be "given in marriage," to her brother-in-law. Therefore, this does not concern people in general as is wrongly expressed in some translations, but that Jesus is really saying that at the resurrection, and therefore in the Kingdom, **this kind of marriage arrangement—Levirate marriage—would not be necessary**, and the reason is that they "are like angels in heaven."

But is Jesus here saying that angels don't marry and therefore resurrected Christians won't marry either? This does not seem to be the case because the parallel account in Luke indicates that Jesus' statement that they "are like angels in heaven" concerns their immortality, rather than their marital status. Here Jesus is reported as saying that:

> *"those who are considered worthy to share in that age and in the resurrection from among the dead neither marry nor are given in marriage, because **they can no longer die**. In being children of God they are like angels; and so they are sons of the resurrection"*
> *(Luke 20:35-36).*

Therefore, the key reason given for these ones as not being required to marry at the resurrection is, "because they can no longer die" i.e.,

214

they are immortal and so are like the angels in this particular respect. Now angels were sometimes called "sons of God" (Job 38:7) throughout the Scriptures, so Jesus connected that fact to Christians in the resurrection as also being called "sons" or "children of God." However, Jesus said this in the context of their future immortality; so, he was not here saying that angels do not marry, and therefore resurrected Christians will not marry in the Kingdom. Indeed, Jesus' statement that *"they neither marry nor are given in marriage"* in Matthew 22, Mark 12:24, and Luke 20:35 is not a broad statement that means that everyone in the first resurrection will never marry or be given in marriage. Instead, it is **in the narrow confines of the regulations of the Mosaic Law** applicable only to a specific Jewish situation at the time, namely, Levirate marriage. This law never concerned Gentile marriages or even Jewish marriages in general. Indeed, this issue concerned the very particular situation of the application of the Levirate law detailed in Deuteronomy 25:5-10. So, Jesus is showing that it is this law of Levirate marriage that will not apply to resurrected Christians because they will be immortal and so have no need to procreate. Indeed, there will be no Christian widows from the time of the resurrection onward and so no need for any widow's "brother-in-law" to "perform his duty as a brother-in-law with respect to her" (Deut. 25:5). Further to this is the fact that the brother, if he was "considered worthy," to be in the first resurrection would be resurrected and would never die.

So rather than making a grand theological statement, Jesus was simply destroying the basis for the faulty argument the Sadducees presented against the teaching about the resurrection. So, having shown up the Sadducees misapplication of their illustrative story, based on the Levirate law of marriage in Deuteronomy 25:5-10, in their attempt to disprove the resurrection, Jesus then goes on to show that God will resurrect Abraham, Isaac, and Jacob because He is the God "of the living." So here Jesus shows that the Sadducees have failed to see that the resurrection is pointed to even within the five books of Moses that they did accept as valid.

Objection to This View from Galatians 3:28

The question may be asked: how can there be marriage in the Kingdom when one takes into consideration that the Apostle Paul said that: *"There is no longer Jew or Greek, there is no longer slave or* *free, there is no longer **male and female**; for all of you are one in Christ Jesus" (Gal. 3:28 NRSV).*

RESPONSE:

Firstly, please note that, as correctly rendered in the NRSV, from the Greek Paul uses the phrase taken from Genesis 1:27 "male <u>and</u> female" rather than 'male <u>or</u> female' as wrongly rendered in many versions of Galatians 3:28. Then please note that Paul is saying that this is an existing condition for Christians in the first century, and yet there was no actual change in the genders of male and female. So, in analysing this text one must take account of the considerable restrictions and very bad attitudes that Jewish male freemen of the time had toward Gentiles, slaves, and women. Therefore, Paul's point concerns the rebalancing of '**the worth**' of people from oppressed backgrounds so that God sees them all as of equal worth. Their nationalities as Jew/Gentile or their roles as husband/wife or their social status as slave/free do not necessarily change. Indeed, James Dunn makes the comment on this verse that:

> these distinctions have been relativised, not removed. Jewish believers were still Jews (Gal. 2:15). Christian slaves were still slaves (1 Cor. 7:21)...wives were still wives. These racial, social, and gender differentiations, which as such were often thought to indicate relative worth or privileged status before God, no longer had that significance. But, as so often with Paul's vision of ministry, the social realities conditioned the practice of the principle. *The Theology of Paul the Apostle* p.593.

Certainly, many of the privileges previously and traditionally granted only to men in the Jewish and Gentile systems of the first century were now to be granted to women in the Christian system of things, and so raising the status of women. Hence, Galatians 3:28 does not refer to a change in the physical, hormonal or emotional makeup of the two sexes, and so the phrase "no longer male and female" does not mean that there will be any change in the male and female genders in the future resurrection or indeed mean that marriage will cease from the time of the first resurrection.

Conclusion

The answer Jesus gave to the Sadducees that, "at the resurrection they neither marry nor are given in marriage," does not apply to marriage in general. This conclusion is arrived at when we take account of the context and the background rather than taking a surface reading. From this it seems evident that the purpose of Jesus' answer was specifically to destroy the basis for the Sadducees' faulty argument against the resurrection. He did this by showing that there would be no need of Levirate marriages in the resurrection. So, Jesus showed that at the resurrection there would be a change to immortality which involves having a changed body (1 Cor. 15:36-49), and so meaning that, for resurrected Christians, there would be no need for procreation, the very point of the Levirate marriage arrangement. However, procreation is only one of several very significant reasons a Christian might marry.

In view of the additional fact that God's perfect arrangement for Adam and Eve, in their perfection, was for a loving marital arrangement, and which Jesus himself confirmed (Matt. 19:4-6), it seems evident that Jesus did not give this answer to the Sadducees to show that no marriages would happen for resurrected persons in the coming kingdom.

Note on the Several Reasons for Marriage

Although the procreation mandate given to Adam and Eve was needed for populating the earth, that doesn't cover all the reasons for marriage. Indeed, the Song of Solomon has much to say on loving, romantic, sexual relationships in marriage—but nothing about procreation. These aspects of marriage beyond simple procreation are explained by Duanne Garrett in *The New American Commentary* on The Song of Solomon Volume 14, p. 366. He notes that:

> It may seem strange to some readers that the Bible should contain love poetry. While the marriage relationship is meant to be a partnership and friendship on the deepest level that does not mean that the sexual and emotional aspects of love between a man and a woman are themselves unworthy of the Bible's attention. Sexuality and love are fundamental to the human

217

experience; and it is altogether fitting that the Bible as a book, meant to teach the reader how to have a happy and good life, should have something to say in this area.

Indeed, it is primarily and sadly within the faulty thinking of Roman Catholicism that marriage has been viewed as only for procreation.

———— ❑ ————

Index of Theological, Hebrew, and Greek Terms

Agamos (Gk) — "unmarried" p.171, 180, 210

An *a fortiori* argument — an argument from the lesser to the greater. p.44.

Any cause — a technical legal term used by the Hillelite rabbis to promote the right of arbitrary divorce pp. 74-76, 82-84, 97, 107, 114, 123

Aphiemi (Gk) — to release or dismiss. In divorce contexts meaning divorce-by-dismissing pp.29, 82

Apoluo (Gk) — "to send away, dismiss, divorce" p.29, 206

Apostasion (Gk) — Certificate of divorce pp.31, 53-54, 98, 202, 206

Cairo Geniza contracts: Jewish marriage contracts found in the synagogue room for storing documents p.58, 77

Chera (Gk)— "widow" p.171

Chorizo (Gk) — to separate. In divorce contexts meaning divorce-by-separating from. pp.29, 82, 131

Dabag (Heb.) — "joined together." Not necessarily permanently so p.102

Ezer (Heb.) — "strength" or "power." p.8.

Erwat dabar (Heb.) — Original Hebrew for "nakedness of a thing." A vague catch-all and non-specific term i.e., "*something offensive or indecent*" as practices that could lead to adultery. The later rabbis interpreted it as "extramarital sexual intercourse" pp. 46-48, 73, 86, 98, 106, 201, 204.

For the sake of peace — The rabbinic pragmatic solution for peace after a turbulent marriage p.175

gezarah shavah — The rabbinic exegetical technique whereby two texts are linked into one thought p.100

Kairite Judaism — a back-to-scripture movement started in the seventh century A.D. p.77

Kephale (Gk) — Greek for "head" and metaphorically meaning 'taking priority over,' 'source,' or 'origin' as well as 'authority' pp.11-13.

Ketubah (Heb.) — Conditional contract/<u>covenant</u>. This specified the conditions that both parties agreed to fulfil. p.5.

K'rithuth (Heb.) — "certificate of divorce." Also called the *get* p.29

Lelusai apo gunaikos (Gk) — *"Are you free<u>d</u> from a wife?"* p.176

Love Definitions *(Gk)*: pp.20-21
Agape: Godly unconditional, self-sacrificing love shown to a person.
Phileo: The showing of tender affection toward one's partner or friend.
Storge: Physical showing of affection
Eros: Physical/sexual love

Mias gynaikos andra (Gk) — "a one-woman man" p.198

Mohar (Heb.) — Bride Price. The Price paid by the groom to the bride's father p.3.

Moichia (Gk)— "to commit adultery" pp.30, 84, 162-3, 206, 208

Nedunyah (Heb.) — Dowry. The amount paid into the marriage by the father pp.3, 63

Non-sexual adultery — e.g., *"adulterous [Gk moichalis] generation"* p.31, 163, 208

Ou dedoulotai — "no longer bound" pp. 173, 179

<u>*Porneia* (Gk)</u> — Greek term for 'sexual immorality' pp.82, 84, **92-95**, 98, 162-3, 206

Proskallao (Gk) — "joined together." Not necessarily permanently so p.102

Qol vahomer — The Hebrew exegetical rule: "if this is true, then surely this is also true" pp. 44, 200

Shalach (Heb.) — "divorce-by-sending away" or "putting away" p.29

Shana (Heb.) — *"he hates and divorces" pp. 66-67*

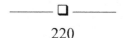

Suggested Reading

Not Under Bondage—Biblical Divorce for Abuse, Adultery, & Desertion .... Barbara Roberts

Divorce and Remarriage in the Bible .... David Instone-Brewer
Divorce and Remarriage in the Church .... David Instone-Brewer

1 Corinthians 7 in the Light of the Graeco-Roman Marriage and Divorce papyri Tyndale Bulletin 52 .... David Instone-Brewer

Marriage, Divorce, and Children in Ancient Rome (see Divorce Roman Style: How Easy and How Frequent was it? .... Susan Treggiari)

Divorce and Remarriage—Recovering the Biblical View .... William F. Luck

...And Marries Another: Divorce and Remarriage in the Teaching of the New Testament .... Craig keener

Something Happened on the Way to Happily Ever After .... Rick Walston
The Bible and Homosexual Practice .... Robert Gagnon
Restoring Sexual Identity .... Anne Paulk

OTHER HELPFUL BOOKS
Divorce and the Bible – What Does the Bible Really Say? .... Ralph Woodrow

Divorce/Remarriage: A Primer for Christians .... David L. Smith

Divorce, Remarriage, and Abuse .... Jeff Crippen
Unholy Charade .... Jeff Crippen
The Divorced and Happy Christian .... Nicole Huffman
You Can Survive Divorce: Hope, Healing...for Your Journey .... Jen Grice

HELPFUL WEBSITES
Not Under Bondage blog .... Barbara Roberts

Divorce—A Gift of God's Love .... Walter Callison

Divorce: God's Will? .... Steven Gola

Divorce Care .... Steve Grissom

Three Positions on Divorce .... Tim Conway on YouTube

The Silent Killer of Christian Marriages ... Amy Wildman-White. This paper is found in *Healing and Hurting* by Catherine Clark-Kroeger and James beck.

Because it Matters—Freedom from Abuse in Christianity .
.... Danni Moss

You Can Survive Divorce website .... Jen Grice

Mending the Soul .... Renee Malina

Sounds of Encouragement .... Barrington Brennan

Biblical Divorce and Remarriage .... Frank L. Caw

Christian Marriage Today.com – 20 Signs of Marriage Problems

———— ❑ ————

Scripture Index

Genesis

1:26, 27....... male and female he created them 10, 99
2:18 .... not good for the man to be alone 7, 166
2:23 .... bone of my bones, and flesh of my flesh 8
2:24 .... cleave unto his wife...one flesh 4, 99, 101
3:16 .... your husband...will rule over you 8

Exodus

20:13 .... you must not murder 152
20:15 .... you must not steal 152
21:10-11 .... first wife...food, clothing, intimacy 54, 111
21:26-27 ..... strikes the eye of his slave...the slave go free 44, 147, 151

Leviticus

18:16 .... you shall not uncover the nakedness of your brother's wife 97
18:22 .... not have sexual intercourse with a man 195
20:10 .... adulterer/adulteress...put to death 29, 53, 115
21:14 .... divorced and widowed treated the same 170

Deuteronomy

21:10-14 ..... become your wife...not delight in her...let her go 44
22:8 .... build a new house...railing around the edge of the roof 40
22:13-19 ..... proof of my daughter's virginity...the cloth 40
22:22 .... death by stoning for an adulteress 37
22:28, 29 .... rapes her...He can never divorce her 40
24:1-4 .... some indecency... a letter of divorce 46
25:4 .... not muzzle an ox while it's treading out the grain 152
25:5-10 ...... brother-in-law shall have sex with her... as a wife 213

2 Samuel

14:5 .... I'm a widow; my husband is dead 170
20:3 .... David's concubines...lived like widows 170

Ezra

10:2 .... broken faith with our God...married foreign women 69

Nehemiah

13:23-27 ..... marriages of certain Jews to pagan women 68

Psalm

82:3-4 .... Defend the defenseless 191

Proverbs

5:19 .... rejoice in the wife of his youth 22
6:16-19 ...... six things Yahweh hates...seven things 65

12:18 .... the words of wise people bring healing 153
18:4: .... who can bear a crushed spirit 149
21: 19 .... better to live in a desert, than with a quarrelling woman 24
31:10-31 ... Who can find a wife with a strong character 17

Song of Solomon
5:16 .... not only as "my lover" but "my friend 22

Isaiah
50:1 .... divorce document of your mother's divorce 61

Jeremiah
3:6-8 .... I divorced her and gave the letter of divorce to [Israel] 61
8:10 .... I will give their wives to others 69

Ezekiel
11:19; 36:26 I will give you a new heart, and a new spirit 190
16:8-13 .... lovemaking...clothed you...costly fabric...ate finely 61
16:16, 19-20 garments...played the whore...my bread 62
44:22 .... the divorced and the widowed together 180

Hosea
2:8, 9 .... gave her the grain...wine...oil...wool...flax 60
2:16, 19-20 . I will take you as my wife 62
6:6 .... I desire mercy and not sacrifice 110, 167

Malachi
2:14-16 ..... The man who hates and divorces his wife 66

Matthew
1:19 .... Joseph...intended to divorce her 63
5:20 .... unless your righteousness exceeds that of the Pharisees 40
5:17-20....... Law or the Prophets. I did not come to destroy 39, 89, 101, 109
5:31-32 .... except "a cause of sexual immorality" 83, 87, 89, 116
7:3 .... speck in your brother's eye...beam in your own eye 25
7:12 .... treat people the same way you want them to treat you 92
9:13 .... 'I desire mercy, and not sacrifice' 109
11:29 .... Take my yoke on you and learn from me...you will find rest 14
12:7 .... I desire mercy and not sacrifice 153, 167
12:31 .... the unforgivable sin 168
12:39 .... adulterous generation 31, 93, 163
14:4 .... John said to Herod, "It is not lawful for you to be having her 97
15:3-6 .... God's commandment...leaders had nullified God's word 38
17:5 .... listen to him 153
18:22 .... forgiveness up to "seventy times seven 122

19:4-6 .... man shall leave...and <u>hold fast to</u> his wife...one flesh 99
19:3-9 .... divorce a wife for "any cause"...certificate 83, 104, 114
19:8 .... hardheartedness. From the beginning **it** hasn't been this way ... 105
19:9 .... except for "sexual immorality," and marries another 92
19:10-12 ..... eunuchs who were born that way.............…................. 120, 198
19:17-19 ..... practice keeping the commandments 38, 97
20:26 .... to serve, and to give his life as a ransom 14
22:24-28 .... So, in the resurrection...whose wife will she be 213
22:29-30 .... in the resurrection they neither marry...like angels 212, 214
28:19 .... teaching [new disciples] everything I have commanded you 132

Mark
7:15 .... it's what comes out from a person that contaminates them 37
7:19 .... he declared every kind of food clean 37
8:38 .... adulterous and sinful generation 163
10:2-12 .... certificate of divorce...hard-heartedness 84, 104, 114, 115
10:11 .... commits adultery against her 135
12:24 .... in the resurrection they neither marry...like angels 212

Luke
2:51-52 .... continued under that law fully obedient to his parents 37
16:18 .... divorcing for the purpose of marrying another 83
20:35-36 ..... resurrection...neither marry...no longer die 212
22:27 .... But I am among you as one who serves 14
24:27 .... explained...things written about himself in all the Scriptures 39

John
4:16-18 .... had 5 husbands...one now living with isn't your husband 167
5:20 .... The Father loves (Gk *phileo*) the Son 20
8:3-11 .... woman caught in adultery 37
13:14 .... If I your Lord...washed your feet...wash one another's feet 14
14:27 .... my peace I'm giving you...stop being so distressed 145
16:27 .... the Father Himself loves (Gk *phileo*) you 21

Acts
8:12 .... good news about the kingdom and everything about Jesus 129
20:35 .... help the weak...It is more blessed to give than to receive 14

Romans
1:26-27 ...... exchanged their natural sexual function ....….….............. 196
3:27 .... the law of faith 91
3:31 .... Do we then nullify the Law?...we establish the Law 39
5:8 .... God confirms His love (Gk *agape*) for us...while... sinners 20
7:1-4 .... adulteress...her husband lives...becomes another man's 158

7:2 .... the law concerning the husband 15
7:6 .... serve in...spirit, and not in oldness of a written code 90
7:12 .... the Law is holy and the commandment is holy and right 90
7:14 .... the Law is spiritual 90
8:2 .... the law of the spirit 91
12:18 .... live at peace with everyone 174
13:10 .... love is the fulfilment of the law 40
15:3-5 .... Christ did not please himself...insults...have fallen on me 14

1 Corinthians
6:16 .... the "one flesh" union with a prostitute 102
7:1-9 .... sexual immorality...sexual relations with his wife 129
7:5 .... get back together again, in case the Satan should tempt you 130
7:8-10 .... the unmarried...the widows...[and] the married 171
7:9 .... better to marry than to burn with sexual desire 179
7:10-11 ...... separating herself...unmarried/ reconciled 136-139
7:12-14 ...... content to live with him, he shouldn't divorce her 142
7:15 .... no longer bound...called to peace 116, 141-145, 171, 173
7:21 .... if indeed you are able to become free...use the opportunity 153
7:25-28 .... released from a wife...marry haven't sinned 174-175
7:26, 28 ...... in view of the present crisis...will face a difficult time 169
7:32-35 .... those who have the gift for singleness 198
7:33-35 ...... anxious about the worldly things...please his wife 57, 128, 150
7:39 .... husband dies, she is free to be married 6, 52, 170-172, 198
9:8-11 .... not muzzle an ox while it's treading out the grain 44, 152
9:20 .... I am not under the law 37, 39
11:3 .... the head of a wife is her husband 11
11:7 .... image...of God, but woman is the glory of man 9
13:4-7 .... Love...doesn't...insist on its own way 23, 150

Galatians
3:28 .... no longer male and female 215
4:4 .... Jesus was "born under law" 37
5:13-15 .... serve each other through love 25, 150
6:2 .... the law of Christ 91

Ephesians
4:26 .... not let the sun go down while [they] are still angry 24
4:32 .... be kind to each other, compassionate, forgiving one another 24
5:11 .... keep away from the fruitless deeds of darkness 103
5:21 .... out of reverence for Christ 14
5:21-24 .... submissive to one another Wives...to...husbands 13, 14, 17
5:25-33 .... Husbands, love (Gk *agapate*) your wives 22, 127
5:28-29, 33 . love...body...he nourishes it and cherishes it 15

Philippians
3:13 .... forgetting the past...forward toward what is ahead 25
4:7 .... Let your reasonableness be obvious to everyone 152

Colossians
2:14 .... erased the written record with its legal regulations 37
3:18 .... Wives...be subject to your husbands ……...............…................. 17
3:19 .... love your wives, and stop being bitterly harsh with them 24

1 Thessalonians
5:23 .... the God of peace...dedicated 19

1 Timothy
3:1-2, 12 ..... overseer...must be a husband of one wife 198
4:1-3 .... deceiving...teachings of demons...forbid marriage ... 166, 186, 189
5:3 .... Support widows...children...to repay their parents 171
5:8 .... not provide for his relatives...worse than an unbeliever 136, 171
5:9 .... "wife of one man" i.e., a one woman man 199
5:14 .... the younger widows should marry 180, 189

2 Timothy
3:16 .... all Scripture profitable...for training in uprightness 31, 95, 112

Titus
2:4-5 .... submissive to their own husbands ……….............…................. 17

Hebrews
3:5-6 .... Moses...a servant...Messiah...over God's house as a son 37

James
1:5 .... short in wisdom, let them ask God...given to them 25
1:27 .... Pure, uncontaminated religion...to look after...widows 171
4:4 .... adulterous people...friendship...world...enmity with God 163
5:16 .... practice confessing [our] offences to each other 23

1 Peter
3:1-2, 5-6 ... willingly submitting to their husbands. Sarah …......…....... 14, 17
3:14, 17 ...... if you should suffer for doing what is right...blessed for it 153

——— ❏ ———

Subject Concordance

The Christian Attitude to Marriage
1 Cor. 7:39; Eph. 5:22-31; Col. 3:18-19; Heb. 13:4; 1 Pet. 3:1-7.

Grounds for Valid Divorce
1. Sexual Unfaithfulness: Matt. 5:32; 19:9.
2. Material Neglect: Ex. 21:10-11; 1 Cor. 7:32-34; Eph. 5:29.
3. Physical/Emotional/Sexual Neglect or Abuse: **Ex. 21:10-11**, 26; 1 Cor. 7:1-5; 32-34; Eph. 5:25-31,
4.   Desertion - including Constructive Desertion: 1 Cor. 7:15.
The "any cause" issue: Matt. 5:31-32; 19:3-9; Mark 10:2-12; Luke 16:18. Also Romans 7:1-4 as an illustration).
Treacherous Divorce: Mal: 2:14-16
God is a Divorcee: Isa. 50:1; Jer. 3:6-11; Hos. 2; Ezek. 16.
Remarriage: 1 Cor. 7:15, 27-28, 39; 1 Tim. 4:3.

Homosexual Activity
Gen.19:4-8; Judges 19:22-23; Lev. 18:22; 20:13;
Rom. 1:26-27; 1 Cor. 6:9b; 1 Tim. 1:10; Jude 7.

———— ❏ ————

Concise Studies in the Scriptures

Other paperback and Kindle books in this series by Raymond Faircloth are also available from Amazon. These are:

Vol. 1. ---- *Can There Be Three Persons in One God? - Why You Should Question the Trinity Doctrine.* This deals with the main subject of Christianity, namely: who is God? Is Jesus the Almighty God? And is the holy spirit a third person in an essence that makes up the God-head of a trinity? The biblical answers are shown to be that God is ONE person (186 pages).

Vol. 1. (1a) ----- *The True Origin of the Son of God – Did Jesus Literally Pre-exist?* This book examines the traditional church belief that before his conception in Mary Jesus had existed in heaven as either a 'God the Son' or as a spirit being, in particular as the archangel Michael. Here it is shown that these ideas are mistaken. The major misunderstanding concerns a failure to recognize Jesus' many figurative sayings in the Gospel of John along with a failure to note the context of certain statements in Paul's letters and the letter to the Hebrews. When these are all correctly understood it becomes evident that Jesus was a miraculously born human whose existence began in his mother's womb, but uniquely as God's Son (197 pages).

Vol. 2. ---- *How God Works in Human Affairs.* This book answers such questions as: Is God really a total controller of all we think, say, and do? It also deals with the subjects of: God's foreknowledge, Christian salvation, universal salvation, and the 'once saved always saved' teaching (190 pages).

Vol. 3. ---- *Delusions and Truths Concerning the Future Life.* This book answers the questions: Do people really go to heaven or hell after death? Does the Bible really teach that humans have an immortal soul? The book shows that the real future for faithful Christians is the Kingdom of God on a renewed earth (124 pages).

Vol. 4. ---- *Don't Misjudge Who Your Real Enemies Are!* This discussion on the reality of a supernatural personal Satan and real demons shows that the so-called Age of Enlightenment led Christian thinkers away from the truths concerning our most powerful enemies (105 pages).

Vol. 5. ---- *Tongues Will Cease...But When?* This book examines the modern-day phenomenon of 'speaking in tongues' and compares it with the biblical record. The book also gives the biblical answer to the question on the timing for the ending of the miraculous phenomenon (155 pages).

Vol. 7. ---- *The End-Time Events for Jesus' Return.* This book examines the various approaches to prophecy with all the biblical evidence to show that a Futurist and Post-tribulation approach is the correct one. It also includes a detailed examination of the biblical information recorded by the ancient prophets so that we might have a good picture of what to expect at the time of Jesus' return. It further connects these prophecies with what Jesus himself said in his Olivet Discourse along with the end-time prophecy statements of the Apostle Paul. This is the first of two books on this subject - the second is the commentary on the entire Book of Revelation with its connections to the end-time events for Jesus' return (278 pages).

Vol. 8. ---- *Messiah's Future Triumph - A Commentary on the Book of Revelation.* This book is a brief verse by verse commentary on the entire Book of Revelation (280 pages).

Vol. 9. ---- *Be in Awe of Our Creator! – Exploring the Early Chapters of Genesis.* This book provides all the major avenues of evidence for the existence of a personal Creator starting with arguments from logic for His existence, His revelation of Himself, as well as proof because of the miracle of Christ's resurrection. Further evidence is given from the world of nature through science regarding our fine-tuned Universe and the many unique factors about Earth. Lastly, the world of biology/chemistry shows the incredible complexity in proteins, DNA, and cells as well as many amazing factors about animals and humans—all leading us to be in awe of our Creator! This book also shows why the neo-Darwinian hypothesis for evolution does not work and is now on the road to being discarded by a growing number of scientists. Finally, there is exploration into the "Days of Creation" and the extent of the great Flood of Noah's day (249 pages).

Vol. 10. ---- *The Veil Removed by Turning to Christ.* This book shows how Christians should view the Mosaic law based on all that Jesus said and all that Paul said about it. It also shows why all Christians must be in the New Covenant and what the benefits are for those in this covenant. (155 pages).

Vol. 11. ---- *Living the Christian Life According to Jesus.* This book shows what Jesus and his emissaries stated is required for a person to become a Christian, including baptism as full immersion in water and the keeping of the Lord's Supper. It also shows the many ways that love is to permeate the Christian community as well as answering concerns over whether or not women can teach in the church. For caring for the interests of the Christian community it is important to know what the role of elders and deacons is and how they are to be qualified to do this care-giving work for all members of each congregation. Two major issues which the book deals with concern that of homosexuality and that of how far Christian may go in terms of defence of self, family, and community (251 pages).

Vol. 12. ---- *Christ Died for Us While We Were Still Sinners – How God, Through Christ, Dealt with Sin.* This book analyses the many models proposed over the centuries to explain why Jesus had to die i.e., the Atonement and describes the multifaceted approach that is necessary and has been put forward by N.T. Wright and other skilled theologians (182 pages).

Vol. 13. ---- *Learning from the Parables of Jesus.* This book shows that the best approach to understanding Jesus' parables is that of limited allegory so that there are often primary figures and subordinate figures from which we gain the application and the secondary meaning. A total of 36 parables and further metaphors and analogies are presented so that the lessons from them are made clear. (156 pages).

*

Other books by Raymond Faircloth

The Shackled Mind of the Jehovah's Witness – Why They Surrender Their Lives to the Watchtower Organization. This book looks at the policies of the Watchtower Society which cause the subtle removal of the free will of members, and psychological damage to them. In particular situations certain Watchtower policies cause the break-up of Jehovah's Witness families, and even literal death of members (251 pages).

Waking Up from Watchtower's Distorted Bible Teachings – Analysis of the Organization's Dogma. This book reveals the false teachings of the Watchtower Society in the areas of: the separating of true Christians into two classes, the manner of Jesus' resurrection and of his return, the date setting for his second advent in 1914, and things concerning the future hope of true Christians (300 pages).

The Kingdom of God Version - The New Testament (Fourth edition). This Fourth Edition has been further refined for greater ease of reading and further accuracy of terms. It is a literal-idiomatic version, but without the jargon of many other versions. The significant footnotes on most pages and notes at the back provide the reasons for the various word and phrase choices along with explanatory and interpretive comments which make clear that God is one person and not a triadic trinity as well as giving clarity on many other Bible teachings (473 pages).

A Bible Subjects Concordance. This quick reference book covering 45 Bible subjects are set out in seven parts and covering such issues as the Trinity, the immortality of the soul, Jesus' return, requirements for Christians, and much more. For these subjects the complete or partial Scripture quotations of the relevant texts are given (150 pages and available only as paperback).

~~~~~~~ ❏ ~~~~~~~

email: rcfaircloth@msn.com

232

Printed in Great Britain
by Amazon

13613153R00139